Python
for
Beginners

The Easy Guide to Coding & Data Science

- ✓ *Programming Logic*
- ✓ *Python coding*
- ✓ *String, Tuple, List, Dictionary*
- ✓ *Module & OOP concept*
- ✓ *NumPy*
- ✓ *Data Science & Ensemble*
- ✓ *Pandas*
- ✓ *File Handling*
- ✓ *MySQL Database*
- ✓ *Database connectivity*
- ✓ *AI concept*
- ✓ *Self-management – a key to success*

Dr. Srikumar Mukherjee
MSc | MA | PhD

"Best Teacher" awardee with 25 years of experience

Python for Beginners: The Easy Guide to Coding & Data Science

Copyright © Srikumar Mukherjee

All rights reserved (No. **LD-20250178133**) under the IPR Act, Govt. of India

ISBN **9798896996330**

Brief quotations may be used for review, academic, or educational purposes, provided proper acknowledgement of the source is given. Any unauthorised use or reproduction of this work is a violation of the Copyright (IPR) Act and may result in legal action.

An
IndoAryan School of Human Resource Development (ISHRD)
Publication
In association with Notion Press & Amazon
Date: May 1, 2025

Price: Rs 499 ($ 29)
Hardcover: Rs 675
Courtesy: Google image
These contributions will be served for 3M

DEDICATED

To my father

Sri Barendra Nath Mukherjee

(15.01.1928 – 22.05.2011)

"Education is to edit,
the experience and knowledge
- that nurtures our existence
with every progressive push."

---Sree Sree Anukulchandra

The first copy of this book has been handed over to the Hon'ble Chancellor (Governor) of the state (Jharhand), Shri Santosh Kumar Gangwar, by the author on Dec. 23, 2025, at the Governor's House

Index

AKNOWLEDGEMENT

We stand for Digital Global Citizenship

*In solidarity with the Open-Source Software (OSS)
movement, we urge promoting technology by the people
and for the people, to advance equitability and
interdependence in the world.*

Forewords

When Dr Srikumar Mukherjee asked me to write a foreword for his book 'Python for Beginners', I was taken by surprise. During December 2025, me and my team was busy organising the International Conference on Computational Management for Decision Making. He had visited my office and had a long discussion with my colleagues and me. During that conversation, this proposal came up surprisingly. He presented a paper at the conference and had a long discussion with me. We have known each other since our childhood days (he is my senior, but playing cricket developed the camaraderie), and I said yes.

As an individual's role changes in one's life, I am no exception. At BIT Mesra, Ranchi, I have the opportunity to interact with a variety of students and faculty colleagues. AI has been my area of interest, and I have been dealing with it for the last 28 years with students from the undergraduate to the Doctoral level.

One issue that I have come across is that communicating with the computer system is key to further growth. The sooner you learn, the better it is. Somewhere, you must break the ice.

Python is a high-level language that allows us to write the program the way we think, perceive and act. With a little bit of practice, it is easy to learn and execute. Nowadays, it has become a foundation stone for developing Artificial Intelligence-based systems.

I went through the book (took time) and found it very helpful. The language in which the book is written is very much Indian; it is aligned with the way we talk, do our work and think. This is not only meant for young students of senior secondary or undergraduate levels, but also for those who wish to learn the language to develop systems based on Artificial Intelligence.

Dr Srikumar Mukherjee is himself an avid learner and writer. The number of books that he has written is proof of his thinking and ability to pen down his thoughts. His love for students and being in the profession for over 25 years takes him closer to understanding the psychological and behavioural aspects of young minds.

The book has 17 chapters focused on relevant aspects of Python. The book is well-suited for all those who are willing to learn Python and Data Science lucidly. The readers will be enriched by the information they will get from the book; moreover, they will enjoy reading and using the book for their self-development.

Prof (Dr.) Bhaskar Karn

Professor of Information Science, Dept. of Management

Head, Department of Humanities and Social Sciences

Former Dean of Students' Welfare & Exam Controller

Birla Institute of Technology (BIT)

Mesra, Ranchi - 835215

Date: March 1, 2026

Introduction

This book is written for complete beginners, with no prior knowledge of programming, to help them grow in confidence step by step. It provides clear explanations and solutions to common problems faced by the students of +2, BCA, MCA and BTech, based on the challenges I once faced in my IT education and also during teaching as well.

My journey with computers began unexpectedly. In the late 1990s, during my science graduation, I was more interested in social change than 'career' prospects, so I joined the movement. One day, I was reading 'Dialectical Materialism' - the Marxist philosophy authored by Maurice Cornforth. Suddenly, I heard a gentle yet heart-pounding voice: 'What do you think of pursuing after graduation?' My father stood behind, his penetrating and anxious eyes fixed on me. Looking at him, I had no ready answer. I lowered my eyes and closed the book.

My father, an educator at a renowned engineering college, envisioned the same path for me to secure my future. With his stand, I earned a post-graduate diploma in IT, followed by Microsoft Certified Professional (MCP) with distinction, and eventually built a future where survival met the search for truth.

Over time, I realised IT was not just a livelihood, but also a force for education, creativity, and empowerment. I had an MSc in IT, and later on, my passion to explore cultural spirit led me to pursue an MA and a PhD in Sociology, where I found an all-inclusive vision, 'IndoAryan Existentialism'. In that technology, under the existential science, i.e. 'Dharma'(upholds existence), and 'Education' (that nourishes potential), builts liberal and innovative society. Here, my profession and passion jointly began to fly with two wings: Education and Spirituality.

So, I chose teaching, and for the last 25 years I have been teaching at the Sr Secondary level, guiding thousands of students through FoxPro, Python, Oracle, and MySQL, and learning from them. My inspiration to write this came from my mentor, Rev. Dr Buddhadev Chakraborty, ex-professor and grandson of my master, Sree Sree Anukulchandra, who once asked me, "Can't you write a book on the subject you teach?" These words motivated me to share my achievements with the nation's youth and the tech world, in favour of the Man Making Mission (3M).

This book begins with the basics of program-logic and gradually builds a foundation in Python, covering essential concepts like Strings, Tuples, Lists, Dictionaries, Modules & OOP concept, NumPy and File handling. Learners would explore Data Science and Ensemble with Pandas, Database of MySQL, and even get a glimpse of Artificial Intelligence.

To complete the journey, I have included a final chapter, "Self-Management – A Key to Success," designed to help students, teachers, and parents nurture their inner potential and develop the qualities needed to succeed in a global environment.

I think youth should be more creators rather than consumers, employers rather than employees, leading society toward social and cultural liberty. With knowledge and values, they can shift economic control into the hands of people and move humanity toward true global citizenship.

I hope this book will serve as both a guide to mastering technology and a companion for personal growth and social transformation to uphold equitability, and if so, then it could be a small contribution to my nation. I warmly welcome ideas from readers to improve future editions.

I'm truthfully grateful to Dr Bhaskar Karn, Professor, HOD and Dean in BIT Mesra, for writing his encouraging 'Foreword'.

Before concluding, I would like to thank Dr Itu Singh, Prof. of Computer Science, BIT Mesra, Dr Manorama Patnaik, faculty of Computer Science, Amity University, Sanjiv Sinha, formar HOD of Computer Science, DPS Ranchi, for their valuable suggestion and motivation.

I'm also thankful to my wife, Smt. Debjani Mukherjee for always providing me with all the required mental and moral support.

Finally, I dedicate this book to my beloved father, whose love, vision and encouragement made computer science my essential companion.

Srikumar Mukherjee,   May 1, 2025
Ranchi,
srikumar[dot]hrm@gmail[dot]com
Cell# +91-9470932544 / 8210137153

Chapter 1

Software
and
Programming Logic

Chapter Objective

- Software & its Evolution

- Relation of Binary to ASCII

- Evolution of Software

- Programming Concept

- Algorithm – as problem-solving logic

- Flowchart – as problem-solving logic

Software as Defined:

The human body is the best machine of nature's evolution out of her 'existential urge'. Now, humans wanted a similar man-made machine to make their work easier. The human body has visible components like the brain, heart, lungs, kidneys, etc., which can be called hardware. But to activate, it needs power, energy, and impulses that pass through its neural system, which is invisible; it can be compared to software.

Similarly, Computer Software is a collection or set of electronic instructions to perform specific tasks. It is a non-physical (intangible) part of a computer that tells its hardware what to do. It is written in Binary or Machine Language, the only language that the computer understands. The binary is composed of power-on (True), i.e., 1s, and power-off (False), i.e., 0s. Any task we take from a computer in the form of text, numbers, pictures, music, or video is a combination of 0s and 1s and gets converted into human-readable ASCII code.

Relation of Binary, Decimal and ASCII code:

Binary Code:
- Binary code uses **base-2** (0 and 1) to represent information.
- Computers natively process and store data in binary format.
- Each binary digit (bit) represents an exponential power of 2.

Decimal Code:
- Decimal code uses **base-10** (0 to 9) to represent numbers.
- It is the system humans commonly use for counting.
- Conversion between binary and decimal involves interpreting binary digits as powers of 2 and summing them:
  Example: $1011 = 1 \times 2^3 + 0 \times 2^2 + 1 \times 2^1 + 1 \times 2^0 = 11$ in decimal

ASCII Code:
- ASCII (American Standard Code for Information Interchange) is a character encoding standard.
- Each character (e.g., letters, numbers, symbols) is assigned a unique decimal value (0–127 in the standard ASCII).
- These decimal values are then converted into binary format for computer processing.

Character in ASCII	Decimal	Binary
A	65	01000001
a	97	01100001

Binary Controls Hardware and Software:

Binary instructions control various hardware components as follows:

Central Processing Unit: It works in the CPU by fetching, decoding, and executing binary code.

Memory: Stores binary data as electrical states.

Input/Output Devices: Interprets binary signals to perform actions (e.g., showing images on a screen).

Storage Devices: Save data in binary format for retrieval.

High-Level Programming Languages: High-Level Languages (HLL) like Python, Java, and C++ are used by humans to write code in a readable form, and compilers or interpreters convert this code into binary (machine code) so the computer can understand and execute it.

Conversion into Binary: 2GL (Assembly language) is translated into Binary (1GL) or Machine Language by an Assembler, but Compilers translate the entire program into machine code before execution (e.g., C, C++). Interpreters translate and execute code line-by-line at runtime (e.g., Python, JavaScript). Some languages use a mix of both.

Evolution of Software:

1GL: First-generation language (Machine Language)
    Examples: 11000110   10101011

2GL: Second-generation language (Low-level Assembly Language)
    Examples: PRINT, END, SAVE, GOTO….

3GL: Third-generation language (Procedural/Programming Languages)
    Examples: C, C++, C#, VB, Java, Python…

4GL: Fourth-generation language (Database Query Languages like SQL)
    Examples: MySQL, SQL Server, Oracle, FoxBase, etc.

5GL: Fifth-generation language (Logic-based languages)
    Example: AI, Robotics

Programming Concept:

The programming concept is divided into two:

- **Logical** Concept
- **Coding** Concept

The logical concept is again divided into two: Algorithm and Flowchart.

    ✓**Algorithm**: Step-by-step expression of the logic of the program in simple English language

    ✓**Flowchart**: Pictorial representation of the logic.

Algorithm: *Textual problem-solving logic*

The algorithm is the Presentation of programming logic in steps in simple English, as the best a writer could express to a programmer.

 # Write an Algorithm (WAA) to find the sum of two numbers:

Step-1: Read a value in x

Step-2: Read a value in y

Step-3: Read sum of x & y [or Get x+y]

Step-4: Print / Show the result

 # WAA to take two values and exchange: *(using 3rd variable)*

Step-1: x Gets a value (i.e. Red pen)   # x=10

Step-2: y Gets a value (i.e. Blue pen)   # y=20

Step-3: z Gets no value (i.e. having no pen)   # z=0

Step-4: z Gets the Red pen from x   # z = x

Step-5: x Getes the Blue pen from y   # x=y

Step-6: Now y Getes Red pen from z   # y=z

 # WAA To take 2 values in two variables and exchange: (Swapping NOT using 3rd variable)

Get x=10

Get y=20

Find X=(X+Y)

Find Y=(X-Y)

Find X=(X-Y)

Sow the values of X & Y

Not Using 3rd variable		Using 3rd variable		
X	Y	X	Y	Z
10	20	10	20	0
30	20	10	20	10
30	10	20	20	10
20	10	20	10	

 # WAA to find Simple Interest (SI), whereas P, T, R will be inputs:

STEP-1: Get PRINCIPAL As P

STEP-2: Get RATE As R

STEP-3: Get TIME As T

STEP-4: CALCULATE SI=(P * T * R)/100

STEP-5: DISPLAY "SIMPLE INTEREST=>" SI

 # WAA to take 2 numbers and find the greater number. *assume X ≠ Y*

STEP-1: Get 1st no into X [10]

STEP-2: Get 2nd no into Y [5]

STEP-3: COMPARE X & Y || CHECK X is greater than Y?

STEP-4: IF X > Y : GOTO STEP-6

STEP-5: IF X<Y : GOTO STEP-7

STEP-6 DISPLAY/PRINT "GREATER NO=>" X : END

STEP-7: DISPLAY/PRINT "GREATER NO=>" Y

Flowchart: *Pictorial problem-solving logic*

A flowchart is a Graphical or Pictorial representation of programming logic. Here are some of the common symbols used in a flowchart.

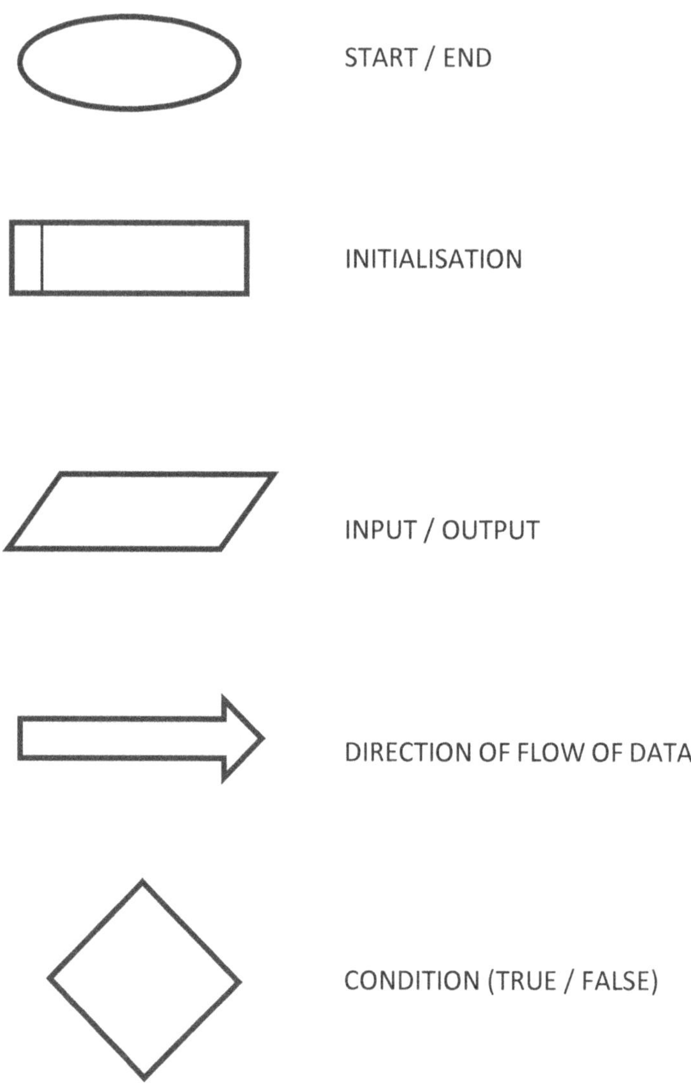

 # _Draw A Flowchart_ (DAF) to enter Principal, Time & Rate and print Simple Interest.

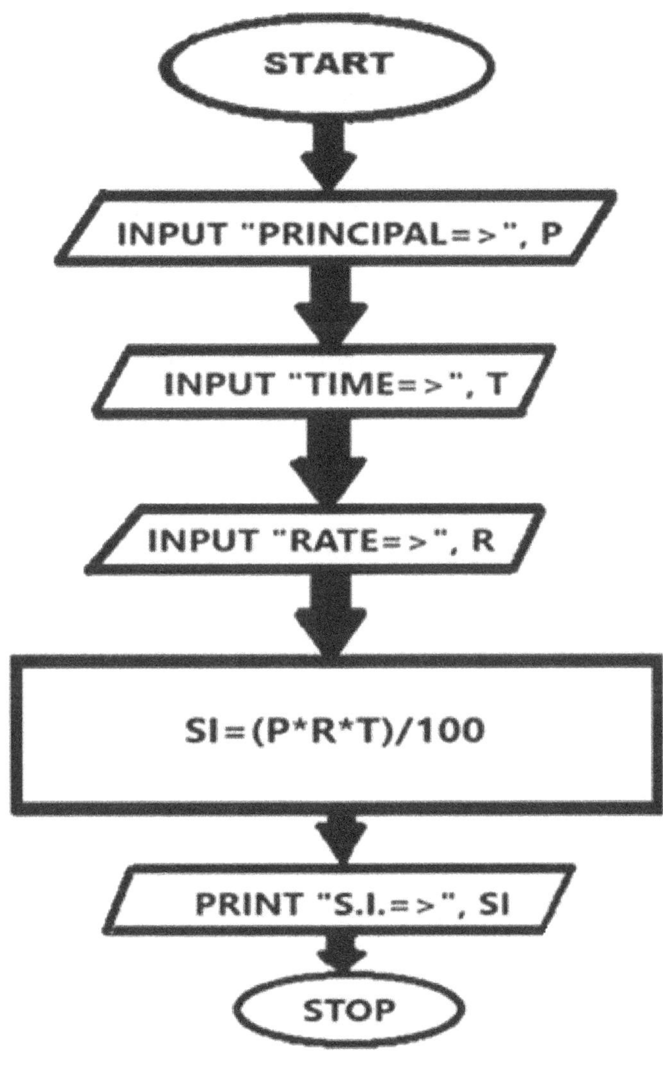

Note: _Here, it is based on 'simple data flow', following the order (1) Initialization, (2) Input, (3) Calculation/processing, (4) Output._

 # DAF to enter Length & Breadth and find the Area & Perimeter of a rectangle:

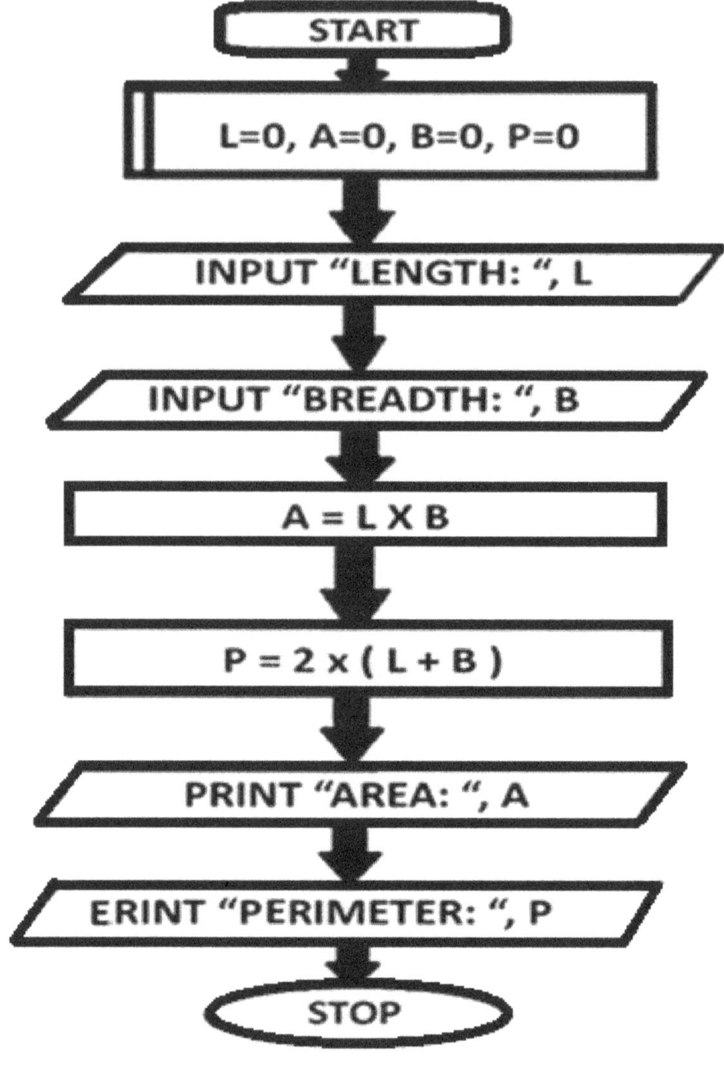

> **Note:** *Here, it is also based on 'simple data flow', following the same order (1) Initialization, (2) Input, (3) Processing, & (4) Output.*

 # DAF to enter 2 numbers and swap using 3rd variable:

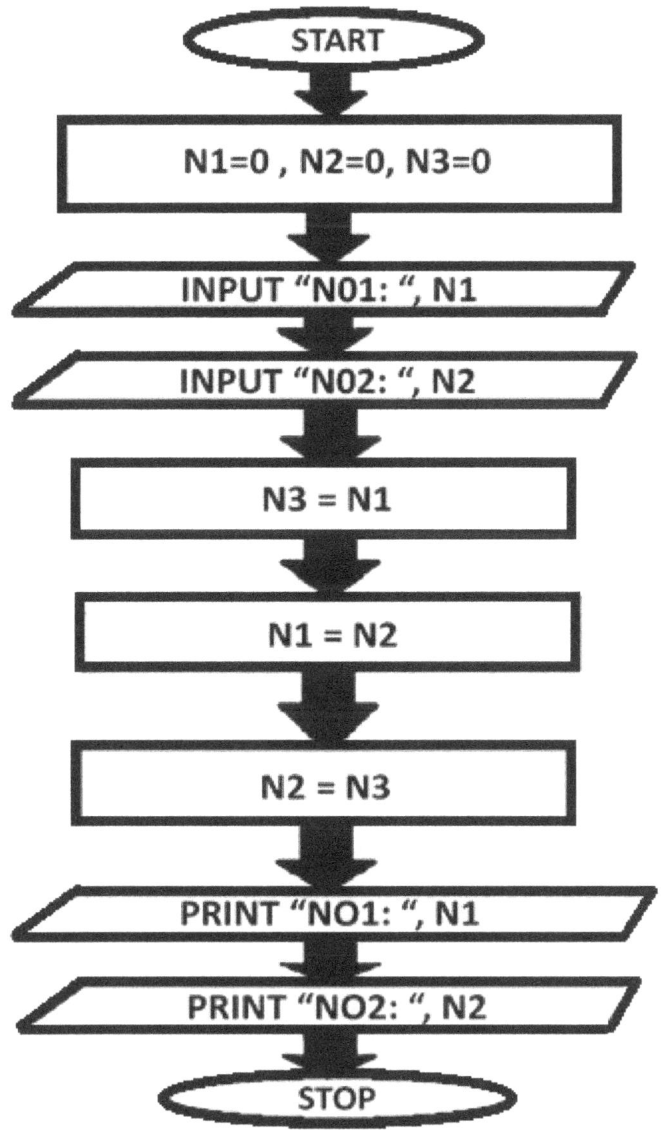

Note*: It is also following the same orders. Here, Values are assigned from right to left variables; i.e. 1st to 3rd Var., then 2nd to 1st Var., finally 3rd to 2nd Var. to interchanges of N1 & N2.*

DAF to input 3 numbers and determine the largest number
(Technique-1)

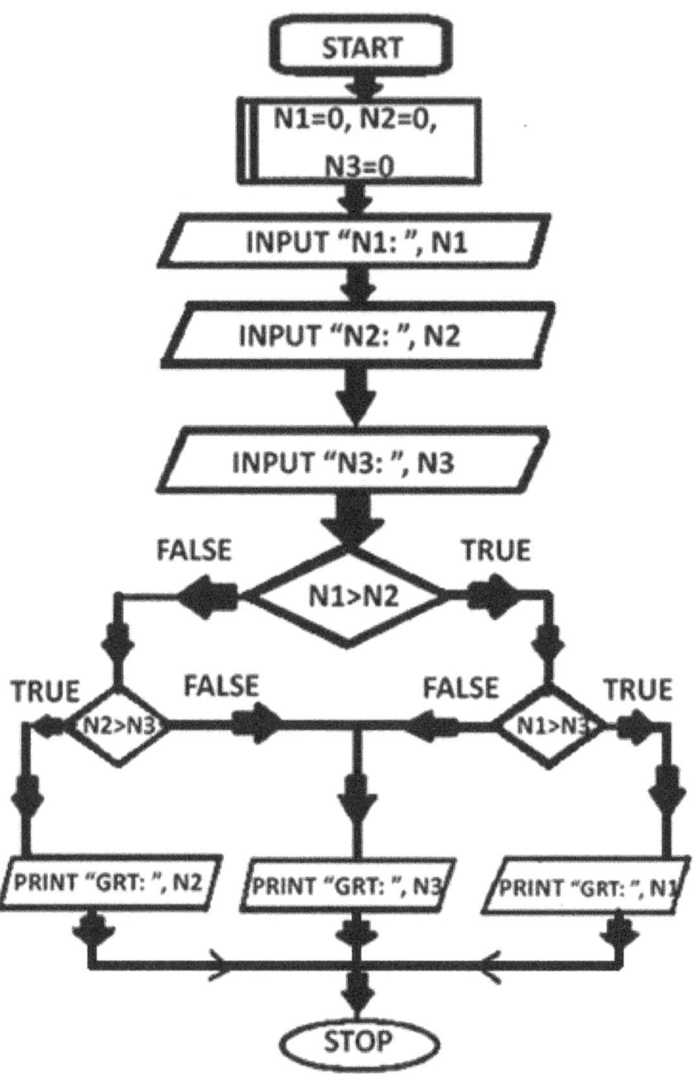

Note: *Here, the greater number of the first 2 numbers is compared with the 3rd numeer. For example, assume it as a triangular knock-out football tournament, winner of the first 2 teams, plays with the 3rd team, to be the champion.*

 # DAF to input three numbers and determine the largest number
(Technique-2)

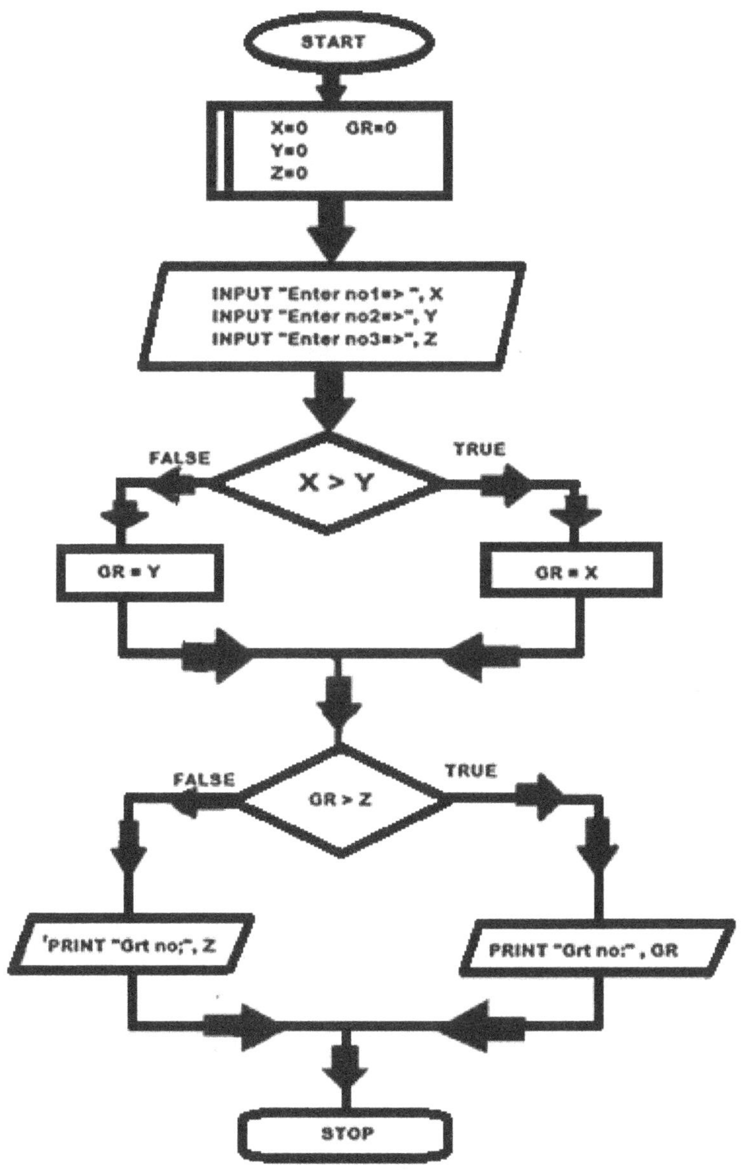

> **Note:** *For the same problem given above, here the Greater value of the first 2 values is stored in a variable (GR), then the variable (GR) is compared with the 3rd value.*

DAF to enter average marks and print Grade (A/B/C/D) as given:

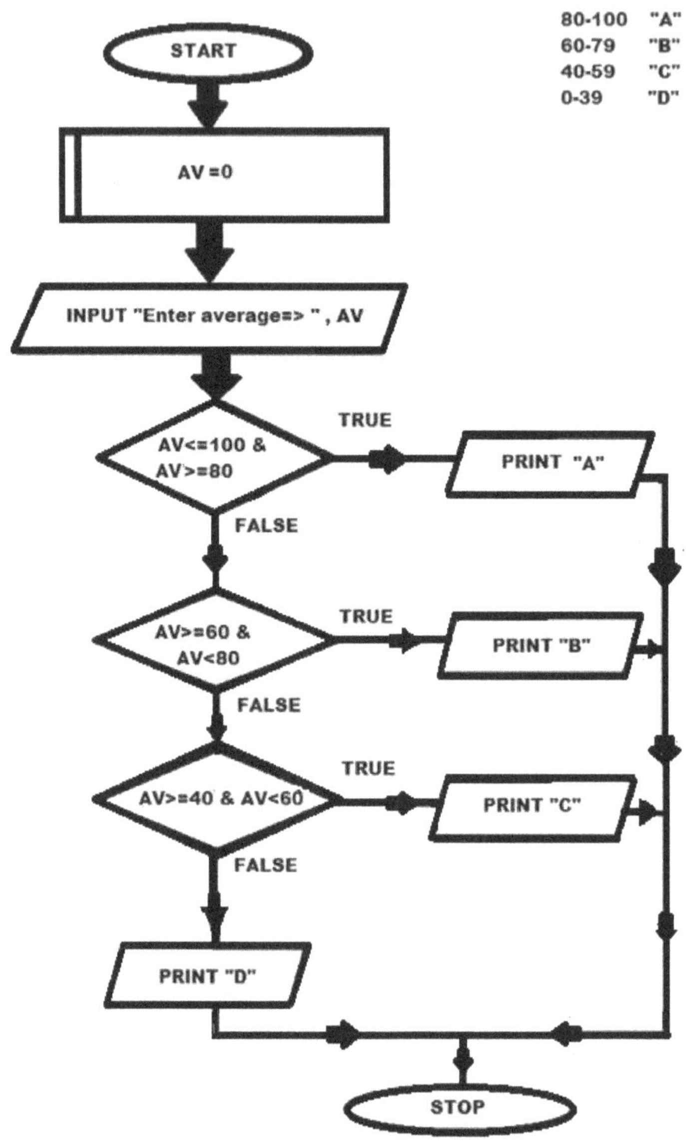

Note: Here, the problem is based on multiple conditions or choice or menu-based, so at a time <u>only one</u> output will be printed according to the choice, and after all the outputs, all the flow directions will meet at STOP only, to end.

 # DAF to print the first 5 natural numbers.

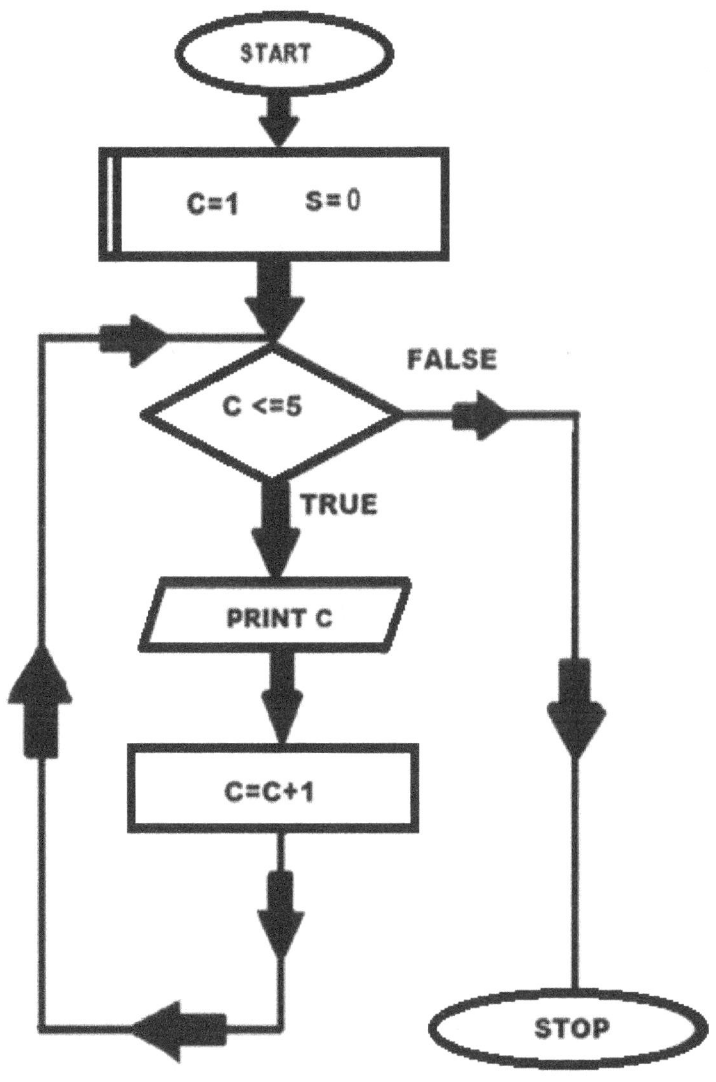

Note: *Here, the Print statement is located inside the loop, i.e. before the condition is FALSE, because output has to be shown <u>multiple</u> times.*

DAF to print the Sum of the first 5 natural numbers.

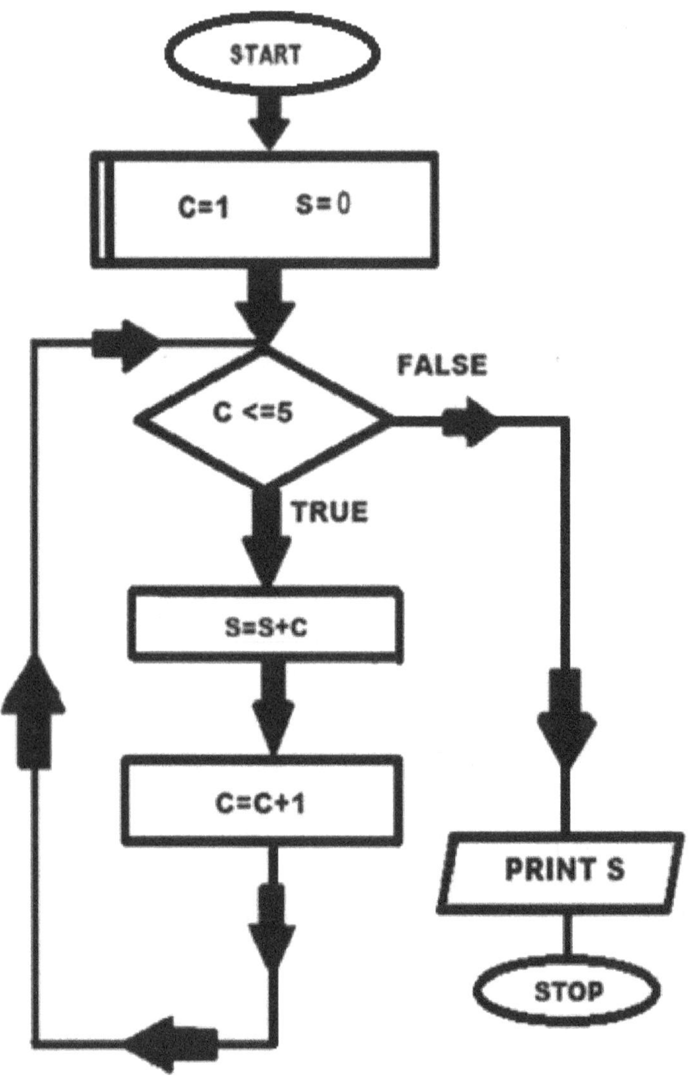

> **Note:** *Here, the Print statement is located out of the loop, i.e. after the condition becomes FALSE, because output has to be shown only <u>once</u>.*

DAF to print the Multiplication Table of a given number

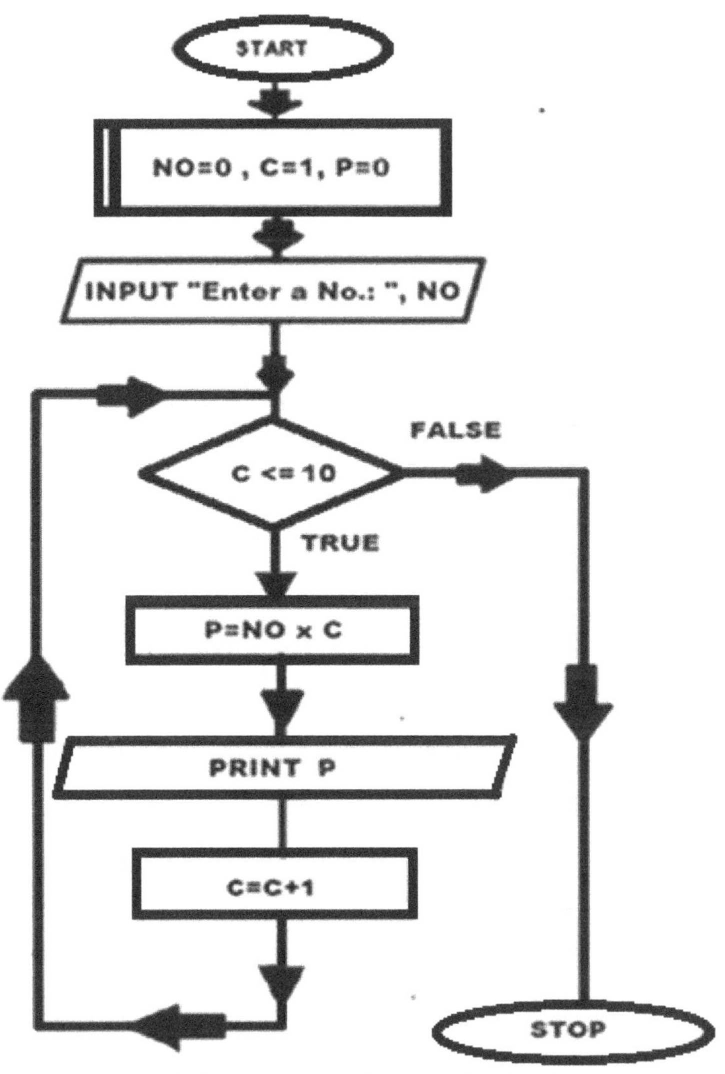

> **Note:** *Here, the Print statement is located within the loop, i.e. before the FALSE condition takes place, because the output is to be printed repeatedly. P (product) can be printed in a formatted form, in the following statement:* **PRINT (NO, "X", C, "=", P) i.e. 5X1=5...** *instead of* **PRINT P** *as given in the flowchart.*

DAF to find the factorial of a number, say 3, as 3!=1 x 2 x 3

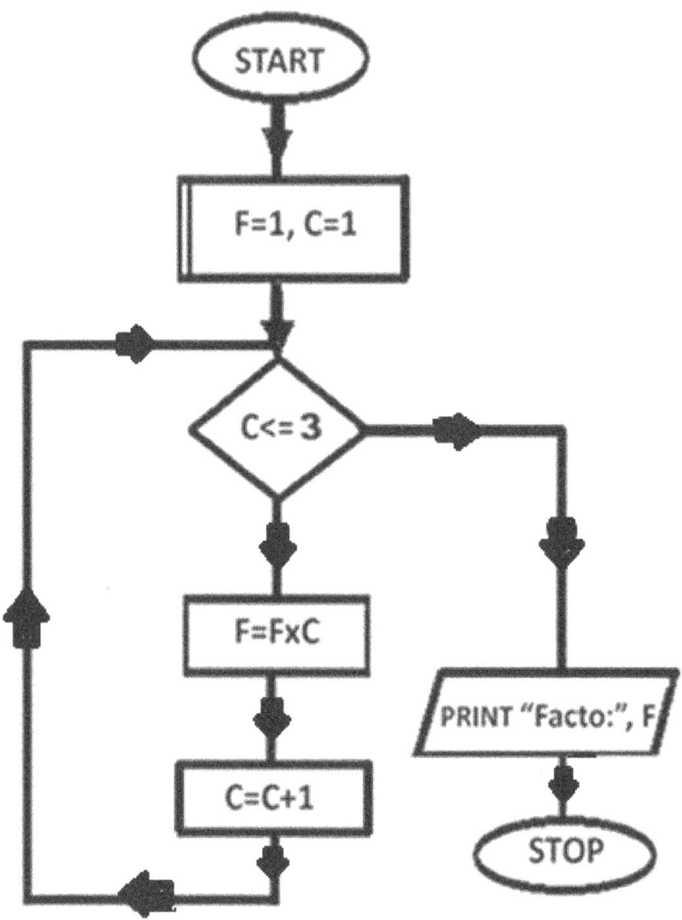

Dry run of the Flowchart to find the factorial of a no.

NO	F	C	C<=NO?	F=FXC	C=C+1
3	1	1	True	1	2
	1	2	True	2	3
	2	3	True	6	4
	6	4	False	-	-

DAF to find S=1/2 + 2/3 + 3/4……..Nth term.

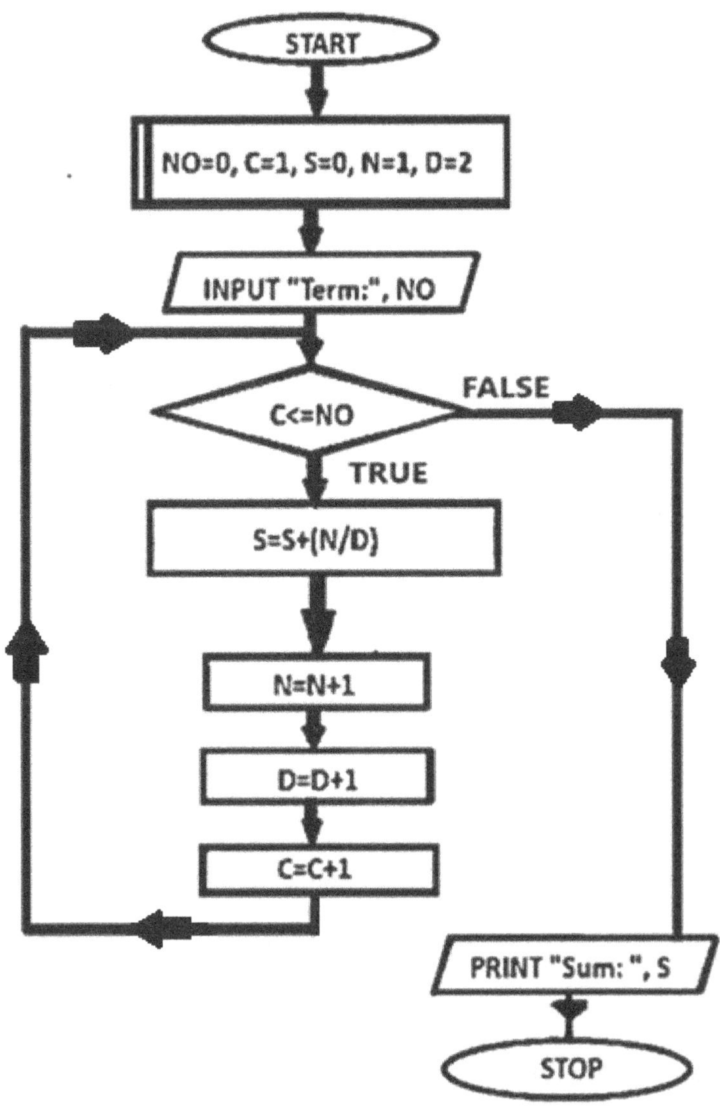

Note: *Here, the print statement is written out of the loop, i.e. after the condition False, because we need to print the sum only once.*

DAF to find S=1 + 4 + 9 + 16 .... Nth term.

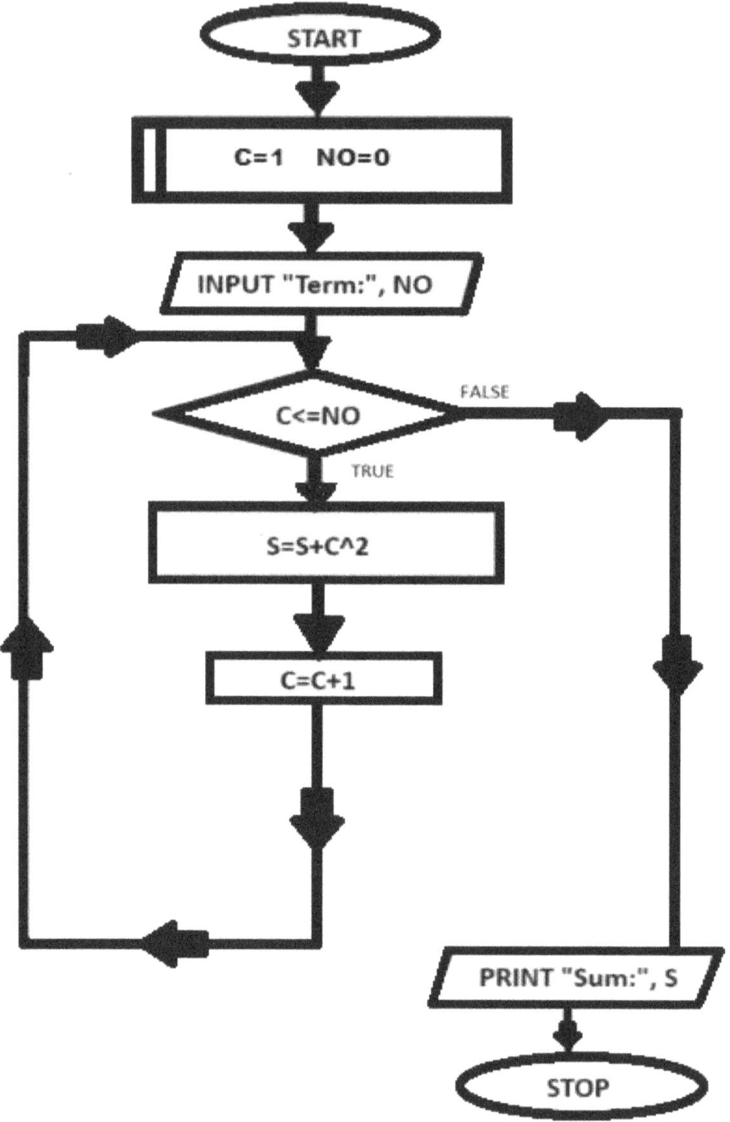

> **Note:** *Here, in series cases, first we have to find out 3-points, (1) what is the base of the series elements, (2) how it is increasing, (3) how the power is increasing, (4) what is the final term & accordingly what is counting.*

 # DAF to find S=(1)+(1+2)+(1+2+3)+(1+2+3+4)+........Nth term.

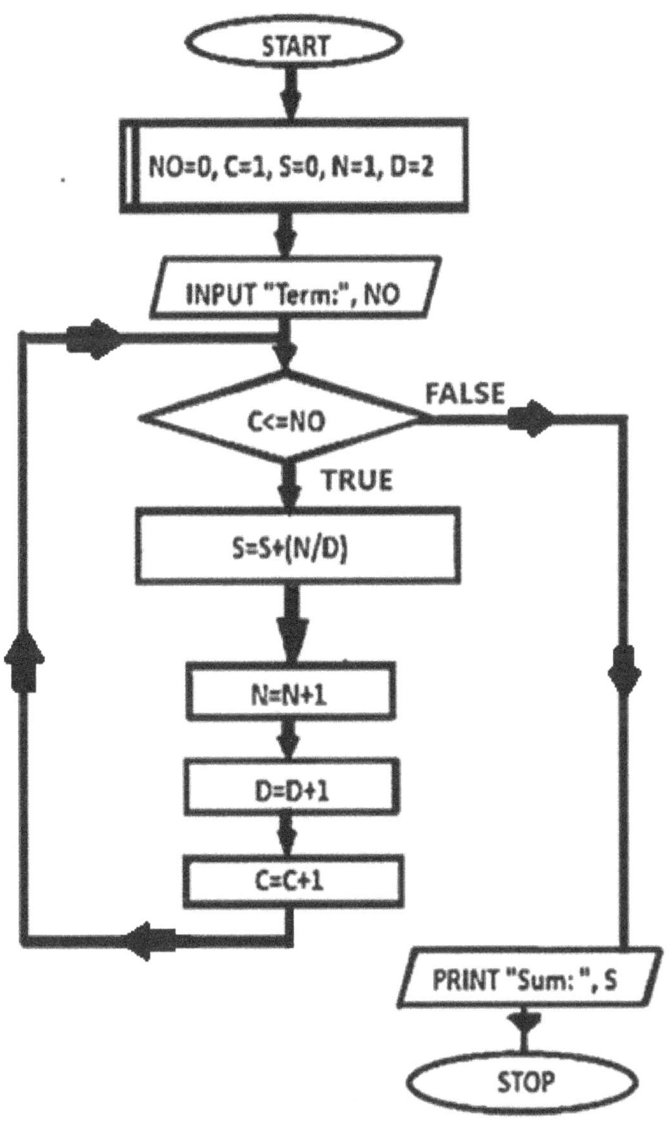

> **Note:** *Here, it is based on nested-loop, i.e. inner loop (C<=K) within an outer loop (K<=NO) & each time (i.e. value of K) inner loop starts from the beginning, i.e. C=1, S=0 & its sum (S) is added with TOT*

DAF to find S=1! + 2! + 3! +....... Nth Term.

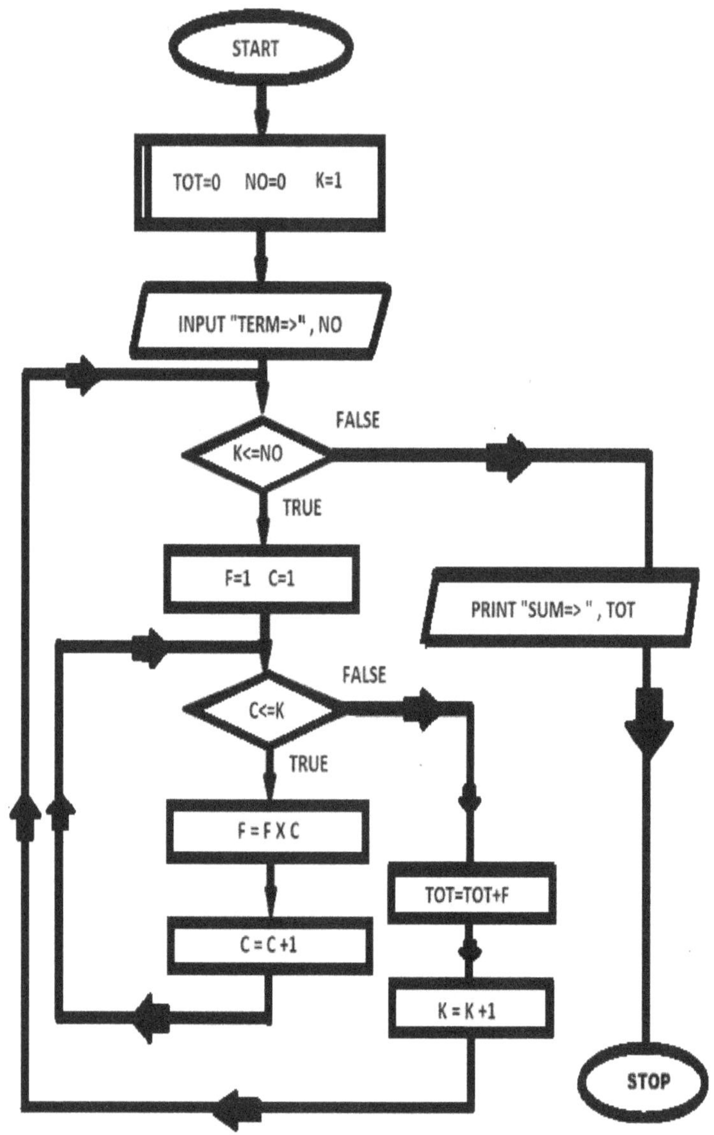

> **Note:** *It is also a nested-loop, i.e. inner loop (C<=K) within an outer loop (K<=NO) & each time inner loop starts from the beginning, i.e. F=1, C=1 & each time its Factorial (F) is getting added with TOT.*

DAF to find whether the number is Prime or not.

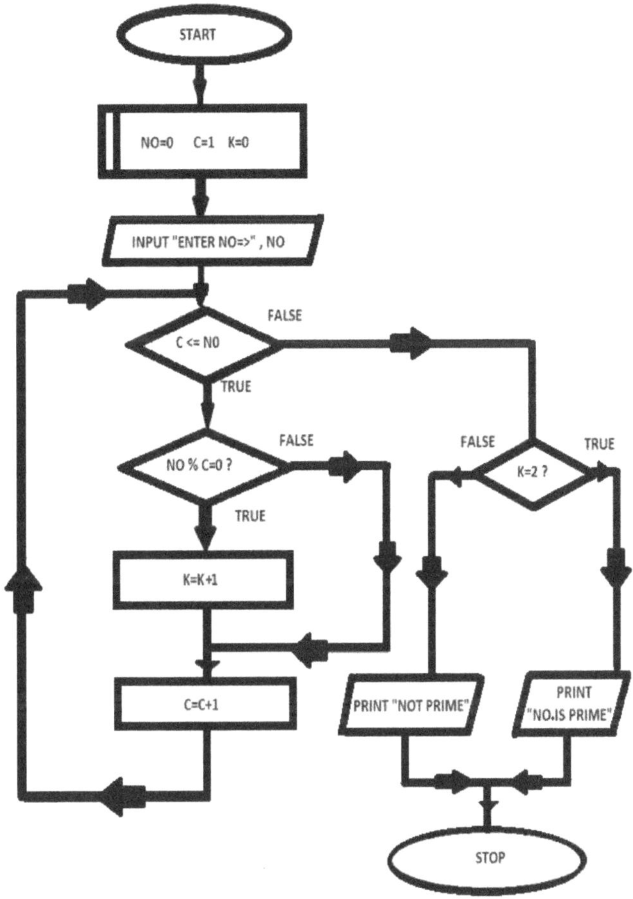

Dry/manual run to check whether the No is Prime?

NO	C	K	C<=NO?	NO%C=0?	K=K+1	C=C+1	K=2?
3	1	0	True	True	1	1	-
3	2	1	True	False	-	3	-
3	3	1	True	True	2	4	-
3	4	2	False	-	-	-	True i.e. It's Prime

 # DAF to enter a number and find the reverse of the same.

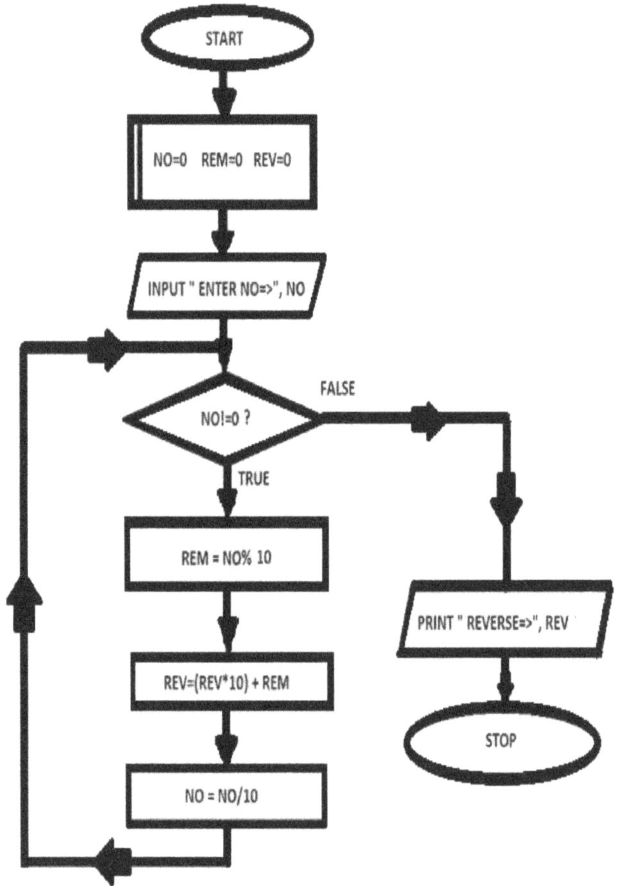

Dry-run to find the reverse of the Number:

NO	No!=0	REM	REV
123	True	3	3
12	True	2	32
1	True	1	321
0	False	-	*Prints 321*

Chapter 2

Data
and
Data Processing

Chapter Objective:

- Data as Defined
- Types of Data
- Digital Data-set
- Importance of Data
- Structured & Unstructured Data
- Big Data
- Data Processing
- Statistical Methods to Understand Data
- Boolean Algebra
- Logic Gates

Data as Defined:

Data refers to raw, unprocessed facts, figures, or observations collected for analysis, processing, and decision-making. Data is collected to provide meaningful insights and support informed decision-making. It consists of distinct pieces of information, typically formatted and stored for a specific purpose. In general, data is a set of characters stored and transformed for analysis, which eventually becomes information. If data is not put into context, it serves no meaningful purpose for either humans or computers.

Types of Data:

- Single character
- Text (string)
- Number (integer or floating-point)
- Boolean (True or False)
- Picture/Graphic
- Sound/Audio
- Video/Animation

Again, the data is divided into two:

- **Qualitative Data:** It tells 'what kind' - that describes its character. Fundamentally, it is non-numeric data. Such as Eye colour: blue, brown, Customer feedback: "excellent", "poor", Types of fruits: apple, mango, banana. Qualitative Data is used for understanding patterns, categories, opinions, or behaviours, which usually represent Text, labels, or categories.

- **Quantitative Data:** It tells 'how much' - that gives the measurement. Fundamentally, it represents measurable quantities or amounts. Its nature is numerical, which can be counted or measured. Such as Age: 25, 40, Temperature: 23.5°C, Sales figures: Rs 100000, $ 8000. It is used for calculations, statistical analysis, and data modelling and usually represents Numbers, charts, and graphs.

Digital Data Set:

In a computer's storage, digital data is represented as a sequence of bits (binary digits, i.e., 0 and 1). The Central Processing Unit (CPU) processes this data through logical operations to produce new data (output) from source data (input).

Examples:

Let's convert "IndoAryan" to its binary representation! First, each character is turned into its ASCII value, then represented in 8-bit binary:

```
I →    ASCII 73 →      01001001
n →    ASCII 110 →     01101110
d →    ASCII 100 →     01100100
o →    ASCII 111 →     01101111
A →    ASCII 65 →      01000001
r →    ASCII 114 →     01110010
y →    ASCII 121 →     01111001
a →    ASCII 97 →      01100001
n →    ASCII 110 →     01101110
```

Final binary representation of "IndoAryan":
01001001 01101110 01100100 01101111 01000001 01110010
01111001 01100001 01101110

Importance of Data:

- Empowers to make informed decisions
- Helps identify problems
- Helps to develop accurate theories
- Gives back-up arguments
- Approaches strategic/decision-making
- Helps to get hands-on funding
- Tells what is going well
- Saves time and money
- Improves the quality of life

Structured Data:

Structured data has a fixed format or pattern, making it meaningful, easily trackable, and analyzable. It is usually stored in relational databases (RDBMS).

Example: Data stored in banking systems, educational records, business databases, etc.

Unstructured Data:

Unstructured data lacks a predefined format or pattern, making it difficult to analyse using traditional relational databases. It is not organised in a predefined manner, so it is not stored in the RDBMS.

Examples: Word processor, PDF files, Media files, Satellite images, Scientific data, Sensor data, Surveillance pictures and video, Chat, IM, Phone recordings, Collaboration software, Data from social media, etc.

Big Data:

Big Data refers to extremely large and complex sets of data that are difficult to process using traditional data processing tools. It includes structured, semi-structured, and unstructured data that keeps growing rapidly, based on **Cloud Computing** – a global open-source internet-based platform for processing and analysing Python-based applications such as Pandas, RDBMS, etc., which we shall cover here.

The 5 Vs of Big Data are:

Volume Huge amounts of data (e.g., terabytes, petabytes)
Velocity Data is generated and processed very fast
Variety comes from different sources and formats
Veracity Refers to the accuracy and reliability of the data
Value Usefulness in decision-making, predictions, etc.

Sources of Big Data:

It collects data from the most modern technology-based people's platforms, such as Social media, which generates billions of posts daily, E-commerce sites tracking user behaviour and transactions, Sensor data from IoT (Internet of Things) devices, Education and Healthcare records from millions of students and patients, and Traffic data from smart cities

Importance of Big Data:

Big Data allows businesses, governments, and researchers to discover hidden patterns, make smarter decisions, predict trends, improve products and services, and personalise user experiences

Data Processing:

Data holds valuable facts, and processed information becomes useful for decision-making. However, by examining a large amount of data, one cannot conclude. Rather, data needs to be processed to get results, and after analysing those results, conclusions or decisions are made.

Example:

Automated data processing in situations like online bill payment, registration of complaints, booking tickets, etc. The following illustrates the basic steps used to process data and generate output. Here is the relation of Data, Processing and Information.

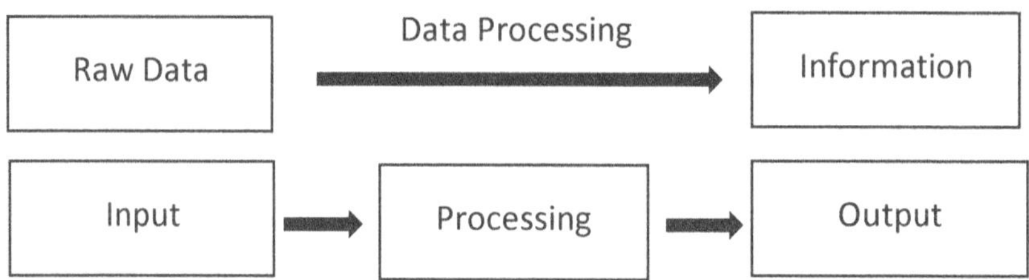

Basic Statistical Methods to Understand Data:

Mean: it is the average of the numeric values of an attribute, so the Mean is also called the average. Suppose there are marks data of 40 students in a class. Instead of looking at each individual's values, we can calculate the average of the students in that class.

Example:

Assume that the marks of students in a class are as follows [90,102,110,115,85,90,100,110,110]. The mean or average marks of the class are:

=> (90+102+110+115+85+90+100+110+110)/9

=> 912/9

=> 101.33

> **Note:** *Mean is not a suitable choice if there are outliers in the data, if so then median is a better choice. To calculate the mean, the outliers or extreme values should be removed from the data, then calculate the mean of the remaining.*

Median: The median is also computed for a single attribute/variable at a time. When all the values are sorted in ascending or descending order, the middle value is called the Median. When there is an odd number of values, then the median is the value at the middle position. The median represents the central value at which the given data is equally divided into two parts.

Example: Consider the data on the marks of students to calculate the mean. Now, to compute the median, **(i)** Sort data - the marks, in ascending (or descending) order as [85, 90, 90, 100, 102, 110, 110, 110, 115] **(ii)** Count the values, is: 9 (is an odd number), **(iii)** Find the median value at 5th position, that is 102, whether counted from left to right or reverse. The median represents the actual central value where the data is equally divided into two parts.

Mode: The mode is the value that appears most frequently (the greatest number of times) in a dataset, it is called the mode. It is computed based on the frequency of occurrence of distinct values in the given data. A data set has no mode if each value occurs only once. There may be multiple modes in the data if more than one values have the same highest frequency. Mode can be found for numeric as well as non-numeric data.

Example: In the list of marks of students, the mode is 110 as its frequency of occurrence in the list is 3, which is larger than the frequency of the rest of the values.

Range: The range is a measure of dispersion that calculates the difference between the maximum and minimum values in a dataset. It describes the spread of numerical data and is influenced by outliers since it relies on the two extreme values. Examples include differences in salaries, marks, or prices.

Let M be the largest or maximum value and S be the smallest or minimum value in the data, then Range is the difference between the two extreme values, i.e. (M - S) or Maximum *minus* Minimum.

Example: In the above example, the minimum mark value is 85, and the maximum mark value is 115. Hence, the range is: 115-85 = 30.

Standard Deviation: Standard deviation measures the spread of data by considering how much each value differs from the mean. Unlike the range, which only uses the extreme values, standard deviation accounts for all data points. It's calculated as the positive square root of the average squared differences from the mean. A smaller standard deviation indicates less spread, while a larger one indicates greater spread.

Example: Let us compute the standard deviation of the marks of the nine students that we used while calculating the Mean. The Mean (x) was calculated to be 101.33. Subtract each value from the mean and take the square of that value. Dividing the sum of square values by the total number of values and taking its square root gives the standard deviation in the data.

Variance: Variance is a measure of variability that describes the degree of spread in a dataset. It measures the spread of data by calculating the average of the squared deviations from the mean. A larger variance indicates more dispersed data, while a smaller variance means data points are closer to the mean. There are five main steps for finding the variance as follows:

Finding Variance:

Step 1:
To find the mean, add up all the scores, then divide them by the number of scores.
$\bar{x} => (46 + 69 + 32 + 60 + 52 + 41) / 6$
$\bar{x} => 50$

Step 2: Find each score's deviation from the mean, then subtract the mean from each score to get the deviations from the mean.
Since $\bar{x} = 50$, take away 50 from each score.

Score	Deviation from the mean
46	46 − 50 = -4
69	69 − 50 = 19
32	32 − 50 = -18
60	60 − 50 = 10
52	52 − 50 = 2
41	41 − 50 = -9

Step 3: Square each deviation from the mean. This ensures all values are positive, preventing negative differences from cancelling out.

$=> (-4)^2 => -4 \times -4 => 16$
$=> (19)^2 => 19 \times 19 => 361$
$=> (-18)^2 => -18 \times -18 => 324$
$=> (10)^2 => 10 \times 10 => 100$
$=> (2)^2 => 2 \times 2 => 4$
$=> (-9)^2 => -9 \times -9 => 81$

Step 4: Find the sum of squares. Add up all of the squared deviations. This is called the sum of squares.
Sum of squares: 16 + 361 + 324 + 100 + 4 + 81 = 886

Step 5: Divide the sum of squares by n−1, where n=6.

Variance:
$=> 886/(6−1)$
$=> 886/5$
$=> 177.2$

Basics of Boolean Algebra and Logic Gates:

Boolean algebra is a branch of algebra that deals with binary variables and logical operations. It's fundamental in digital electronics, computer science, and mathematical logic. Boolean algebra is named after George Boole, who introduced it in 1847. This algebraic system uses only two values:

0 (False)

1 (True)

Boolean algebra forms the basis of **Logic Gates**. Logic gates are the physical components that implement Boolean logic in digital circuits. They take one or more binary inputs and produce a single binary output logic gate, which is the electronic circuit in a digital system.

Boolean Operations:

AND (·) — Output is True, i.e. 1, if both inputs are True, i.e. 1.

Boolean expression: $A{\cdot}B$ or $A{\wedge}B$

Truth Table:

A	B	A AND B
0	0	0
0	1	0
1	0	0
1	1	1

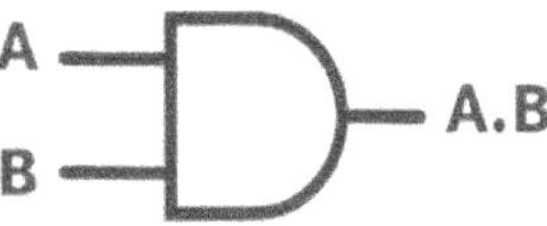

OR (+) — Output is True, i.e. 1, if at least one input is True, i.e. 1.

Boolean expression: A+B or $A{\vee}B$

Truth Table:

A	B	A OR B
0	0	0
0	1	1
1	0	1
1	1	1

NOT (') — Inverts the value, i.e. True becomes False, and vice versa.

Boolean expression: A' or $\bar{A}$

Truth Table:

A	NOT A
0	1
1	0

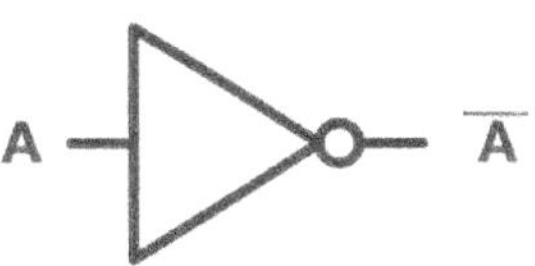

NAND (NOT AND): It gives output False, i.e. 0, only when both inputs are True, i.e. 1. It is the negation or complement of the AND operation.

Boolean expression: $A \uparrow B$ or $\overline{A \cdot B}$

Example: If A=1 and B=0, A↑B=1.

Truth Table:

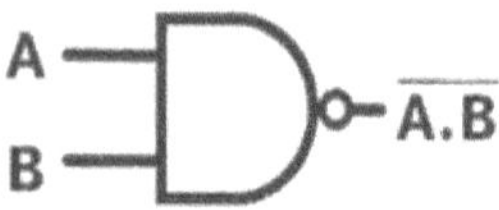

A	B	A AND B	A NAND B
0	0	0	1
0	1	0	1
1	0	0	1
1	1	1	0

NOR (NOT OR): Output True (1) only when both inputs are False (0).

Boolean Expression: $A \downarrow B$ or $\overline{A + B}$ or A↓B=¬(AVB)

Truth Table:

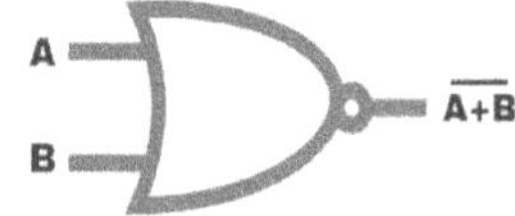

A	B	A OR B	A NOR B
0	0	0	1
0	1	1	0
1	0	1	0
1	1	1	0

Example: If A=0 and B=0, A↓B=1.

XOR (Exclusive OR): This gives the outputs True (1), otherwise False (0)

Boolean expression: A.B+$\bar{A}.\bar{B}$ or Y=A⊕B

Truth Table:

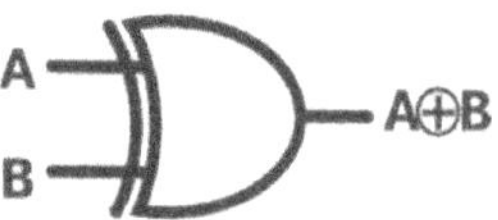

A	B	Y
0	0	0
0	1	1
1	0	1
1	1	0

Exclusive-NOR Gate (XNOR Gate):

The output is True, i.e. 1 when both inputs are the same, and False, i.e. 0 when they are different.

Boolean expression: A⊕B=A.$\bar{B}$+$\bar{A}$.B Or A⊕B=(A·B)+(A·B)

Truth table:

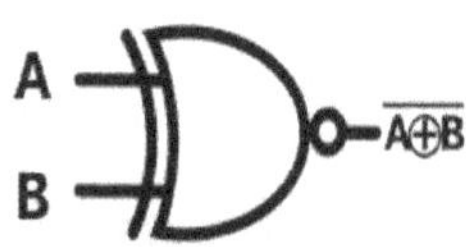

A	B	Y
0	0	1
0	1	0
1	0	0
1	1	1

Chapter 3

Programming with Python

Chapter Objective:

- Introduction
- Why programming with Python
- Uses of Python
- Installation of Python
- Understanding Data Types
- Operators
- Comments
- Indentation
- Errors in Programming
- Type Conversion
- Types of Programming
- Break & Continue

Introduction:

The Python language was developed by Guido van Rossum and released in 1991 with version 0.9.0. It is used for: Web development on the server side, Software development, Advanced Mathematical operations, System scripting, etc. Due to its simple and readable syntax and efficiency, Python is widely used and has gained popularity over many other languages.

Why programming with Python:

- **Easy to learn** - Python has a very simple and elegant syntax. It's much easier to read and write Python programs compared to other languages like C++, Java, C#, etc.
- **Free and open-source** - One can freely use and distribute Python, even for commercial use.
- **Portable** - One can move Python programs from one platform to another, such as Windows, Mac, Linux, Raspberry Pi, etc., and run them without any modification.
- **Excellent Interpreter** - Python runs on an interpreter system, executing code line by line, which makes development and debugging easier. However, interpreted languages are generally slower than compiled languages like C or Java.
- **Reliable, Efficient and Accessible** - Python is made for web development, desktop applications, mobile applications, hardware, and more with less effort and less coding. Python is truly easy to learn and user-friendly. It's one of the most accessible programming languages presently available.

Uses of Python:

- AI and machine learning
- Data Analytics
- Data visualisation
- Programming applications
- Web development
- Game development
- Language development
- Finance
- Search Engine Optimisation (SEO).
- Graphic Design

Installation and Execution of Python:

One may download and install a suitable Python compiler from:
https://www.python.org/downloads

After installation, a Python development environment is created. Its name is an acronym for "Integrated Development Environment" (IDLE). It has a Python shell window, which provides access to the Python interactive mode on **>>>** prompt called 'Shell'. It also has a file editor that lets one create and edit existing Python source code files, which saves the file in **.py** extension.

Token: The building block of a programming language, such as keywords, identifiers, literals, operators, and symbols

Variable/Identifire: This holds values and gets stored in the memory.

DataType: Data has various types, such as:

- Numeric Types: int, float, complex
- Sequence Types: str, list, tuple, range
- Mapping Type: dict
- Boolean Type: bool (True/False)
- Set Types: set, frozenset
- Binary Type: bytes, byte-array, memory-view
- None Type: Null

Operators:
- Mathematical: + , - , * , / , // , % , **
- Relational: > , < , >= , <= , == , !=   ⎫
- Logical and, or, not   ⎭ **TRUE/FALSE**

Keywords: These reserved words have a specific role in programming, so they can't be taken as a variable.

Rules for Python variables:
- A variable name must <u>start with a letter</u> or the <u>underscore</u> character.
- A variable name <u>can't</u> start with a <u>number</u>.
- A variable <u>can only</u> contain alpha-numeric characters and underscores (A-Z, a-z, 0-9, & _)
- Variables are case-sensitive (i.e. name, Name, and NAME are three different variables)

Understanding Data Types:

The type of data or value that a variable has is called a Data Type.

```
x =10                          # int or Integer Data Type
z=199.90                       # float or Float Data Type
y = "World United States"      # str or String Data Type
k=True                         # bool or Boolean Data Type
a = [1, 2, 3]                  # list
b = (4, 5, 6)                  # tuple
c = {"key": "value"}           # dict
d = {7, 8, 9}                  # set
f = None                       # NoneType
```

Integers:

In Python, there is effectively no limit to the length of an integer value; the length of an integer can be as long as one needs, i.e. **int**

Example: x=10

int is a whole number, positive or negative, without decimals, of unlimited length.

```
x = 1
y = 35656222554887711
z = -3255522
print(type(x))         # <class 'int'>
print(type(y))         # <class 'int'>
print(type(z))         # <class 'int'>
```

Floating-Point Numbers:

The float type in Python designates a floating-point number. **Float** values are specified with a decimal point.

```
z=199.90
y=1.0
x=-35.59
print(type(x))         # <class 'float'>
print(type(y))         # <class 'float'>
print(type(z))         # <class 'float'>
```

Sequence: *str*

Strings are sequences of character (alphanumeric) data. The string type in Python is called **str**.

Example: y = "The World United States 4K295X"

Sequence: *list*
Example: Ordered, mutable items: *[1, 2, 3], ["a", "b", "c"]*

Sequence: *tuple*
Example: Ordered, immutable items: *(1, 2, 3), ("x", "y", "z")*

Sequence: *range*
Example: A sequence of numbers, used in loops: *for i in range(5):*

Mapping: *dict*
Example: Key-value pairs of a dictionary: *{"name": "Alice", "age": 25}*

Boolean Type: *Ture* or *False*
Python 3 provides a Boolean data type. Objects of Boolean type may have one of two values, True or False: ***bool.***

```
Example:
x=True
print(x)
print(type(x))
```

Output:
```
True
<class 'bool'>
```

Operators: There are three types: Arithmetical, Relational, Logical

Arithmetical Operators where a=7, b=23

+   **Addition** - adds values on either side of the operator: **a + b = 30**

-   **Subtraction** - subtracts right-hand operand from left-hand operand: **a − b = -16**

*   **Multiplication**, multiplies values on either side of the operator: **a * b = 161**

/   **Division** - divides left-hand operand by right-hand operand and gives decimal quotient: **b/a=3.285714**

//   **Floor Division** - The division of operands where the result is the quotient, in which the digits after the decimal point are removed, i.e. non decimal. But if one of the operands is negative, the result is floored, i.e. rounded from zero (towards −ve infinity): **b//a=3**

%   **Modulus** - divides left-hand operand by right-hand operand and returns remainder: **b % a = 2**

**   **Exponent** - performs exponential (power) calculation on the operator: **5**3 = 125** *(5 to the power 3, equals 125)*

Relational Operator:

== If the values of two operands are equal, then the condition becomes true; else (a==b) is not true.

!= If the values of two operands are not equal, then the condition becomes true; else (a!= b) is true.

\> If the value of the left operand is greater than the value of the right operand, then the condition becomes true; else (a > b) is not true.

< If the value of the left operand is less than the value of the right operand, then the condition becomes true, i.e. (a < b) is true.

\>= If the value of the left operand is greater than or equal to the value of the right, then the condition becomes true, i.e. (a >= b) is true.

<= If the value of the left operand is less than or equal to the value of the right, then the condition becomes true, i.e. (a <= b) is true.

Logical Operator Description Example:

and Returns True if both statements are true x < 5 and x < 10

or Returns True if one of the statements is true: x < 5 or x < 4

not Reverse the result, returns False if the result is True, not(x < 5 and x < 10)

Rules of Logical Operators		
	TRUE	**FALSE**
and	Both of the conditions are TRUE	Any one of the conditions is FALSE
or	Any one of the cond. Is TRUE	All of the cond. are FALSE
not	Cond. is FALSE	Cond. is TRUE

 # Uses of logical & relational operators:

Assuming x=10, y=5, z=20, then let's find the output of the statement:
not (((x>=y) or (x==z)) and ((z>=x) and (y<x)))
not ((T   or   F) and (T   and   T))
not (T   and   T)
not (T)
F

Mathematical Operators:

```
x=5, y=17
s1=x+y        # 22
s2=y-x        # 12
s3=x*y        # 85
s4=y/x        # 3.4    (Float)
s5=y // x     # 3      (Integer)
s6=y%x        # 2      (Reminder)
s7=3**2       # 9      (To the power)
```

Python first code (in shell):

```
>>> print("Hello, Be blessed!")
```

Output:
Hello, Be blessed!

> **Note:** *Python code gets saved in **.py** file & it runs on the shell (>>>)*

Comments:

Python has a commenting capability for in-code documentation. For **a single-line comment**, it starts with # (hash) and the Python interpreter ignores the line following the hash (**#**), for example:

```
print("Hello, World!")   # This is a comment, which doesn't affect the code.
```

For **multiple-line comments**, it starts with ''' (triple quotes) before the code line and also ends with ''' after the code line, for example:

```
'''
print("Welcome to learn Python")
print("Let's begin")

'''
```

Output:
Hello, World!

Taking input value from a user:

Example:
x=int(input ("Enter your age: "))

The variable x stores the user-inputted value in memory. The = operator assigns this value to x. The **int** type-casting converts the input (received as a string) into an integer. The **input()** function allows the user to enter a value, and any text within quotes inside input() is displayed as a prompt on the screen as a user interface.

Indentation in Python: *A very important factor*

Indentation refers to the spaces (a tab) at the beginning of a code line. In Python, it is very important to indicate a block of code.

Example:

if (5 > 2)**:**

        print("Five is greater than two!")

> **Note:** *After any condition followed by : (colon), the next line of the statement will begin within four blank/white spaces or a tab stroke.*

Following is a <u>Syntax Error</u> for the wrong indentation:

if (5 > 2):

print("Five is greater than two!")

> **Note:** *Here print function began with NO indentation (tab or 4 blank spaces) and it gives a syntax error.*

Example (with correct syntax):

if (5 > 2):
->->->->print("Five is greater than two!")   *# There is an **indent** (a tab->)*

Errors in Programming:

Beginners make coding mistakes due to inexperience, while experienced programmers may err due to carelessness or flawed logic. These errors fall into three categories: Syntax errors, Run-time errors, and Logic errors.

Syntax Errors:

The Python interpreter executes valid programs by translating source code into machine code. If it encounters an invalid program, it reports a syntax error, which is similar to a grammatical mistake in English. Similarly, the Python statement **a=b+5** is syntactically correct because it obeys the rules for the structure. Consider replacing this assignment statement with a slightly modified version: **b+5=a**

If a statement like this is a grammatical mistake in a program, the interpreter can't understand it, and it raises an error message.

Run-time Errors:

A syntactically correct program still can have problems. Some errors depend on the execution; such errors are called **run-time errors** or exceptions. The interpreter may raise an error, which is a run-time error. For example:

```
a=0
a=y+5
print(a)
```

Here, variable y has not been assigned; the compiler will inform us as an error message: *name 'y' is not defined.*

Logical Errors:

The interpreter detects syntax and runtime errors, while the compiler catches syntax errors but not logic errors, which only become apparent through incorrect output or behaviour.

A **logical error** happens when a program runs without crashing but gives the wrong result. If we accidentally swap the **divisor** with the **dividend**, the program won't show an error, but the output will be incorrect, except when both values are the same. The interpreter can't catch this mistake because the code is syntactically correct, but the logic is flawed, as:

```
c=10 , d=3
s=d/c
print(s)
```

Type Conversion: *One datatype to another datatype*

You can convert from one type to another with the int(), float(), and complex() methods:

Example: Conversion of data type

```
x = 5            # int
y = 2.8          # float

# Convert from int to float:
a = float(x)

# Convert from float to int:
b = int(y)
print(a)                 # Prints 5.0
print(b)                 # Prints 2
print(type(a))           # Prints class float
print(type(b))           # Prints class int
```

Output:
5.0
2
<class 'float'>
<class 'int'>

 # Convert string-to-int:
int("10")   *# gives 10*

> **Note:** *int("10a") would raise an error, as it has mixed characters.*

Triple Quotes (Printing multiple lines):

If we need to display a long message, we can use the triple-quote symbol ("'' '''" or """ """) to span our message over multiple lines. This helps to increase the readability of a message.

For example:
print ('''Hello World.
Let's unite for Global peace.''')
Output:
Hello World.
Let's unite for Global peace.

Types of Programming:

There are two ways to run a program using the Python interpreters: (i) Interactive mode and (ii) Script mode:

- **Interactive mode:** In the interactive mode, the Python code is written on the **>>>** prompt directly, and by pressing enter, the interpreter executes the statement and prints the result(s).

- **Script mode:** In the script mode, the Python program is written in a file, then saved, and then used as an interpreter to execute the program from the file. Such program files have a .py extension, and they are also known as scripts.

Again, the programming is divided into three types:

Simple Flow of Data	Branching/Cond.	Looping
Input->Processing->Output	if():	for():
	if():...... else:	while():
	if():.......elif():.... else:	

Programming of Simple Flow of Data:

 # WAP to get the sum of 2 integers:

```
x=10
y=20
s=0                       # Optional
s=x+y                     # s is dynamically assigned
print("SUM=>", s)
```

Output:

```
SUM=> 30
```

 # WAP to find the Simple Interest:

```
si=0
p=int(input("ENTER PRINCIPAL=>"))
r=int(input("ENTER RATE=>"))
t=int(input("ENTER TIME=>"))
si=(p*r*t)/100
print()                   # Prints a blank line
print("SI=>", si)
```

Output:

```
ENTER PRINCIPAL=> 500
ENTER RATE=> 5
ENTER TIME=> 6

SI=> 150.0
```

 # WAP to swap 2 integers using 3rd variable:

```
z=0
x=int(input("ENTER no1=>"))
y=int(input("ENTER No2=>"))
z=x
x=y
y=z
print(" ")                # Prints an empty string followed by a new line
print("1st val after swapping=>",x)
print("2nd val after swapping=>",y)
```

Output:

```
ENTER no1=> 5
ENTER No2=> 7
1st val after swapping=> 7
2nd val after swapping=> 5
```

x	y	z
5	7	0
5	7	5
7	7	5
7	5	5

 # WAP to swap 2 integers, Not using 3rd variable:

```
x=int(input("ENTER no1=>"))          # 10
y=int(input("ENTER No2=>"))          # 20
x=x+y
y=x-y
x=x-y
print("1st val after swapping=>",x)
print("2nd val after swapping=>",y)
```

x	y
10	**20**
30	20
30	10
20	**10**

Output:

```
ENTER no1=> 10
ENTER No2=> 20
1st val after swapping=> 20
2nd val after swapping=>10
```

Programming of Branching:

 # WAP to enter age and show the eligibility to cast a vote (Using if)

```
age=0
age=int(input("Enter Age=> "))
if (age>=18):           # Here colon (:) is used after every cond. for a block
        print("Eligible to cast Vote")
```

Output:

```
Enter Age=> 19
Eligible to cast a Vote
```

 # Enter an age & show the eligibility to cast a vote (Using if…. else)

```
age=0                   # Optional
age=int(input("Enter Age=>"))
if (age>=18):           # after a condition: (colon) is a MUST
        print("Eligible") # after condition INDENT (Tab) is a MUST
else:
        print("NOT Eligible")
```

Output:

```
Enter Age=> 17
NOT Eligible
```

 # WAP to enter 2 nos and find the greater one:

```
x=int(input("ENTER no1=>"))
y=int(input("ENTER No2=>"))
print("")        # To insert a line space (blank row)
if (x>y):
        print("Greater No=>", x)
else:            # after any condition: (colon) should be given
        print("Greater No=>", y)
```

Output:
ENTER no1=> 7
ENTER No2=> 8
Greater No=> 8

 # WAP to enter 3 numbers and find the greatest one

```
grt=0
x=int(input("ENTER no1=>"))
y=int(input("ENTER No2=>"))
z=int(input("ENTER No3=>"))
print()                     # To insert a line space (blank row)
if (x>y):                   # After a condition: (colon) is given
     grt=x
else:                       # After last condition: (colon) is given
     grt=y
if (grt>z):
     print("The greatest is=>", grt)
else:
     print("The greatest is=>", z)
```

Output:

ENTER no1=> 5
ENTER No2=> 6
ENTER No3=> 8

The greatest is=> 8

 # WAP to enter the Average marks and print the Grade

```
grd=' '
av=float(input("ENTER Average=> "))
if (av>=80 and av<=100):      # First condition starts with if()
     grd='A'
elif (av>=60 and av<80):      # Second condition starts with elif()
     grd='B'
elif (av>=40 and av<60):      # Third condition starts with elif()
     grd='C'
else:                         # After all conditions else
     grd='D'
print("")
print("The Grade is=>", grd)
```

Avg	Grd
100-80	A
79-60	B
40-59	C
39-0	D

Output:
ENTER Average=> 60.4
The Grade is=> B

Definition and usage of *range()* function:

The **range()** function returns a sequence of numbers, starting from 0 by default, increments by 1 (by default), and stops before a specified number, i.e., the last value is n-1. Syntax: ***range(start, stop, step)***

Parameters of range() function:

Parameter	Description
Start (Optional)	An integer number specifying at which position to start. Default is 0
Stop (Required)	An integer number specifying at which position to stop (not included).
Step (Optional)	An integer number specifies the increment or decrement. Default is 1

Programming of Looping:

 # WAP to display 1st 3 integers

```python
c=1
while (c<=3):          # Colon (:) should be given after condition
      print(c)
      c=c+1            # or c+=1
```

Output:
```
1
2
3
```

 # WAP to print your name 3 times:

```python
n=input("Enter your name=> ")
for i in range(0,3,1):    # range() function is explained below
      print(n)
```

Output:
```
Enter your name=> Srijit Roy

Srijit Roy
Srijit Roy
Srijit Roy
```

 # WAP to display 1 to 5 using the range() function:

```python
for x in range(1,6,1):  # range(StVal , MaxVal , increment) function
      print(x)
```

Output:
```
1
2
```

3
4
5

WAP to display natural numbers up to 5 using range() function:

```
for n in range(6):       # range(StVal, MaxVal, increment) is function
        print(n)
```

Output:
0
1
2
3
4
5

> **Note:**
> - *By default starting value of range() fn. is 0*
> - *By default increments in range() fn. by 1*
> - *The last value generated in range() fn. is **MaxVal-1***

WAP to display the odd integers up to integer 10:

```
for x in range(1,10,2):  # range(StVal, MaxVal, increment) is function
        print(x)
```

Output:
1
3
5
7
9

WAP to display all the even integers up to 10

```
for x in range(2,10,2):  # range(StVal, MaxVal, increment) is function
        print(x)
```

Output:
2
4
6
8

WAP to display all the integers up to integer 10, incremented by 3

```
for x in range(1,10,3):  # range(StVal, MaxVal, increment) is function
        print(x)
```

Output:
1
4
7

WAP to display the first 10 even numbers using the range() function

```
for x in range(2,21,2):  # range(StVal, MaxVal, increment) is function
        print(x)
```

Output:
```
2
4
6
8
10
12
14
16
18
20
```

 # WAP to find the sum of 10 even numbers using range() function.
```python
e=2
s=0
for i in range(0,10,1):
      s=s+e
      e=e+2
print("SUM=>", s)              # Out of the block, runs once
```

Output:
```
SUM=> 110
```

 # WAP to find the factorial of N
```python
f=1
n=int(input("Enter a No=>"))
for i in range(1,n+1,1):
      f=f*i
print("Factorial=>", f)
```

Output:
```
Enter a No=> 5
Factorial=> 120
```

 # WAP to find the factorial of a number using while() loop
```python
f=1
i=1
n=int(input("Enter a No=>"))
while (i<=n):                  # 5!=1X2X3X4x5
      f=f*i
      i=i+1                    # i+=1
print("Factorial=>", f)
```

Output:
```
Enter a No=> 5
Factorial=> 120
```

WAP to find the factorial of a number, as 5! =5x4x3x2x1

```
f=1
n=int(input("Enter a No=> "))  # 5
for i in range(n, 0, -1):
        f=f*i
print("Facto=>", f)
```

Output:
```
Enter a No=> 5
Facto=> 120
```

WAP to show the table of a given number

```
p=0
i=1
n=int(input("Enter a No=>"))   # 5
while (i<=10):
        p=n*i
        print(n , "X" , i , "=" , p)
        i=i+1                       # or i+=1
```

Output:
```
Enter a No=> 5
5 X 1 = 5
5 X 2 = 10
5 X 3 = 15
5 X 4 = 20
5 X 5 = 25
5 X 6 = 30
5 X 7 = 35
5 X 8 = 40
5 X 9 = 45
5 X 10 = 50
```

WAP to find: S=1 + 4 + 9 + 16 + ... Nth term.

```
s=0
n=int(input("Enter Term=>"))  # Say  5
for i in range(1, n+1, 1):
        s=s+(i**2)
print("SUM=>", s)
```

Output:
```
Enter Term=> 5
SUM=> 55
```

WAP to find s=1/2 + 2/3 + 4/5 .....nth term

```
s = 0
n=int(input("Enter number: "))
for i in range(1, n+1):
        s=s+(i/(i+1))
print("Sum: ", s)
```

Output:
Enter number: 5
Sum: 3.5500000000000003

 # WAP to find s= 1 + 4 + 27 + 256 + ...nth term
```
s = 0
n=int(input("Enter number: "))
for i in range(1, n+1):
        s += i**i
print("Sum: ", s)
```

Output:
Enter number: 5
Sum: 3413

 # WAP to find s=(1) + (1+2) + (1+2+3) + ... nth term
```
sum=0
c=1
n=int(input("Enter number: "))
while(c<=n):
        s=0
        k=1
        while(k<=c):
                s=s+k
                k=k+1
        sum=sum+s
        c=c+1
print("Sum: ", sum)
```

Output:
Enter number: 5
Sum: 35

 # WAP to find s= 1! + 2! + 3! + 4! + ...nth term
```
sum=0
c=1
n=int(input("Enter number: "))
while(c<=n):
        f=1             # f is initilised by 1 before entering the loop
        k=1             # k is initilised by 1 before entering the loop
        while(k<=c):
                f=f*k
                k=k+1
        sum=sum+f
        c=c+1
 print("Sum: ", sum)
```

Output:
Enter number: 5
Sum: 153

 # Enter a number, and check if the number is prime or not
```
k=0
c=1
n=int(input("Enter a number: "))
while(c<=n):
      if(n%c==0):
                 k=k+1               # Counts the times of exactly divisible
      c=c+1
if(k==2):                           # Checks whether it is divided 2 times
     print("Number %d is Prime" %n)
else:
     print("Number %d is not Prime" %n)
```
Output:
Enter a number: 5
Number 5 is Prime

 # Enter a number, reverse it and check if it is* a *Palindrome or not
```
rem=0
rev=0
no=int(input("Enter a number: "))
n=no                        # Original number no is copied to n
while(no!=0):               # Run the loop unless no becomes 0
      rem=no%10             # Finds the reminder
      rev=(rev*10)+rem      # Calculating reverse
      no=no//10             # Finds the quotient
print("The reverse of the no %d is :" %n, rev)

if (n==rev):
     print("The number %d is a Palindrome" %n)
else:
     print("The number %d is not a Palindrome" %n)
```
Output:
Enter a number: 1234
The reverse of the no 1234 is: 4321
The number 1234 is not a Palindrome

 # WAP to find s=1+1+2+3+5+8+13. . . . . nth term:
```
t1=1
t2=1
s=t1+t2
n=int(input("Enter term: "))
```

```
for i in range(1,n-1,1):        # while(c<=n-2)
        t3=t1+t2
        s=s+t3
        t1=t2
        t2=t3
print("Sum:", s)
```

Output:
Enter term: 5
Sum: 12

Write Programs to Display Patterns (using a loop):

Output	Program

*
*
*
	```c=1```
	```while (c<=3):```
	``` print("*")```
	``` c=c+1```

* * *	```c=1```
	```while (c<=3):```
	``` print("*" , end=" ")```
	``` c=c+1```
	# end=" " *means <u>no new line</u>, prints in the same row*

* * *
* * *
* * *
	```n=1```
	```while (n<=3):```
	``` c=1```
	``` while (c<=3):```
	``` print("*" , end=" ")```
	``` c=c+1```
	``` print("\n")```
	``` n=n+1```
	
	Note: *"\n" Gives a new line or line-break, but '\n' within print() fnc. prints double new lines, because print() also prints a blank line.*

``
*
* *
* * *
``
	``python
	c=1
	while (c<=3):
	        n=1
	        while (n<=c):
	            print("*", end=" ") # No of elements per row
	            n=n+1
	        print("\n") # New line
	        c=c+1
	``

```python
y=1     # for *
x=2     # for " "
c=1     # for row
while (c<=3):
  n1=1
  while (n1<=x):
        print(" ", end=" ")
        n1=n1+1
  n2=1
  while(n2<=y):
        print("*", end=" ")
        n2=n2+1
  print("\n")
  x=x-1
  y=y+1
  c=c+1
```

> **Note:** In the outer loop (3), 2 more loops are running for printing spaces & stars simultaneously, where the no of spaces is decreasing by 1 & the no of stars is increasing by 1.

```
" " *
" * *
* * *
```

```python
y=1             # Using for loop
x=2
c=1
for k in range(c , 4, 1):
    n1=1
    for i in range(n1 , x+1, 1):
        print(" ", end=" ")
    n2=1
    for j in range(n2 , y+1, 1):   # As y-1 is last value so +1
        print("*", end=" ")
    print("\n")
    c=c+1
    x=x-1
    y=y+1
```

<pre>   *
  ***
*****</pre>
	``python
	y=1
	x=2
	c=1
	while c<=3:
	  n1=1
	  while (n1<=x):
	        print(" ", end=" ")
	        n1=n1+1
	  n2=1
	      while (n2<=y):
	            print("*", end=" ")
	            n2=n2+1
	 print("\n")
	 c=c+1
	 x=x-1
	 y=y+2
	``
	
	Note: *Here outer loop is running as it is, but to print spaces no of spaces is decreasing by 1 & for stars (*) no is increasing by 2.*

<pre>1
12
123</pre>
	``python
	c=1
	while (c<=3):
	      n=1
	      while (n<=c):
	            print(n , end=' ')
	            n=n+1
	      print('\n')
	      c=c+1
	``

<pre>1
12
123</pre>
	``python
	y=1
	x=2
	c=1
	while (c<=3):
	      n1=1
	      n2=1
	      while (n1<=x):
	            print(" ", end="")
	            n1=n1+1
	      while(n2<=y):
	            print(n2, end="")
	            n2=n2+1
	      print('\n')
	      x=x-1
	      y=y+1
	      c=c+1
	``

<table>
<tr><td>

1
22
333

</td><td>

```python
y=1
x=2
c=1
while (c<=3):
        n1=1
        n2=1
        while (n1<=x):
                print(" ", end="")
                n1=n1+1
        while(n2<=y):
                print(c, end="")
                n2=n2+1
        print('\n')
        x=x-1
        y=y+1
        c=c+1
```

</td></tr>
<tr><td>

Row1 Sum: 1
Row2 Sum: 3
Row3 Sum: 6

</td><td>

```python
c=1
while (c<=3):
        n=1
        s=0
        while (n<=c):
                s=s+n
                n=n+1
        print('Row%d Sum:' %c, s)
        c=c+1
```

</td></tr>
</table>

Break and **Continue:**

<table>
<tr><td>

Note: *Break terminates the immediate innermost loop/block, and **Continue** returns the counter to the condition.*

 # Break
```python
for i in range(1, 10, 2):
    if (i==7):
        break   # Terminates loop
    else:
        print(i)
```
Output:
```
1
3
5
```

</td><td>

 # Continue
```python
for var in range(5):
    if(var==2):
        print("Before Continue...")
        continue    # Jumps to range()
    print("Current value: ", var)
    # The above print() is part of the loop
```
Output:
Current value : 0
Current value: 1
Before Continue...
Current value: 3
Current value: 4

</td></tr>
</table>

Chapter 4

String

and

Tuple

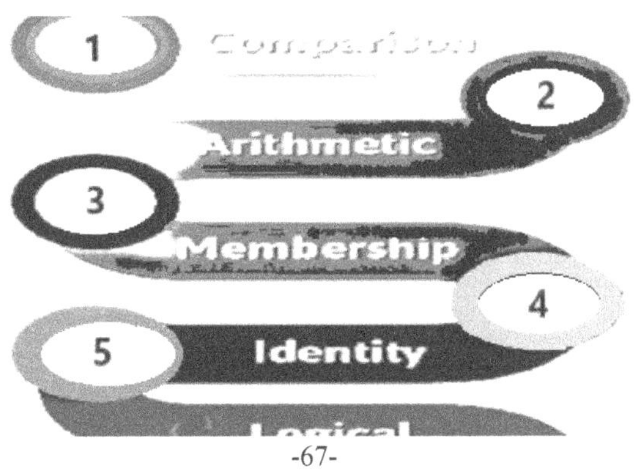

Chapter Objective:

- String as Defined
- Accessing elements of String
- Traversing of String
- Tuple as Defined
- Accessing elements of Tuple
- Traversing of Tuple
- Conversion in Tuple

String

String as Defined:

A String is a collection of characters that works as an array. It is immutable, i.e. once it is created, it can't be modified, but a new one can be created. The String is kept within single or double quotes and can be accessed by the index with square brackets. For example:

x="IndoAryan"

0	1	2	3	4	5	6	7	8
I	n	d	o	A	r	y	a	n
-9	-8	-7	-6	-5	-4	-3	-2	-1

index (+ve) / *index (-ve)*

```
x="IndoAryan"
print(x[0])
print(x[5])
print(x[-4])
print(x[-5])
print(x[0 : 4])   # To get a substring from the starting index up to (last index - 1)
print(x[-9:-5])   # The output is from (starting-index i.e., -9) to (lastindex-1, i.e.-5 -1)
print(x[4 : ])    # Prints value of St. index up to the last character
print(x[-5: ])    # Prints value of St. index up to the last character, prints the same
```

Output:
```
I
r
r
A
Indo
Indo
Aryan
Aryan
```

Formatted String Literals (f-strings):

```
user="Rohan"
item=3
tot= 45.60
res=f"User {user} purchased {item} items for ${tot:.2f}"
print(res)      # Variable is put within {} & .2f decimal values
```

Output:
```
User Rohan purchased 3 items for $45.60
```

Traversing of String:

```
x="IndoAryan"
for i in x:
        print(i)
```
Output:
```
I
n
d
o
A
r
y
a
n
```

String	Output
s="IndoAryan"	
print(s[4])	A
print(s[-5])	A
print(s[3])	o
print(s[-3])	y
print(s[0:4])	Indo
print(s[-9:-5])	Indo
print(s[4:])	Aryan
print(s[:4])	Indo
print(s[:-1])	IndoArya
print(s[:])	IndoAryan
print(s[4:])	Aryan
print(s[4:8])	Arya
print(s[-5:-1])	Arya
print(s[4:-1])	Arya
print(s[-5:8])	Arya

 # Write a program to print the First name only of the full name
```
n=input("Enter your name=> ")
for i in range(len(n)):
        if(n[i] != " "):              # Checks the space after First name
                print(n[i], end="")
        else:
                break
```

Output:
```
Enter your name=>  Sridhar Kumar Pandey
Sridhar
```

 # Program to apply split() function to convert String into List
```
x="Indo Aryan Existentialism"
y=x.split()                     # Splits a string into a list of words
print(y)
```

Output:
```
['Indo', 'Aryan', 'Existentialism']
```

Tuple

Tuple as Defined:

A tuple is an ordered, immutable collection and is faster than lists and can hold multiple items of various data types. However, since it is immutable, we can't make any changes to the Tuple. We create a tuple within round brackets **()** to declare multiple values, which are separated by a comma. For example: week = **(**"Sunday", "Monday", "Tuesday", "Wednesday", "Thursday", "Friday", "Saturday"**)**

We can access the individual values of a tuple using their indices. There are +ve and –ve indexes as we discussed in String.

Values of **+ve** indexes	Values of **-ve** indexes
week[0]="Sunday"	week[-7]="Sunday"
week[1]="Monday"	week[-6]="Monday"
week[2]="Tuesday"	week[-5]="Tuesday"
week[3]="Wednesday"	week[-4]="Wednesday"
week[4]="Thursday"	week[-3]="Thursday"
week[5]="Friday"	week[-2]="Friday"
week[6]="Saturday"	week[-1]="Saturday"

Access elements of Tuple:

week = ("Sunday", "Monday", "Tuesday", "Wednesday", "Thursday", "Friday", "Saturday")
print(week[5])
Output: Friday
print(week[-2])
Output: Friday
print(week[1:4])
 # Prints values from indexes 1 to 3 (i.e. 4-1)
Output: ('Monday', 'Tuesday', 'Wednesday')
print(week[-5:-2])
 # Prints values of the indexes from -4 to (-2-1), i.e. -4 to -3
Output: ('Tuesday', 'Wednesday', 'Thursday')

Traversing of Tuple:

for i in week:
    print(i)
	x=(123, 456, 60.65, 88.89, "Mon", "Tue")
	 for i in range(len(x)):
	    print(x[i])

Output:	Output:
Sunday	123
Monday	456
Tuesday	60.65
Wednesday	88.89
Thursday	Mon
Friday	Tue
Saturday	*# len() fn. counts the no of elements in obj*

Conversion of String & List into Tuple:

```
T1=()
print("Empty Tuple: ")
print(T1)

# Converting a string into a tuple
T2=("IndoAryan", "Existentialism")
print("\nTuple from String: ")
print(T2)

# Use of built-in function
T3 = tuple('IndoAryan')
print("\nTuple from Function: ")
print(T3)

# Converting a list into a tuple
L = [10, 20, 30, 40, 50, 60]
print("\nTuple from List: ")
print(tuple(L))
```

Output:

Empty Tuple:
()

Tuple from String:
('IndoAryan', 'Existentialism')

Tuple from Function:
('I', 'n', 'd', 'o', 'A', 'r', 'y', 'a', 'n')

Tuple form List:
(10, 20, 30, 40, 50, 60)

> **Note:**
>
> ***Difference between String & Tuple:***
>
> ***String:*** *It is designed to represent sequences of characters, forming textual data.*
>
> ***Tuple:*** *It holds elements of any data type, including integers, floats, strings, other tuples and lists.*

Chapter 5

List

0	1	2	3	4	+ve index
22	23	24	21	25	*List of data*
-5	-4	-3	-2	-1	-ve index

Chapter Objective:

- List as Defined
- Accessing and Slicing data
- Searching element
- Sorting elements
- Two-Dimensional (2-D) Array of List
- Applications of Lists in Programming
- Built-In Functions

List as Defined:

List holds the list of values or a single-dimensional (1-D) Array of values of various data-types (heterogeneous data), and is put into square brackets ([ ]). The list is mutable (update existing data).

```
y=[ ]                  # Empty list
x=["Sudhir",  11, "A", 20, 96.98]        # List of heterogeneous data
temp=[22, 23, 24, 21, 25]                # List of numbers
lst1=[10, 12, 14, 16]
```

0	1	2	3	4	+ve index
22	23	24	21	25	List of elements
-5	-4	-3	-2	-1	-ve index
1234	3323	4532	2334	5432	memory address of data

```
print(temp[1])      # Output: 23
print(temp[-4])     # Output: 23
```

Example:

```
L=[10,30,20]
for item in L:
      print(f"Element: {item}, Memory Address: {id(item)}")
```

Output:

```
Element: 10, Memory Address: 140655596077584
Element: 30, Memory Address: 140655596078224
Element: 20, Memory Address: 140655596077904
```

> **Note:** *To get Memory Address of each element we can use **id()***

```
# Slicing: list[start:end] (end is exclusive)
print(temp[1:4])        # Output: [23, 24, 21]
print(temp[-4:])        # Output: [23, 24, 21, 25]
print(temp[1:])         # Output: [23, 24, 21, 25]
print(temp[:3])         # Output: [22, 23, 24]
print(temp[:])          # Output: [22, 23, 24, 21, 25]
```

> **Note:** *Slicing a list with [start : end] returns elements from start to end-1. Omitting start defaults to 0, and omitting end includes all elements till the end. So, while taking range (n1: n2) of values returns the value of 1st index to last index minus 1*

```
# Step slicing: list[start : end : step]
print(temp[0:4:2])      # Output: [22, 24]
print(temp[0::2])       # Output: [22, 24, 25]
print(temp[::2])        # Output: [22, 24, 25]
print(temp[::])         # Output: [22, 23, 24, 21, 25]
print(temp[:: -1])      # Output: [25, 21, 24, 23, 22]
print(temp[:: 2])       # Output: [22, 24, 25]
print(temp[:: -2])      # Output: [25, 24, 22]

# Concatenation:
print(temp + lst1)      # Output: [22, 23, 24, 21, 25, 10, 12, 14, 16]

# List is mutable/editable/can add value to the existing list:
temp=[22, 23, 24, 21, 25]
print(temp)             # [22, 23, 24, 21, 25]
print(temp[0])          # 22
temp[0]=111             # Assignment of value to list
print(temp)             # [111, 23, 24, 21, 25]
```

Output:
```
[22, 23, 24, 21, 25]
22
[111, 23, 24, 21, 25]
```

```
# Create a new list from an existing list
lst1=[10, 12, 14, 16, 18, 20]
lst2=lst1[1:4]
print(lst2)
```

Output:
```
[12, 14, 16]
```

```
# Traversing of the list:
temp=[22, 23, 24, 21, 25]
for i in temp:          # i takes element by element from the object, temp
    print(i)
```

Output:
```
22
23
24
21
25
```

```
# Print the elements of L using the +ve index
L=[10,20,30,40,50]
for i in range(5):
    print(L[i])         # Prints the 5 values of 0 to 4 index
```

Output:
10
20
30
40
50

 # Print the elements of L using the -ve index
```
L=[10,20,30,40,50]
for i in range(-5, 0, 1):
        print(L[i])        # Prints the 5 values of -5 to -1 index
```

Output:
10
20
30
40
50

 # Accessing values of a list using range()
```
temp=[22, 23, 24, 21, 25]
n=len(temp)             # len() Returns the no of elements present in the list
for i in range(0 , n, 1):
        print(temp[i])
```

Output:
22
23
24
21
25

 # Write a program to search if a user-taken value is present in the list
```
x=[22, 23, 24, 21, 25]
for i in x:
        print(i, end=" ")
no=int(input("Enter an element to search=> "))
c=0
for i in x:
        if (i ==no):
                c=1
                break    # Terminates/breaks to loop & goes out of this block
```

```
if (c==1):
        print ("Element is present")
else:
        print("Element is Not present")
```

Output:
```
22 23 24 21 25
Enter an element to search=> 22
Element is present
```

 # Write a program to search (Linear) for a user-given element present in the given list, and also find the +ve index (position) of the very element. The given list is: lst=[10, 20, 30, 40, 50]

```
lst=[10, 20, 30, 40, 50]
for i in lst:
        print(i, end=" ")
no=int(input("Enter an element to search=> ")) # 30
c=pos=0
f=False
while (c<len(lst)):
        if (lst[c]==no):
                pos=c
                f=True
                break
        c=c+1
if (f==True):
        print ("Element is present")
        print ("Position of %d is: %d "  %(lst[c] , pos) )
# Output: Position of 30 is 2
else:
        print("Element is Not present")
```

Output:
```
Position of 30 is: 2
```

 # Write a program using Binary Search to find an entered element that is present with its +ve index, in the list created by the user.

```
L=eval(input("Enter a list of elements with commas within []: "))
L.sort()
print(L)                    # After sorting in ascending order
no=int(input("Enter an element to search=> "))
l=len(L)
```

```python
f=False
first=0
last=l-1
while (first<=last):
        mid=int((first+last)/2)    # Finds the middle index
        if(L[mid]==no):            # Change of the middle index of the 1st half
                f=True
                break
        if(no<L[mid]):             # Checks element in 1st half
                last=mid-1         # Change of the middle index of the 1st half
        else:                      # Checks element in 2nd half
                first=mid+1        # Change of the middle index of the 2nd half
if (f==True):
        print ("Element is present & its position is: %d" %(mid+1))
else:
        print("Element is Not present")
```

Output:
Enter a list of elements with commas within []: [6,3,8,2,9,3]
[2, 3, 3, 6, 8, 9]
Enter an element to search=> 6
Element is present & its position is: 4

 # Write a program to create a list using the Selection-Sort technique.
```python
n=int(input("Enter no of elements=> "))
L=[0 for i in range(n)]            # Create a list of n elements with 0
print(L)
l=len(L)                           # Length of the list
for i in range(l):                 # Filling the list
        L[i]=int(input("Enter element no%d: " %(i+1)))
for i in range(l-1):
        min=i
        for j in range(i+1, l):
                if(L[j]<L[min]):
                        min=j
        temp=L[i]
        L[i]=L[min]
        L[min]=temp
print("Sorting in ascending order: ")
for i in range(l):
        print(L[i])
```

Output:

Enter no of elements=> 3	Sorting in ascending order:
[0, 0, 0]	2
Enter element no1: 5	5
Enter element no2: 2	7
Enter element no3: 7	

 # Write a program to create a list and the Bubble Sort technique

```python
n=int(input("Enter no of elements: "))
L=[0 for i in range(n)]
print(L)
for i in range(n):
    L[i]=eval(input("Enter element no-%d:" %(i+1)))
for i in range(n-1):
    for j in range(n-1-i):
        if(L[j]>L[j+1]):
            temp =L[j]
            L[j]=L[j+1]
            L[j+1]=temp
print("Sorting in ascending order: ")
for i in range(n):
        print(L[i])
```

Output:

Enter no of elements=> 5	Sorting in ascending order:
[0, 0, 0, 0, 0]	2
Enter element no-1: 5	3
Enter element no-2: 3	5
Enter element no-3: 8	6
Enter element no-4: 6	8
Enter element no-5: 2	

 # Use of random() function

```python
import random as rnd  # importing
lst=[rnd.randint(2,9) for r in range(5)]
print(lst)
```

> **Note:** *Under the random module, functions **random(), randint(), choice()**, etc., are present.*

Output:

[3, 5, 4, 9, 4]   *# Creating random integers between 2-9*

Algorithm of Bubble Sort:

- *Start with a list (array) of n elements.*
- *Iterate through the list n-1 times.*
- *In each pass, compare adjacent elements:*
  - ✓ *If the current element is greater than the next element*
  - ✓ *Swap them.*
- *After each pass, the largest element moves to its correct end position.*
- *Repeat this process for the remaining unsorted elements.*
- *If no swaps occur, the array is sorted, and then it terminates early.*
- *End.*

Example:
For an input array [5, 3, 8, 6, 2]:
Pass 1: Compare and swap adjacent elements

[5, 3, 8, 6, 2] → [3, 5, 8, 6, 2]
[3, 5, 8, 6, 2] → [3, 5, 8, 6, 2] (no swap)
[3, 5, 8, 6, 2] → [3, 5, 6, 8, 2]
[3, 5, 6, 8, 2] → [3, 5, 6, 2, 8]

Pass 2: [3, 5, 6, 2, 8] → [3, 5, 6, 2, 8] → [3, 5, 6, 2, 8] → [3, 5, 2, 6, 8]
Pass 3: [3, 5, 2, 6, 8] → [3, 2, 5, 6, 8]
Pass 4: [2, 3, 5, 6, 8] (Sorted!)

 # Write a Python program in a method to sort a list of values taken by the user, applying Insertion Sort.

```
# <-----------------Below here is the Called Method------------------>
def insertion_sort(L1):
    n=len(L1)
    for i in range(1,n):
        k=L1[i]
        j=i-1
        while(j>=0 and k<=L1[j]):
            L1[j+1]=L1[j]
            j=j-1
        L1[j+1]=k
    return L1
# <-----------------Below here is the Calling Method------------------>

L= list(map(int, input("Enter numbers separated by space: ").split()))
print("Original List:", L)
x=insertion_sort(L)
print("Sorted List:", x)
```

> **Note:** *.split()* function breaks the input into elements, and *map()* function makes the elements iterable, i.e., can be accessed element by element.

Output:
Enter numbers separated by space: 5 3 8 6 2
Original List: [5, 3, 8, 6, 2]
Sorted List: [2, 3, 5, 6, 8]

Algorithm of Insertion Sort:

- *Start with an array of n elements.*
- *Assume the 1st element is already sorted.*
- *Iterate from the 2nd element (index 1) to the last element (index n-1).*
  - ✓ *Let the current element be key.*
  - ✓ *Compare the key with the elements before it in the sorted array.*
- *Shift larger elements one position to the right until the correct position for a key is found.*
- *Insert the key in its correct position.*
- *Repeat until all elements are sorted.*
- *End.*

Example:
For an input array [5, 3, 8, 6, 2]:
Step 1: [5] (sorted), [3, 8, 6, 2] (unsorted)
Insert 3 → [3, 5, 8, 6, 2]
Step 2: [3, 5] (sorted), [8, 6, 2] (unsorted)
Insert 8 → [3, 5, 8, 6, 2] (no change)
Step 3: [3, 5, 8] (sorted), [6, 2] (unsorted)
Insert 6 → [3, 5, 6, 8, 2]
Step 4: [3, 5, 6, 8] (sorted), [2] (unsorted)
Insert 2 → [2, 3, 5, 6, 8]
Here, the array is sorted!

 # Write a program to create a list initialised by 0, then fill it with user-given values, and find the sum of the elements.

```python
s=0
n=int(input("Enter no of elements=> "))
L=[0 for i in range(n)]          # Create a list of n elements with 0
print(L)
for i in range(n):
    L[i]=int(input("Enter element no%d=> "  %(i+1)))
for i in range(n):
    s=s+L[i]
print("Sum of Elements=> ", s)
```

Output:
Enter no of elements=> 3
[0, 0, 0]
Enter element no1=> 11
Enter element no2=> 22
Enter element no3=> 33
Sum of Elements=> 66

 # Find the longest word in a string and words in reverse order
```
max_word=" "
s="Indo Aryan Soviet Socialist Republic"
lst=s.split()            # split() fn. breaks each word into elements
print(lst)
print()
for i in lst:
    if (len(i)>len(max_word)):
        max_word=i
print(max_word)          # Prints the longest element
```

 # Printing the reverse
```
s=s.split()[::-1]        # Elements are placed in reverse order
print(s)
```

Output:
['Indo', 'Aryan', 'Soviet', 'Socialist', 'Republic']

Socialist

['Republic', 'Socialist', 'Soviet', 'Aryan', 'Indo']

Two-Dimensional (2-D) Array (values are stored in row-col):

Assume the name of the following 2-D array is: **Mtx**
Then the location of the value 70 is Mtx[1][2], i.e., at Row index 1 and
Column index 2.

	0	1	2	3
0	10	20	30	40
1	50	60	70	80
2	90	100	110	120
3	130	140	150	160

Mtx[1][2]

Program to print a nested list in 2D format

```
Mtx= [ [1, 2, 3] , [4, 5, 6], [7, 8, 9] ]
print(Mtx)                # Prints the list

for i in range(3):
      for j in range(3):
             print(Mtx[i][j] , end="\t")
      print("\n")
```

> **Note:**
> *A List can't be a Matrix, i.e. it can't be in a 2D format. Here, it virtually looks like a 2D, but it is actually 1D.*

Output:

```
[ [1, 2, 3] , [4, 5, 6] , [7, 8, 9] ]
1       2       3
4       5       6
7       8       9
```

Write Python code to generate a 4X4 2D array and fill it with # (hash)

```
r=3
c=4
# To create an 2D array of list
Mtx = [['#' for col in range(c)] for row in range(r)]
print(Mtx)
print()
for i in range(r):
      for j in range(c):
             print(Mtx[i][j] , end="\t")
      print("\n")
```

Output:

```
Enter No of Rows  3
Enter No of Columns  4
[['#', '#', '#', '#'], ['#', '#', '#', '#'], ['#', '#', '#', '#']]
#       #       #       #
#       #       #       #
#       #       #       #
```

Write Python code to generate a 2D array and fill it with the entered values by the user

```
r=int(input("Enter No of Rows "))      # 3
c=int(input("Enter No of Columns ")) # 2
# To create an 2D array of list
Mtx = [[0 for col in range(c)] for row in range(r)]
```

```
# To display the initial format of the matrix filled with 0
for i in range(r):
        for j in range(c):
                print(Mtx[i][j] , end="\t")
        print("\n")
# Taking values from the user
for i in range(r):
   for j in range(c):                # Input with positions using %d
      Mtx[i][j]=int(input('Enter for Mtx [%d][%d]  => ' %(i, j) ))
# Print the final output
print()
for i in range(r):                   # r=3
   for j in range(c):                # c=2
      print(Mtx[i][j] , end="\t")
   print("\n")
```

Output:

```
Enter No of Rows   2
Enter No of Columns   2
0       0
0       0
Enter for Mtx [0] [0]  => 1
Enter for Mtx [0] [1]  => 2
Enter for Mtx [1] [0]  => 3
Enter for Mtx [1] [1]  => 4
1       2
3       4
```

> **Note:**
> A **Nested list can't** be **sliced column-wise**, because it is not a Matrix (2D format), but rather 1D

 # Write a program to enter the average marks of the students of a class, and after displaying the marks in a 2D array, also calculate and print the Average, maximum and minimum marks of the class.

```
k=1
s=av=mx=mn=0          # One value is assigned to many variables
no=int(input("Total no of students  "))
r=int(input("Enter No of Rows  "))
c=int(input("Enter No of Columns  "))
Mtx = [[0 for col in range(c)] for row in range(r)]
for i in range(r):
    for j in range(c):
```

```python
        Mtx[i][j]=int(input('Enter average marks for Mtx [%d][%d] of roll %d => ' %( i,j, k) ))
    s=s+Mtx[i][j]
    k=k+1
print("Average marks of the class=> ")
print("=========================")
for i in range(r):
        for j in range(c):
                print(Mtx[i][j] , end="\t")
        print("\n")
av=s/no
mx=max(max(Mtx))
mn=min(min(Mtx))
print("Class Average ", av )
print("Maximum Class Average=> ", mx)
print("Minimum Class Average=> ", mn)
```

Output:

```
Total no of students   9
Enter No of Rows   3
Enter No of Columns   3
Enter average marks for Mtx [0][0] of roll 1 => 88
Enter average marks for Mtx [0][1] of roll 2 => 99
Enter average marks for Mtx [0][2] of roll 3 => 77
Enter average marks for Mtx [1][0] of roll 4 => 66
Enter average marks for Mtx [1][1] of roll 5 => 55
Enter average marks for Mtx [1][2] of roll 6 => 76
Enter average marks for Mtx [2][0] of roll 7 => 78
Enter average marks for Mtx [2][1] of roll 8 => 94
Enter average marks for Mtx [2][2] of roll 9 => 67

Average marks of the class=>
========================
88      99      77
66      55      76
78      94      67
Class Average  77.77777777777777
Maximum Class Average=> 99
Minimum Class Average=> 55
```

 # Replace the Vowels with the next character

```python
tx=input("Enter a Text: ")
print("The Vowels are: ", end=""))
L=list(tx)                              # Converting string into a list
```

```
for i in range(len(L)):
    if(L[i]=="A" or L[i]=="a" or L[i]=="E" or L[i]=="e" or L[i]=="I" or
    L[i]=='i' or L[i]=="O" or L[i]=="o" or L[i]=="U" or L[i]=="u" ):
        print(L[i], end="")        # Prints vowels
        s=chr(ord(L[i])+1)         # Next char incremented by 1
        L[i]=s                     # Replacement of the vowel(s)
print("\nAfter replacement of Vowels by its next character:")
for i in L:
    print(i, end="")
```

Note: *chr()* converts ASCII code into a character, and *ord()* vice versa, i.e., Character to ASCII, numeric operations work here.

Output:
Enter a Text: Srikumar
The Vowels are: iua
After the replacement of Vowels by their next character:
Srjkvmbr

Built-In Functions *(pre-defined code for a specific job)*:

- list()
- append()
- insert()
- extend()
- reverse()
- reversed()
- enumerate()
- index()
- len()
- sort()
- sorted()
- count()
- clear()
- del()
- remove()
- pop()
- max()
- min()
- sum()
- all()
- any()
- zip()

Note: *sort()* function sorts the values in the object itself, but *sorted()* function retains the original values in its object, and returns/assigns the sorted values to a new object.

Uses of the functions:

```
x = list("IndoAryan")   # Coverts String into list
print(x)
```

Output:

['I', 'n', 'd', 'o', 'A', 'r', 'y', 'a', 'n']

```
lst=[]
lst.append(60)          # append() the value as the last element of the list
print(lst)
```
Output:

[10, 20, 30, 40, 50, **60**]

```
lst.insert(2, 25)       # insert() posts the value in the index position
print(lst)
```

Output:

[10, 20, **25**, 30, 40, 50, 60]

```
l1=[100,200]
lst.extend(l1)          # extend() joins a list at the end
print(lst)
```

Output:

[10, 20, 25, 30, 40, 50, 60, **100, 200**]

```
lst1=[10,30,50,20,40]
lst1.reverse()          # Reverses the order of the elements
print(lst1)
x=list(reversed(lst1))
print(x)
```

Output:

[40, 20, 50, 30, 10]
[10, 30, 50, 20, 40]

```
nos = ['zero', 'one', 'two', 'three' ]
for index, n in enumerate(nos):   # prints index position and its value
    print(index, n)
```

Output:

0 zero
1 one
2 two
3 three
lst2=[10,30,50,40,20]

> **Note:** *Sorting can't take place in string & numeric together*

```
lst2.sort(reverse=False)        # By default, it orders in ascending order
print(lst2)
```
Output:
```
[10, 20, 30, 40, 50]
```

```
lst2.sort(reverse=True)         # Arrange the elements in descending order
print(lst2)
```
Output:
```
[50, 40, 30, 20, 10]
```

```
str= ['India', 'Pakistan', 'China', 'Russia', 'Germany']
str.sort()
print(str)
```
Output:
```
['China', 'Germany', 'India', 'Pakistan', 'Russia']
```

```
str= ['India', 'UK', 'China', 'Russia', 'Germany']
s=sorted(str, reverse=True)     # Sorted values get assigned to object
print(s)
print(str)
```

> **Note:** *sorted()* fn. retains the original values

Output:
```
['UK', 'Russia', 'India', 'Germany', 'China']     # Sorted output of s
['India', 'UK', 'China', 'Russia', 'Germany']     # Original values of str
```

```
x=len(lst2)              # Counts the no of elements present in the list
print(x)
```
Output: 5

```
lst2=[10,30,50,10 ,40,20, 30, 10 ]
lst2.count(10)           # Times of Occurrence of the element in the list
```
Output: 3

```
x=['Amit', 'Sumit', 'Hamid', 'Ajit', 'Hamid', 'John', 'Hamid']
print(x.index('Hamid') )  # Returns the index value of the element of the 1st case
```
Output: 2

```
x.clear()                # Clears all elements present in the list
print(x)
```
Output: [ ]

```
y=['India', 'Pakistan', 5000, 98.55, 'Bangladesh']
del y[2]                 # Deletes the element at the index value
print(y)
```
Output:
```
['India', 'Pakistan', 98.55, 'Bangladesh']
```

```
y=['India', 'Pakistan', 5000, 98.55, 'Bangladesh']
del y[-2]                   # Deletes the element at the -ve index value
print(y)
```
Output:
['India', 'Pakistan', 5000, 'Bangladesh']

```
# Removes/deletes the element mentioned in the function remove()
y=['India', 'Pakistan', 5000, 98.55, 'Bangladesh']
y.remove('Pakistan')           # Deletes the element itself
print(y)
```
Output: ['India', 5000, 98.55, 'Bangladesh']

```
y=['India', 'Pakistan', 5000, 98.55, 'Bangladesh']
y.pop()                        # By default, it deletes the last value of the list
print(y)
```
Output:
['India', 'Pakistan', 5000, 98.55]

```
y.pop(1)                       # It also deletes an element of the index value
print(y)
```
Output:
['India', 5000, 98.55]

```
z=[10 ,20, 25, 30, 40, 50, 60, 100,200]
n1=min(z)                  # Returns the minimum value of the list
n2=max(z)                  # Returns the maximum value of the list
n3=sum(z)                  # Returns the sum of values of the list
print(n1 , " ", n2, " ", n3)
```
Output:
10   200   535

```
names = ['Anamika', 'Biswajit']
scores = [85, 90]
res = list(zip(names, scores))   # Combines lists into tuples.
print(res)
```
Output:
[('Anamika', 85), ('Biswajit', 90)]

```
nos = [1, 0, 3]
print(all(nos))                # Returns True if all are True (non-zero).
```
Output:
False

```
val = [3, 0, 1]
print(any(val))                # Returns True if any one element is True.
```
Output:
True

Chapter 6

Dictionary

Chapter Objective:

- Dictionary as Defined
- Dictionary from nested list
- Traversing of the Data
- Accessing data of the dictionary through Coding
- In-built Functions

Dictionary as Defined:

The concept of a dictionary is similar to a telephone directory, where each name (key) maps to a phone number (value). A dictionary is **mutable,** i.e. values can be edited or added, and it is **heterogeneous,** i.e. values of various data types.

x={} *#Empty dictionary*
z={ 1 : 'India' , 2: 'Pakistan' , 3: 'Sri Lanka' , 4: 'Bangladesh', 5: 'Nepal'}
y={'Rohan' : 489 , 'Kaushik' : 477 , 'Kritika' : 488 , 'Sujit' : 465 }

KEY   **VALUE**
(Numeric/String)   (Numeric/String)

 # Addition, Updation, Deletion of values in Dictionary:
x={ 1 : 'India' , 2: 'Pakistan' , 3: 'Sri Lanka' }
x[60]='China'   *# Adding a new item (Key& Value) to x dictionary*
print(x)

Output: {1: 'India', 2: 'Pakistan', 3: 'Sri Lanka', 60: 'China'}

y={'Rohan' : 489 , 'Kaushik' : 477 , 'Kritika' : 488 }
y['Rahim']=478   *# Adding a new item (Key& Value) to y dictionary*
print(y)
y['Rohan']=490   *# Updating the value of an item to y*
print(y)

Output:
{'Rohan': 489, 'Kaushik': 477, 'Kritika': 488, 'Rahim': 478}
{'Rohan': **490**, 'Kaushik': 477, 'Kritika': 488, 'Rahim': 478}

y={'Rohan' : 490 , 'Kaushik' : 477 , 'Kritika' : 488 , 'Rahim' : 478 }
print(y['Kritika'])   *# Prints the value of a key of y as 488*
del y['Kaushik']   *# Deletes the item that returns the value*
print(y)
print(y.**pop**('Rohan')) *# Deletes the item & returns the deleted value*
print(y)
print(y.**popitem**())   *# popitem() deletes the last item*
Output:
488   *# del deletes the item & returns the value of key ('Kaushik')*
{'Rohan': 490, 'Kritika': 488, 'Rahim': 478}
490   *# pop() deletes the item & returns the deleted value*
{'Kritika': 488, 'Rahim': 478}
('Rahim' , 478)   *# popitem() deletes the last item*

> **Note:** *The difference between del & pop are:* ***(1)*** *pop uses dot(.) operator with the object, but del doesn't, as **del** is not a function but a statement **(2)** pop uses () bracket, but del doesn't. **(3)** pop returns the deleted value **(4)** pop() needs an argument (key), but del doesn't*

Converting a nested list into a Dictionary:

```
L=[ [10, 'USA'] , [20, 'China'] , [30, 'UK'], [50, 'India'] ]

print(L)

d={}

# Converting a list into a Dictionary

for i in L:
    d[i[0]]=i[1]

print(d)
```

Output:

```
[[10, 'USA'], [20, 'China'], [30, 'UK'], [50, 'India']]
{10: 'USA', 20: 'China', 30: 'UK', 50: 'India'}
```

Traversing the data of the dictionary:

```
y={'Rohan' : 490 , 'Kaushik' : 477 , 'Kritika' : 488 , 'Sujit' : 465 , 'Rahim' : 478}
for i in y:                 # Prints the keys only of the items
      print(i)

print()

for i in y:                 # Prints the Keys & corresponding values
      print(i , ":" , y[i])
# Here i prints the Key & y[i] prints the corresponding values
```

Output:

```
Rohan
Kaushik
Kritika
Sujit
Rahim

Rohan : 490
Kaushik : 477
Kritika : 488
Sujit : 465
Rahim : 478
```

 # Write a Python program to create a Dictionary 'subj' of n times, by inputting Section as key and 5th subject as corresponding value, and finally display the items under a caption: 'SECTION & 5th SUBJECT'

```python
subj={ }                      # Declaration of an empty dictionary
n=int(input("Enter no of sections=> "))
i=1
while (i<=n):
      s=input("Input Section=> ")
      f=input("Input 5th Subject=> ")
      subj[s]=f             # Creating the dictionary where s is key & f is value
      i=i+1
print("Section" , "\t", "5th Subject")
print("=======================")
for i in subj:
      print(i , "\t", subj[i])
```

Output :

```
Enter no of sections=>  3
Input Section=>  I
Input 5th Subject=>  IP
Input Section=>  J
Input 5th Subject=>  IP
Input Section=>  K
Input 5th Subject=>  EG
```

Section   5th Subject
```
=======================
I                IP
J                IP
K                EG
```

 # A Dictionary of Subject-wise marks, and their sum & average.

```python
d={}
n=int(input("Enter the number of Items: "))
for i in range(n):
     k=input("Enter Name of the Subject no %d: " %(i+1))
     v=int(input("Enter the marks of the subject %s: " %k))
     d[k]=v
print("The Dictionary is==>")
print(d)
print("")
```

```
tot=0
for i in d:
    tot=tot+d[i]
print()
print("The total mark is: ", tot)
av=tot/n
print("The average mark is: ", av)
```

> **Note:** Here, **%d** takes an integer value and **%s** takes string values.

Output:

Enter the number of Items: 3
Enter Name of the Subject no 1: English
Enter the marks of the subject English: 78
Enter Name of the Subject no 2: Maths
Enter the marks of the subject Maths: 90
Enter Name of the Subject no 3: Science
Enter the marks of the subject Science: 89

The Dictionary is==>
{'English ': 78, 'Maths': 90, 'Science': 89}

The total mark is: 257
The average mark is: 85.66666666666667

Dictionary mapping numbers to text forms

```
d = { 0: 'zero', 1: 'one', 2: 'two', 3: 'three', 4: 'four', 5: 'five', 6: 'six', 7:
'seven', 8: 'eight', 9: 'nine', 10: 'ten', 11: 'eleven', 12: 'twelve', 13:
'thirteen', 14: 'fourteen', 15: 'fifteen', 16: 'sixteen', 17: 'seventeen', 18:
'eighteen', 19: 'nineteen', 20: 'twenty' }
```

Get user input

```
no = int(input("Enter a number between 0 and 20: "))
```

Check if the number is in the dictionary

```
if no in d:
    print(f"The number {no} in text form is '{d[no]}'.")
else:
    print("Number is out of range!")
```

Output:

Enter a number between 0 and 20: 18
The number 18 in text form is 'eighteen'.

Conversion from Numbers to Text

```
d={0: 'Zero', 1: 'One', 2: 'Two', 3: 'Three', 4: 'Four', 5: 'Five', 6: 'Six', 7:
'Seven', 8: 'Eight', 9: 'Nine'}
```

```
n=input('Enter a number (multiple digits): ')
for i in n:
        print(d[int(i)], end=' ')              # print(d[i], end=' ') also works
```
Output:
Enter a number: 1025
One Zero Two Five

In-built functions/methods of Dictionary:

- del   # Check in the previous example of the list on page no. 91
- pop()   # Check in the previous example of the list on page no. 91
- len()
- clear()
- get()
- items()
- keys()
- values()
- sorted()
- dict()
- update()
- fromkeys()

Applications of the functions:

```
y={'Rohan' : 490 , 'Kaushik' : 477 , 'Kritika' : 488 , 'Sujit' : 465}
print(len(y))              # Number of items
```
Output: 4

```
y.clear()                  # Deletes all items
print(y)
```
Output: {}

```
y={'Rohan' : 490 , 'Kaushik' : 477 , 'Kritika' : 488 , 'Sujit' : 465 }
x=y.get('Rohan')           # Returns/retrieves the value of the key
print(x)
print(y.items())           # Prints all items of the dictionary with dict_items()
print(list(y.items()))     # Prints all items of the dictionary in  a list
```
Output:
490
dict_items([('Rohan', 490), ('Kaushik', 477), ('Kritika', 488), ('Sujit', 465)])
[('Rohan', 490), ('Kaushik', 477), ('Kritika', 488), ('Sujit', 465)]

```
print(y.keys())            # Prints all the keys
```
Output: ['Rohan' , 'Kaushik' , 'Kritika' , 'Sujit']

```
print(y.values())          # Prints the values of the keys of the dictionary
```
Output: dict_values([490, 477, 488, 465])

Ordering Dictionary:

```
y={'Rohan' : 490 , 'Kaushik' : 477 , 'Kritika' : 488 , 'Sujit' : 465}
x=sorted(y)              # Prints the Keys in ascending order
print(x)
print(sorted(y.values()))
print(sorted(y.keys() , reverse=True)) # Prints keys in Descending order
print(sorted(y.items()))
```

Output:
```
['Kaushik', 'Kritika', 'Rohan', 'Sujit']
[465, 477, 488, 490]
['Sujit', 'Rohan', 'Kritika', 'Kaushik']
[('Kaushik', 477), ('Kritika', 488), ('Rohan', 490), ('Sujit', 465)]
```

> **Note:** *The items are sorted by key, not by their values. So, 'Sujit' with value 465 comes last because 'S' comes after 'R', 'K', 'K'.* **sort()** *fn. doesn't work.*

```
z=[ [10, 'USA'] , [20, 'China'] , [30, 'UK'] , [40, 'Germany'], [50, 'India'] ]
k=dict(z)                # Converts the list into a Dictionary
print(k)
```

Output: { 10 : 'USA' , 20: 'China' , 30: 'UK' , 40: 'Germany', 50:'India'}

```
d={'a':100, 'b':200, 'c':300, 'd':400}
d1={'b':500, 'y':1000}
d.update(d1)             # Modifies the dictionary with another dictionary
print(d)
```

Output: {'a': 100, '**b**': **500**, 'c': 300, 'd': 400, 'y': **1000**}

```
d={'a':100, 'b':200, 'c':300, 'd':400}  # Overlapping key(k) got updated
d1=d.fromkeys(d,25) # Creates a new dictionary with a new value
d2=dict.fromkeys([1,2,3,4] , 25)    # formkeys() belong to dict. class
print(d1)
print(d2)
```

Output:

> **Note:** **fromkeys()** creates a new dictionary with the keys of the existing dictionary, but with new value(s); so the original remains as it is.

```
{'a': 25, 'b': 25, 'c': 25, 'd': 25}
{1: 25, 2: 25, 3: 25, 4:25}
```

 # Comprehension creates a dictionary in a single compact line
```
sqr = {x: x*x for x in range(1, 6)}     # A dictionary comprehension program
print(sqr)
```
Output:
```
{1:1, 2:4, 3:9, 4:16, 5:25}
```

Dictionary of Lists:

```python
marks = {       "Rahul": [85, 78, 92],
                "Anita": [88, 76, 95],
                "Vikram": [90, 82, 87]     }

# Printing dictionary
print("Dictionary:", marks)

# Accessing values
print("\nMarks of Rahul:", marks["Rahul"])

# Loop through dictionary
print("\nMarks:")
for name, marks in marks.items():
        print(name, ":", marks)
```

Output:

```
Dictionary:
{'Rahul': [85, 78, 92], 'Anita': [88, 76, 95], 'Vikram': [90, 82, 87]}

Marks of Rahul: [85, 78, 92]

Student Marks:
Rahul : [85, 78, 92]
Anita : [88, 76, 95]
Vikram : [90, 82, 87]
```

List of dictionaries:

```python
stud = [
   {"Name": "Rahul", "Age": 17, "Marks": 85},
   {"Name": "Anita", "Age": 16, "Marks": 90},
   {"Name": "Vikram", "Age": 18, "Marks": 88}  ]

# Printing a list of dictionaries
print("List of Dictionaries:")
print(stud)

# Accessing elements
print("\nFirst Student:", stud[0])
print("Name of second student:", stud[1]["Name"])
```

```
# Loop through list
print("\nStudent Details:")
for s in stud:
      print(s["Name"], s["Age"], s["Marks"])
```

Output:

```
#List of Dictionaries:
[{'Name': 'Rahul', 'Age': 17, 'Marks': 85},
 {'Name': 'Anita', 'Age': 16, 'Marks': 90},
 {'Name': 'Vikram', 'Age': 18, 'Marks': 88}]

First Student: {'Name': 'Rahul', 'Age': 17, 'Marks': 85}
Name of second student: Anita

Student Details:
Rahul 17 85
Anita 16 90
Vikram 18 88
```

Dictionary of Dictionaries

```
stud = {
      "101": {"name": "Rahul", "grade": "A"},
      "102": {"name": "Anita",  "grade": "B"},
      "103": {"name": "Vikram", "grade": "A+"}
        }
# Printing the dictionary
for roll, info in stud.items():
      print("Roll No:", roll)
      print("Name:", info["name"])
      print("Marks:", info["grade"])
```

Output:

```
Roll No: 101
Name: Rahul
Grade: A

Roll No: 102
Name: Anita
Grade: B

Roll No: 103
Name: Vikram
Grade: A+
```

> **Note:**
>
> *Here,*
>
> *roll → key of outer dictionary*
>
> *info → whole inner dictionary*
>
> *info["name"] → value inside inner dictionary*

Chapter 7

Module
&
Class Concept

Chapter Objective:

- A module as defined

- Simple Module

- Parameterised Module

- Return Type Module

- Scope of Variables

- Class (OOP) Concept:
  - ✓ Class & Object
  - ✓ Encapsulation
  - ✓ Inheritance
  - ✓ Abstraction
  - ✓ Polymorphism

- Class-Based Module

- Summary of OOP Concept

A module is defined:

A module is a file containing Python code, which may include user-defined or built-in functions to solve specific problems. Module breaks down large programs into smaller pieces to manage and organise function files (user-created). Furthermore, modules provide reusability of code. We can define frequently used functions in a module and import them instead of rewriting the code. Here, we shall discuss mainly the **User-Defined Module**.

For example, if **testmod.py** is a Python file (with **.py**), then its name would be **testmod** when importing a module.

Here we divide the Modules into three types: **(1)** Simple module, **(2)** Parameterised module, and **(3)** Return type module.

Simple Module:

Type the following code and save it as a **testmod.py** file. Here, **addnum()** is a user-defined called-function in the file defined using the keyword **def** followed by the function name and : (colon) then followed by code.

```
def addnum():              # Defined addnum()  called function
    a=10
    b=20
    s=0
    s=a+b
    print(s)
```

Now type the following in another **.py** file, say **abc.py** (or in Script >>>) to execute the user-defined function and save it in the same location as **testmod.py**, then run to give its result.

```
>>> import testmod         # importing file of functions
>>> testmod.addnum()       # addnum() is being called from a caller fn.
```
Output: 30

Parameterised Module:

In the **called** function, when values for calculation come from the **caller** function through parameters, it is called a parameterised module. In the following example, values are passed through actual parameters x and y to formal parameters a and b, written in the **testmod.py** file. Here it is:

```
def addnum(a , b):     # a, b are formal parameters, take from x & y
      s=a+b
      print(s)
```

```
# Now type the following code in another .py file or in a Script to execute:
>>> import testmod
>>> x=int(input("Enter 1st number: "))
>>> y=int(input("Enter 2nd number: "))
# x & y are the actual parameters of the caller function passed to addnum()
>>> testmod.addnum(x,y)
```

 # Using Function write print factors of a number:

```
def factor(f):
   print("The factors of", f, " : ")
   for i in range(1, f + 1):
     if (f % i == 0):
        print(i)

num = 20
factor(num)
```

Output:

```
The factors of 20 :
1
2
4
5
10
20
```

 # Program to find the HCF (Highest Common Factor) of Two Numbers:

```
def calc_hcf(n1 , n2):         # This code is saved in "hcfcalc.py" file
      hcf = 1
      for i in range(1, min(n1, n2)+1):
          if ((n1 % i==0) and (n2 % i==0)):
              hcf = i
      print("HCF of", n1, "and", n2, "is", hcf)
```

```
>>> import hcfcalc                # importing the 'hcfcalc.py' file
>>> hcfcalc.calc_hcf(40, 55)    # Caller fnc. Sends values to Called fnc.
```
Output:
HCF of 40 and 55 is**:** 5

Return Type Module, along with a parameter:

When the calculated result of the called function goes back to the caller function for further operations through the ***return*** keyword, the value goes back to the caller method.

*# Here, a & b are the formal parameters that receive values from x,y, which are written in the **testmod.py** file.*
def **addnum**(a , b)**:**

```
    s=a+b              # Indent to be followed
    return s           # Value of s goes to the caller-function of abc.py file
```

*# Now type the following in a file as **abc.py** or in a Script to execute:*
>>> import testmod
>>> x=int(input("Enter 1st number: "))
>>> y=int(input("Enter 2nd number: "))
>>> res=testmod.**addnum**(x,y)

*# **res** variable receives the returned value from the addnum() function*
>>> print("Total=> ",res)   *# Prints the returned value*

Output:
Enter 1st number: 10
Enter 2nd number: 15
Total=> 25

Scope of variables:

A variable's scope defines where it can be used and how long it exists in a program. So, scope => the visibility of a variable. There are two types of variables: Global and Local.

Local Variables:

Definition: Local variables are those that are declared within a function.

Scope: They are accessible only inside the specific function where they are defined and cannot be used or modified directly from outside that function.

Lifetime: A local variable is created when the function is invoked and destroyed once the function finishes execution—either by returning a value or raising an exception. Its memory exists temporarily on the function's call stack during execution.

Global Variables:

Definition: Global variables are declared outside of all functions, usually at the beginning of the code or module.

Scope: They can be accessed and modified from any part of the program, including inside functions (if explicitly referenced as global).

Lifetime: A global variable is created when the program starts and remains in memory until the program terminates, making its data persist throughout the entire program's execution.

```python
# Program to explain Global & Local variables and its Lifetime
a = 10                      # This is a global variable

def fn1():                  # Called function-1
    print('Inside fn1() : ', a)     # Global a is used as there is no local 'a'

def fn2():                  # Called function-2
    a = 20                  # Local variable a is defined as 20
    print('Inside fn2() : ', a)

def fn3():                  # Called function-3
    global a        # The keyword 'global' to modify the global variable a
    a = 30
    print('Inside fn3() : ', a)

# Scopes of Global variables
print('global : ', a)
fn1()                       # Caller function-1
print('global : ', a)
fn2()                       # Caller function-2
print('global : ', a)
fn3()                       # Caller function-3
print('global : ', a)
```

Output:

global: 10
Inside fn1() : 10

global: 10
Inside fn2() : 20

global: 10
Inside fn3() : 30

global : 30   # Global variable a is updated by local a

> **Note:**
> Here, the declaration of the keyword **global** within the function **fn3()** tells Python that inside this function, fn3() refers to the global variable 'a' (which is declared at the top as a=10), not a new local one. Therefore, when a=30 is assigned inside the function **fn3()**, it modifies the global variable and updates it to 30.

Object-Oriented Programming (OOP) Concepts:

OOP is a programming paradigm that organises around **class** and **object**. Here, a class is a blueprint or template that defines the attributes (data) and methods (functions) common to all objects created from it. An object is a specific instance of a class that contains real data and can perform actions defined by the class. Hence, OOP is based on four key principles:

- **Encapsulation:** Combining data and methods within a class and restricting direct access to internal details.
- **Inheritance:** Allowing one class to acquire properties and behaviours of another class, promoting code reuse.
- **Abstraction:** Representing only essential features of an object while hiding complex implementation details.
- **Polymorphism:** Enabling objects of different classes to respond differently to the same method call.

Class: *Object and Encapsulation using Method*

- **Class**: A blueprint for creating objects (a logical structure).
- **Object**: An instance of a class (a physical entity with data and behaviour).
- **Encapsulation**: Encapsulation means "keeping data safe inside a class" and "accessing it only through controlled methods."

```python
# A Class-based programme with Encapsulation
# Defining a class of OOP
class Bird:
    # Constructor to initialise attributes
    def __init__(self, name, colour):
        self.name = name
        self.colour = colour

    # Method (behaviour)
    def sing(self):
        print(f"{self.name} is singing!")    # f"{ }" is formatted string

    def show_details(self):
        print(f"Bird Name: {self.name}, Colour: {self.colour}")
# Creating objects (instances) of the class
bird1 = Bird("Parrot", "Green")
bird2 = Bird("Sparrow", "Brown")
```

 # Calling methods using the object
bird1.show_details()
bird1.sing()

bird2.show_details()
bird2.sing()

Output:
Bird Name: Parrot, Colour: Green
Parrot is singing!
Bird Name: Sparrow, Colour: Brown
Sparrow is singing!

Note:

- ***Class Bird*** *defines the structure (attributes: name, colour) and behaviour (methods: sing(), show_details()).*

- ***Objects bird1*** *and* ***bird2*** *are* ***instances*** *of the class, each having its own data.*

- ***Methods*** *are called using the dot (.) operator, such as bird1.sing() & bird1. show_details()*

- ***Encapsulation:*** *Here, the* ***Bird*** *class keeps both the bird's data (i.e., name, colour) and its actions/functions (i.e., sing(), show_details()) together in one unit and is not accessible outside, making the code organised, reusable, and easier to manage.*

- ***Constructor*** *is that which runs automatically when creating a new* ***Bird*** *object, like:* ***bird1*** *= Bird("Parrot", "Green")*

- ***__init__*** *stands for* ***"initialise"***. *It is called automatically whenever a new object is created. It assigns initial values to the object's attributes (like name and colour).*

- ***self*** *refers to the current object being created or used. It allows you to access attributes and methods of that specific object inside the class. Here,* ***self.name*** *means "the name belonging to this particular bird." Here,*

      self.name = name
      self.colour = colour

Class: *Inheritance*

Inheritance is the process by which a child class (subclass) acquires the properties (attributes) and behaviours (methods) of a parent class (superclass). It allows code reusability, extensibility, and helps establish a hierarchical relationship between classes.

A Class-based programme with Inheritance

```python
class Bird:
    def fly(self):          # 'self' allows access to variables of the class object
        print("Birds can fly.")

# Child class Parrot inherits properties from parent class: Bird
class Parrot(Bird):
    def talk(self):
        print("Parrots can talk.")

# Create an object/instance of the child class Parrot
parrot1 = Parrot()

# The child class can use both its own method and the parent's method
parrot1.fly()               # inherited from Bird
parrot1.talk()              # defined in Parrot
```

Output:
Birds can fly.
Parrots can talk.

> **Note:**
> - **Bird** is the **parent class** with a method **fly()**.
> - **Parrot** is the **child class** that **inherits** from Bird and adds its own method **talk()**.
> - The **object parrot1** can access both methods **fly()** (from parent) and **talk()** (from child).

Class: *Abstraction*

Abstraction means showing only the essential features and hiding complex details. It shows *what* is being done, not *how* it is being done.

A Class-based Programme with Abstraction

```python
# Abstract class
class Bird:
    def fly(self):
        pass                # method to be defined by subclasses
```

```python
# Child class 1
class Parrot(Bird):
    def fly(self):
        print("Parrot can fly.")
# Child class 2
class Penguin(Bird):
    def fly(self):
        print("Penguin cannot fly.")
# Creating objects of child classes
bird1 = Parrot()
bird2 = Penguin()
# Calling the method (abstracted behaviour)
bird1.fly()
bird2.fly()
```

Output:

Parrot can fly.

Penguin cannot fly.

> **Note:**
>
> - Here, **Abstraction** shows only the essential features and hides complex details.
> - The **abstract class Bird** defines **what** actions (like fly() and sound()) every bird must have — but **not how** they work.
> - The **child classes (Parrot, Penguin)** provide their own **specific implementations** of these methods.
> - This hides unnecessary details from the user — they use **fly()** or **sound()** without worrying about how they're implemented.
> - **pass** is a statement in Python which is a placeholder — it means "do nothing". It allows us to define the structure of a class or method without writing its actual code. It's commonly used when designing base classes or abstract methods — where we want subclasses to define specific behaviour. So, here the Bird class defines a method fly(), but doesn't specify how birds fly.

Class: *Polymorphism*

Polymorphism in action — the same method name, but performing different actions based on the object type in different child classes.

A Class-based Programme with Polymorphism

```python
# Parent class
class Bird:
    def sing(self):
        print("Some birds can sing.")

# Child class-1
class Parrot(Bird):
    def sing(self):
        print("Parrot is talking and singing!")

# Child class-2
class Sparrow(Bird):
    def sing(self):
        print("Sparrow is chirping softly.")

# Creating objects of different classes
bird1 = Parrot()
bird2 = Sparrow()

# Calling the same method sing() for different objects
bird1.sing()
bird2.sing()
```

Output:
Parrot is talking and singing!
Sparrow is chirping softly.

Note:

- *Here, in Polymorphism, the same method works in "many forms."*
- *The method **sing()** has **the same name** in all classes, but behaves **differently** depending on the object.*
- *When bird1.sing() is called, it uses the **Parrot** version; when bird2.sing() is called, it uses the **Sparrow** version.*

Class-Based Module:

```
# Save the following code in a file named: myclass.py
```

```python
class Student:
    def __init__(self, name):
        self.name = name

    def show(self):
        print(f"Hello, my name is {self.name}")
```

```
# Save this code in another .py file in the same location, then run
```

```python
# import the class Student from the module written in the 'myclass.py'
# file
from myclass import Student
if __name__ == "__main__":        # Checks if this file runs directly
    s = Student("Rahul")          # Object created of the class
    s.show()                      # Caller method with class-object
```

Output:
Hello, my name is Rahul

Summary of OOP Concept :

Concept	Meaning	Example
Class	Blueprint for objects	class Student:
Object	An instance of a class	s1 = Student()
Attribute	Variable inside a class	self.name = name
Method	Function inside a class	def display(self):
Constructor	Initialises object automatically	def __init__(self):
Inheritance	Child-class gets properties of the Parent-class	class Car(Vehicle):
Polymorphism	The same method behaves differently	animal.sound()
Encapsulation	Protecting data inside the class	__balance
Abstraction	Hiding details, showing only essentials	Shape class example

Chapter 8

NumPy

Chapter Objective

- NumPy as Defined
- Creating Array (1D & 2D) in NumPy
- Accessing Data
- 2-D Array
- Boolean Indexing
- Shaping Dimension
- Joining Array
- Mathematical Functions
- Sorting of the Array

NumPy as Defined:

NumPy is a Python library used for working with arrays. It also has functions for working in the domains of Linear Algebra, Fourier Transform, and Matrices. NumPy was created in 2005 by Travis Oliphant. It is an open-source project, and you can use it freely. NumPy is written partially in Python, but most of the parts that require fast computation are written in C or C++.

In Python, we have lists that serve the purpose of arrays, but they are slow to process. NumPy aims to provide an array object that is up to 50x faster than traditional Python lists. The array object in NumPy is called ndarray (N-dimensional array); it provides a lot of supporting functions that make working with ndarray very easy. Arrays are very frequently used in data science, where speed and resources are very important.

Creating Array (1D & 2D) in NumPy:

 # Create a 0-D array with a value, i.e 42
```
import numpy as np
# The array() function creates a NumPy array from a list.
arr = np.array(42)
print(arr)
```

Output:
```
42
```

 # Create a 1-D array containing the values 1,2,3,4,5:
```
import numpy as np
arr = np.array([1, 2, 3, 4, 5])
print(arr)
```

Output:
```
[1 2 3 4 5]
```

> **Note:** *Unlike a list, there is no comma (,) here in an array*

Accessing Data:

 # Get the first element from the following 1-D array:
```
import numpy as np
arr = np.array([1, 2, 3, 4])
print(arr[0])
```

Output:
```
1
```

 # Create and print the following 2D array:
```
import numpy as np
Lst2=[[10,20,30,40,50] , [11,22,33,44,55]]
x=np.array(Lst2)
print(x)
```

Output: *# NumPy array comes without commas (,)*
```
[ [10 20 30 40 50]
  [11 22 33 44 55] ]
```

 # The row and column indexes of the arrays

```
 0  1  2  3  4          ⟶ Index of 1-D array
[ 10 , 20 , 30 , 40 , 50 ]
```

```
    0  1  2  3  4        ⟶ Column Index of 2-D array
0 | 10 , 20 , 30 , 40 , 50
1 | 11 , 22 , 33 , 44 , 55
```
Row index of 2-D array

 # Selecting and Slicing of the element(s) of the array:
```
import numpy as np
Lst2=[ [10,20,30,40,50] , [11,22,33,44,55]]
x=np.array(Lst2)
print(x)
print(x[1 , 2])              # x[row index , col index] or x[row idx.][col idx.]
```

```
   0   1   2   3   4
0  10 , 20 , 30 , 40 , 50
1  11 , 22 , (33) , 44 , 55
33
```

 # Slice elements from index 1 to index 5 of the following array:
```
import numpy as np
arr = np.array([1, 2, 3, 4, 5, 6, 7])
print(arr[1:5])
```

Output:
```
[2 3 4 5]
```

> **Note:** *While slicing up (range) to the element of last index–1 will be taken*

 # Slice/access elements from index 4 to the end of the array:
```
import numpy as np
arr = np.array([1, 2, 3, 4, 5, 6, 7])
print(arr[4:])
```
Output:
```
[5 6 7]
```

 # Slice/access elements from index 1st element (0th index) to 4th element (3rd index):
```
import numpy as np
arr = np.array([1, 2, 3, 4, 5, 6, 7])
print(arr[:4])
```
Output:
```
[1 2 3 4]
```

 # Slice/access all elements of the array:
```
import numpy as np
arr = np.array([1, 2, 3, 4, 5, 6, 7])
print(arr[ : ])
```
Output:
```
[1 2 3 4 5 6 7]
```

 # Selecting and Slicing of the element(s) together of the array:
```
import numpy as np
Lst1=[10,20,30,40,50]
x=np.array(Lst1)
print(x[2])
print(x[1:4])
```
Output:
```
30
[20 30 40]              # Series prints output without a comma (,)
```

 # Adding a scalar to an array
```
arr = np.array([1, 2, 3])
print( arr + 5)
```
Output:
```
 [6, 7, 8]
```

Joining Array:

Multiple arrays can be joined along rows (axis=0) or columns (axis=1) using concatenation.

 # Joining two arrays:

```
import numpy as np
arr1 = np.array([1, 2, 3])
arr2 = np.array([4, 5, 6])
arr = np.concatenate((arr1, arr2))
print(arr)
```

Output:

[1 2 3 4 5 6]

 # Access the 2nd element on 1st dim:

```
import numpy as np
arr = np.array([1, 2, 3, 4])
print(arr[2] + arr[3])          # Sum of values 3 & 4
```

Output:

7

2-D Array:

 # Selecting and Slicing of the element(s) of the 2D-array:

```
import numpy as np
Lst3=[ [10,20,30,40,50] , [11,22,33,44,55] , [11,12,13,14,15]]
x=np.array(Lst3)
print(x)
print()
print(x[0:2 , 0:1])             # Range using : of rows and columns
print(x[0:2 , 0:2])             # Range using : of rows and columns
```

Output:

```
[[10 20 30 40 50]
 [11 22 33 44 55]
 [11 12 13 14 15]]

[[10]
 [11]]
[[10 20]
 [11 22]]
```

 # Access the 2nd element on 1st dim of 2D array:

```
import numpy as np
arr = np.array([[1,2,3,4,5], [6,7,8,9,10]])
```

```
print('2nd element on 1st row: ',  arr[0 , 1])
```

Output:

2nd element on 1st row: 2

```
        0  1  2  3  4
    0   1  2  3  4  5
    1   6  7  8  9  10
```

 # Access the 5th element on 2nd dim of 2D array:

```
import numpy as np
arr = np.array([[1,2,3,4,5], [6,7,8,9,10]])
print('5th element on 2nd row: ', arr[1, 4])
# Or print(arr[1][4])
```

Output:

5th element on 2nd row: 10

```
        0  1  2  3  4
    0   1  2  3  4  5
    1   6  7  8  9  10
```

 # From the second element of the 2nd row, slice elements from index 1 to index 4 (not included):

```
import numpy as np
arr = np.array([[1, 2, 3, 4, 5], [6, 7, 8, 9, 10]])
print(arr[1,1:4])          # arr(row , col), row has no range
```

Output:

[7 8 9]

```
        0  1  2  3  4
    0   1  2  3  4  5
    1   6  7  8  9  10
```

 # From both elements, return index 2:

```
import numpy as np
arr = np.array([[1, 2, 3, 4, 5], [6, 7, 8, 9, 10]])
print(arr[0 : 2 , 2 ])     # arr(row , col) where col is without range
```

Output:

[3 8]

```
        0  1  2  3  4
    0   1  2  3  4  5
    1   6  7  8  9  10
```

 # From both elements, slice index 1 to index 4 (not included), this will return a 2-D array:

```
import numpy as np
arr = np.array( [ [1, 2, 3, 4, 5] , [6, 7, 8, 9, 10] ] )
print(arr)
print(arr[0:2 , 1:4])
```

Output:

[[1 2 3 4   5]
 [6 7 8 9 10]]

[[2 3 4]
  [7 8 9]]

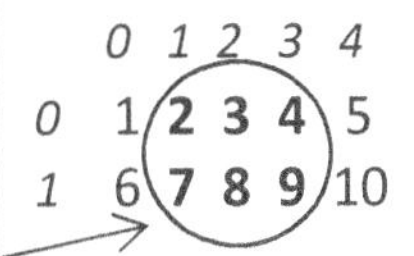

Boolean Indexing in 2D Arrays:

```python
import numpy as np
arr = np.array([[10, 20, 30],
                [40, 50, 60],
                [70, 80, 90]])
print(arr > 50)
# Boolean Indexing to Extract Matching Elements in 1D array
print(arr[arr > 50])
print()

# Filter and Replace Values Using Boolean Indexing
arr[arr > 50] = 0
print(arr)
print()

# Apply Conditions with np.where()
arr = np.array([[1, 2], [3, 4]])
result = np.where(arr > 2, "High", "Low")
print(result)
print()

# Combine Conditions with Boolean Logic
arr = np.array([[10, 20], [30, 40]])
mask = (arr > 10) & (arr < 35)        # both conditions must be true
print(arr[mask])
```

Output:

```
[ [False   False    False]
  [False   False    True ]
  [True    True     True ] ]

[60 70 80 90]

[[10   20    30]
 [40   50     0]
 [ 0    0     0]]

[['Low'  'Low']
 ['High' 'High']]

 [20 30]
```

Shaping Dimension:

 # Print the shape of a 2-D array:
```
import numpy as np
arr = np.array([[1, 2, 3, 4], [5, 6, 7, 8]])
print(arr)
print(arr.shape)              # Displays no of rows & columns
```

Output:
```
[[1  2  3  4]
 [5  6  7  8]]
(2, 4)                        # (Row, Col)
```

 # Convert the following 1-D array with 12 elements into a 2-D array. The outermost dimension will have 4 arrays, each with 3 elements:
```
import numpy as np
L1=[1, 2, 3, 4, 5, 6, 7, 8, 9, 10, 11, 12]
arr = np.array(L1)
print(arr)
print()
newarr = arr.reshape(4, 3)      # Reconstructs the existing array
print(newarr)                   # Number of elements remains the same
```

Output:
```
[1 2 3 4 5 6 7 8 9 10 11 12]

[[1  2  3]
 [4  5  6]
 [7  8  9]
 [10 11 12]]
```

 # Iterate on the elements of the following 1-D array:
```
import numpy as np
arr = np.array([1, 2, 3])
for x in arr:
      print(x)
```

Output:
```
1
2
3
```

 # Iterate on the elements of the following 2-D array:
```
import numpy as np
arr = np.array([[1, 2, 3], [4, 5, 6]])
print(arr)
print()
for x in arr:
      print(x)
```

Output:
```
[[1 2 3]            [1 2 3]
 [4 5 6]]           [4 5 6]
```

 # Iterate on each scalar element of the 2-D array:

```
import numpy as np
arr = np.array([[1, 2, 3], [4, 5, 6]])
for x in arr:                   # Prints elements from each row (of an array)
        for y in x:
                print(y)
```

Output:
```
1
2
3
4
5
6
```

Application of Axis in an Array:

In a 2D array, if **axis=0** then the operation takes place downwards, i.e., summing down rows; and if **axis=1** then it works across, i.e. summing up columns.

 # Applications of axis on 0 & 1

```
import numpy as np

data=[[1,2,3] , [4,5,6] , [7,8,9]]

arr=np.array(data)

print(arr)

print("----------------------")
```

 # axis=0 works through rows on columns
```
res1=arr.sum(axis=0)

print(res1)

print("----------------------")
```

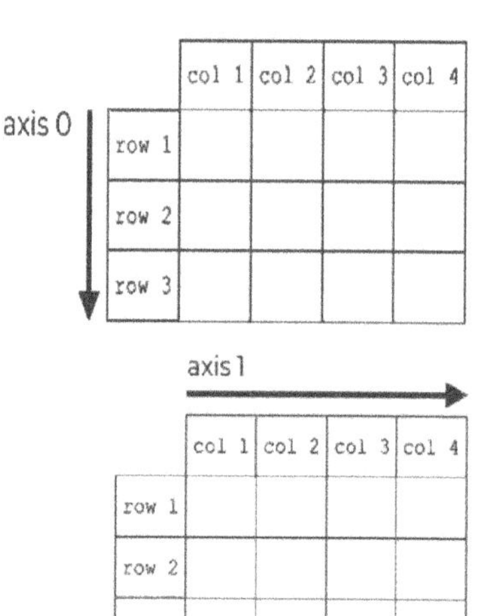

 # axis=1 works through columns on rows
```
res2=arr.sum(axis=1)

print(res2)

print("----------------------")
```

 # When axis=None, the operation on all elements will take place
```
res3=arr.sum(axis=None)

print(res3)
```

Output:

```
[[1 2 3]
 [4 5 6]
 [7 8 9]]
```

```
# Sum across rows on columns (axis=0)
[12 15 18]
```

```
# Sum across columns on rows (axis=1)
[ 6 15 24]
```

```
45
```

 # Joining/concatenation of arrays using axis:
```python
import numpy as np
arr1=np.array([[1, 2], [3, 4]])
arr2=np.array([[5, 6], [7, 8]])
print(arr1)
print("----------------")
print(arr2)
print("\n       # If axis=None : \n")
arr=np.concatenate((arr1, arr2), axis=None)
print(arr)
print("\n       # If axis=0 : \n")
arr=np.concatenate((arr1, arr2), axis=0)    # Rows get joined on same col
print(arr)
print("\n       # If axis=1 : \n")
arr=np.concatenate((arr1, arr2), axis=1)    #Col. Get joined on the same row
print(arr)
```

Output:

```
[[1 2]
 [3 4]]
```

```
[[5 6]
 [7 8]]
```

 # If axis=None :

```
[1 2 3 4 5 6 7 8]
```

 # If axis=0 :

[[1 2]
 [3 4]
 [5 6]
 [7 8]]

 # If axis=1 :

[[1 2 5 6]
 [3 4 7 8]]

Mathematical Functions of NumPy Array:

- add()
- subtract()
- multiply()
- divide()

 # Execution of the functions:

```python
import numpy as np

arr1 = np.array([[1, 2], [3, 4]])
arr2 = np.array([5, 6])
arr3=np.array([[10,20],[30,40]])

add1=np.add(arr1, arr2)
add2=np.add(arr1, arr3)
sub=np.subtract(arr1, arr2)
mult=np.multiply(arr1, arr2)
div=np.divide(arr1, arr2)
modu= np.mod(arr1, arr2)

print("Addition:\n", add1)
print("Addition:\n", add2)
print("Subtraction:\n", sub)
print("Multiplication:\n", mult)
print("Division:\n", div)
print("Modulus:\n", modu)
```

Output:

Addition:	Multiplication:
[[6 8]	[[5 12]
[8 10]]	[15 24]]

Addition: [[11 22] [33 44]]	Division: [[0.2 0.33333333] [0.6 0.66666667]]
Subtraction: [[-4 -4] [-2 -2]]	Modulus: [[1 2] [3 4]]

Sorting of the Array:

 # Use sort() function:
```
import numpy as np
arr = np.array([3, 2, 0, 1])
print(np.sort(arr))
```

Note:
kind='quicksort' is the default sort
kind='mergesort' is a Stable sort
kind='heapsort' is not stable, but good for worst-case

Output:
```
[0 1 2 3]
```

 # Sort the array alphabetically:
```
import numpy as np
arr = np.array(['India', 'China', 'Russia'])
print(np.sort(arr, kind='quicksort'))    # 'quicksort' is by default
```

Output:
```
['China' 'India' 'Russia']
```

 # Sort a 2-D array: Sorting in ascending order row-wise (on column):
```
import numpy as np
arr = np.array([[3, 2, 4], [5, 0, 1]])
print(np.sort(arr, axis=0))      # By default axis=o
```
Output: *# Sorted across row, downwards*
```
[[3 0 1]
 [5 2 4]]
```

 # Sorting in Descending order, Row-wise (on column) when axis=0:
```
import numpy as np
arr = np.array([[3, 2, 4], [5, 0, 1]])
print(-np.sort(-arr, axis=0)      # Descending order by -numpy and -array
```
Output: *# Sorted across rows (top to bottom)*
```
[[5 2 4]
 [3 0 1]]
```

 # Display in Reverse order, Column-wise (on row):
```
import numpy as np
arr = np.array([[3, 2, 4], [5, 0, 1]])
print(np.sort(arr[::-1]))         # Steps back, so row-order is also reversed
```

Output: # *Reversely Sorted across columns (axis=1)*
[[0 1 5]
 [2 3 4]]

 # Sorting in Ascending order Column-wise *(on row)* **when axis=1**
```
import numpy as np
arr = np.array([[3, 2, 4], [5, 0, 1]])
print(np.sort(arr, axis=1))
```

Output: # *Sorted across columns, as axis=1*
[[2 3 4]
 [0 1 5]]

 # Sorting in Descending order Column-wise *(on row)* **when axis=1:**
```
import numpy as np
arr = np.array([[3, 2, 4], [5, 0, 1]])
print(-np.sort(-arr, axis=1))     # Descending order by -numpy and -array
```

Output: # *Sorted in descending order across columns*
[[4 3 2]
 [5 1 0]]

 # NumPy.arange(a,b,c) function:

Syntax: *arange([start], stop, [step], [dtype])*

arange() function generates values from starting value(a) up to before stop value (b-1) incremented by third value(c) where a & c are optional. In the given example below, [**1, 2, 3, 4**] values will be generated for x.

```
import numpy as np
x=np.arange(5)
print(x)
x=np.arange(1,5)
print(x)
x=np.arange(0,5,2)
print(x)
```

Output:
[0 1 2 3 4]
[1 2 3 4]
[0 2 4]

Chapter 9

Data Science:
Python Pandas and Ensemble ML

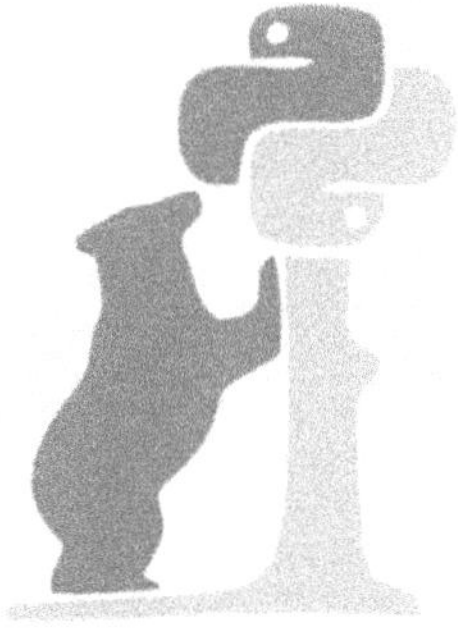

Chapter Objective:

- Python Data Science
- What is Pandas
- The Simple Analogy
- Why Pandas
- Pandas Eco-System
- Environment Setup
- MatPotLib Package
- Data Type
- MatPlotLib
- Data Structure
- Series
- DataFrame
- Overall Functionality of Pandas
- Pandas in a Summary
- What is Ensemble
- How does Ensemble work
- Types of Ensembling
- Why Ensemble Methods are Powerful
- Ensemble in Summary
- Relation between Ensemble and Data Science with Pandas

Python Data Science:

Data Science in Python refers to the process of collecting, storing, cleaning, analysing, and visualising data using Python programming to extract useful insights and support decision-making. It involves applying mathematics, statistics, machine learning, and programming skills to work with real-world data. It has very powerful libraries, such as NumPy, Pandas, Matplotlib, etc.

Pandas as Defined:

Pandas is a foundational Python library for data science, created by Wes McKinney in 2008. Its name is derived from "Panel Data." By making complex data accessible and interpretable, Pandas empowers organisations to make data-driven decisions, solidifying its role as an indispensable asset in the data science toolkit.

The Simple Analogy:

Popular tools like MS Excel or Google Sheets are used for organising data in rows and columns. Pandas can be seen as a more powerful, programmer-friendly counterpart that provides spreadsheet-like flexibility, adding automation, scalability, and the analytical strength of Python.

Why is Pandas so Crucial for Data Science?

Data science projects follow a lifecycle, and Pandas is indispensable for the early and mid-stages:

- **Data Acquisition**: Reading data from various sources (CSV, Excel, SQL databases, JSON, web APIs).
- **Data Cleaning & Munging/Wrangling:** This is Pandas' superpower. Real-world data is messy. Pandas helps you handle:
    - o Missing values
    - o Incorrect data types
    - o Duplicate entries
    - o Irrelevant columns
- **Data Exploration & Analysis (EDA):** Quickly summarising your data to understand its structure, contents, and patterns.
- **Data Transformation:** Reshaping data, creating new columns from existing ones, filtering, and sorting.

- **Preparation for Modelling:** Getting your data into a clean, numerical format required by machine learning libraries like Scikit-learn, TensorFlow, and PyTorch.

Pandas in the Python Data Science Ecosystem:

Pandas doesn't exist in a vacuum. Pandas is the main Python library for handling tabular data. It provides powerful, easy-to-use structures that act as a bridge, turning messy raw data into a clean, organised format ready for analysis. Here are a few of those:

- **NumPy:** Pandas is built on top of NumPy. Its underlying data structures use NumPy arrays, which makes it very fast.

- **Matplotlib:** After analysing data in Pandas, we can directly pass the DataFrames/Series to these libraries for visualisation.

- **Database:** SQL databases and file formats for data input/output.

Installation/Environment Setup of Pandas:

Prerequisites:

Have Python installed (recommended: Python 3.8+).
Open a terminal / PowerShell (Windows) or Terminal (macOS / Linux).

On Windows (PowerShell):

```
python -m venv myenv
.\myenv\Scripts\Activate.ps1
```

On Mac OS / Linux:

```
python3 -m venv myenv
source myenv/bin/activate
```

Install pandas with pip (most common):

```
python -m pip install --upgrade pip        # Optional but recommended
python -m pip install pandas
```

Using Anaconda / Miniconda (alternative):

```
conda create -n ds_env python=3.10 -y     # Creates env (optional)
conda activate ds_env
conda install pandas -y
```

Using Jupyter in the same env:

```
python -m pip install jupyterlab
# or for classic notebook
python -m pip install notebook
```

Matplotlib Package:

Matplotlib is a Python library used to represent data in graphical form. This was developed by John Hunter and many other contributors, enabling the creation of high-quality graphs, charts, and figures. The library is extensive and allows precise control over every detail of a figure. Key concepts and functions in Matplotlib include:

- **Figure and axes:** A figure is the entire plot container, and each plot within it is called an axis.
- **Plotting:** The very first thing required to plot a graph is data. Data can be stored in lists, NumPy arrays, or Pandas DataFrames, which can then be plotted using functions like scatter(), bar(), and pie(), along with other plotting functions.
- **Axis:** The figure and axes obtained using subplots() can be used for modification. Properties of the x-axis and y-axis (labels, minimum and maximum values, etc.) can be changed using Axes.set().

Data Type of Pandas:

- **int64**: For storing integer values
- **float64**: For storing decimal (floating-point) values
- **object**: Used for string (text) data, but can also store mixed types.
- **bool**: Boolean type (True/False) values
- **datetime64**: Used for Date and Time values

Data Structure in Pandas using Series and DataFrame:

- **Series:** 1-D structure to store homogeneous (single data type) and mutable (can be modified/added) data; the index labels themselves are immutable, but the entire index can be replaced with a new one.

- **DataFrame:** 2-D structure to store heterogeneous (multiple data types) and mutable data.

Panadas in Summary:

So, finally, Pandas stands as the primary Python library for working with tabular data. It equips us with robust data structures and practical tools that transform raw, cluttered information into clean, well-organised, and analysis-ready datasets. For anyone pursuing data science in Python, learning Pandas isn't optional - it's fundamental.

Overall, the functionality of Pandas:

Feature	Analogy	Pandas Term	Purpose
Whole Spreadsheet	Excel Worksheet	DataFrame	The primary 2D data structure.
Single Column	Column A, B, C	Series	The primary 1D data structure.
Cells	Individual cells (A1, B2)	Scalar Values	A single data point within a Series/DataFrame.
Formulas & Pivot Tables	Excel Formulas	Pandas Operations	Methods for calculation, grouping, and aggregation.

What is Ensemble:

Ensemble is the process of combining multiple machine-learning (ML) models to learn from experience, improving prediction accuracy, reducing errors, and increasing robustness. It is applied in Data Science and combines the predictions of multiple models to produce a final result that is usually more accurate and reliable than any single model.

How does Ensemble work:

An ensemble is also called a 'teamwork of models'. A model means the reality, and it works in two phases: **(1)** Training and **(2)** Prediction. For example, a Model as a student gets **trained** by solving many different problems, rectifying mistakes, and minimising errors, which predicts the student's ability to solve new critical problems and achieve success. So, the student is trained by feeding **Data** and gaining experience, he builds his ability of **prediction** for solving more problems with accuracy, fewer errors and more robustness.

Thus, in Ensemble, different models (often as part of Artificial Intelligence) make other mistakes, but combining them reduces errors, and overall accuracy improves. Hence, in this model, it takes multiple advices, instead of one and improves prediction accuracy, reduces errors and increases robustness.

Types of Ensembling:

Bagging (Bootstrap Aggregation): Train many models independently, and combine them.
Example: Random Forest

Boosting: Train models one after another, where each new model fixes previous errors.
Example: XGBoost, AdaBoost, LightGBM

Stacking: Combine predictions of many models using a meta-model.
Character: Extremely powerful and often used in competitions

Voting / Averaging: It is a Simple but effective combination of multiple models.
Character: Good baseline and Easy to implement

Why Ensemble Methods are Powerful:

● **They Reduce Errors:**
Every model makes mistakes—but not the same mistakes.
When several models are combined:
- ✓ Their errors cancel out
- ✓ Their strengths add up

This leads to higher accuracy.
Example: 10 weak models → combined → often stronger than 1 strong model.

● **They Reduce Overfitting:**
Many models working together behave more smoothly and predict better on new data.
- ✓ Overfitting = model memorises training data
- ✓ Ensembles = model generalises to future data

Example: Random Forest reduces overfitting that a single decision tree usually has.

● **They Reduce Bias:**

Some models are too simple (high bias).
Boosting methods fix this by learning from previous mistakes.
Boosting = Think step-by-step improvement.
Models like XGBoost and LightGBM are compelling due to this.

- **They Handle Complexity Better**
    Real-world data is messy:
    - ✓ noise
    - ✓ missing values
    - ✓ non-linear patterns

    Ensembles combine different models to capture these patterns more effectively.

- **They Are Very Difficult to Beat**
    In most major data science competitions (Kaggle, analytics challenges):
    Almost all winning solutions use ensemble methods.
    Because they consistently give:
    - ✓ superior accuracy
    - ✓ stability
    - ✓ robustness

Ensemble in Summary:

So, Ensemble technique refers to a method—mostly used in machine learning, statistics, and sometimes in performing arts—where multiple models or performers are combined to produce a better overall outcome than any individual component alone.

Relation of Ensemble and Data Science with Pandas:

Ensemble learning works only when high-quality structured data is provided, and in Data Science, Pandas is the main tool used to create that high-quality dataset.

Hence, Pandas plays a foundational role in Ensemble Learning because accurate and robust predictions depend completely on clean, well-structured, and well-engineered datasets prepared using Pandas before ML models are trained and combined.

So, **Pandas prepares the data → ensemble learning trains models → final prediction improves**.

Chapter 10

Python Pandas:

Series

Chapter Objective:

- Key characters Series
- Series Creating
- Creating a Series with Labels
- Creating a Series with Dictionary
- Creating a Series with a NumPy
- Creating Series with NumPy Function
- Creating index by for loop
- Re-Ordering indexes
- Iteration of Series
- Series from Scalar
- Accessing Data from its Position
- Use of loc and iloc
- Head and Tail functions
- Adding/Updating value
- Re-Indexing
- Renaming Series Label
- Boolean-Indexing
- Access values with Conditions
- Series.where()
- Mathematical Operations
- Delete Data of a Series using del, drop(), pop()
- Concatenation of two Series
- Sorting on Series
- Vector operation

Series as Defined:

A Pandas Series is typically a one-dimensional (1-D) array of homogeneous data type (i.e. integers, strings, floats, or objects) by default. However, Series can also store mixed or heterogeneous data in an object dtype, and the axis labels are collectively called the index.

10   23.3   56   17   52.5   61   73.7   90.2   26   72

Key characters:

- Homogeneous (heterogeneous as well) data
- Size (number of elements) is Immutable (fixed)
- Values of existing elements are Mutable (modified)

A series can be created using various inputs, such as:

- List
- Dictionary
- NdArray
- Scalar or constant value

Create an Empty Series (An example):

import pandas as pd   *# Imports pandas library with an object pd*
s = pd.**S**eries(dtype='float64') *# Creating a series by **S**eries() fn. with pd*
print(s)   *# Printing the series by its object, s*

Output (*of the empty Series*)**:**
Series([], dtype: *float64*)

Create a Series from the List:

If data is a list, then the index passed must be of the same length (no. of data in it). If no index is passed, then by default the index is 0 to the Nth term, and so the range of the index starts from 0 up to N-1.

Example:
x=[10, 20, 30, 40, 50] *# List of 5 elements having default index 0 to 4*
import pandas as pd
s = pd.**S**eries(x)   *# Creates a Series from the list object x*
print(s)   *# Prints the series with default indexes (0...4)*

Output:
0   10
1   20
2   30
3   40
4   50
dtype: int64

Creating a Series with Labels/users' Indexes:

```
import pandas as pd
import numpy as np
x = np.array(['a', 'b', 'c', 'd'])
s = pd.Series(x, index=[100,101,102,103])
print(s)
```

Output:

```
100   a
101   b
102   c
103   d
dtype: object
```

Creating a Series with a Dictionary:

```
import pandas as pd
x = {'a' : 0., 'b' : 1., 'c' : 2.}
s = pd.Series(x)
print(s)
```

Output:

```
a 0.0
b 1.0
c 2.0
dtype: float64
```

Creating a Series with a NumPy Array:

```
import pandas as pd
import numpy as np
x=['a', 'b', 'c', 'd']
data = np.array(x)          # Array created by NumPy
s = pd.Series(data)         # Series
print(s)
```

Output:

```
0     a
1     b
2     c
3     d
dtype: object
```

Note: *Dictionary keys become the indexes of Series.*

Creating Series with NumPy Function arange():

```
import pandas as pd
import numpy as np
a=np.arange(1, 10, 2)          # arange() fn. has single 'r'
s=pd.Series(a , index=[10, 20, 30, 40, 50])
print(s)
```
Output:
```
10   1
20   3
30   5
40   7
50   9
dtype: int64
```

Creating an index using a *for* loop:

```
import pandas as pd
import numpy as np
a=np.arange(1, 10, 2)
s=pd.Series(a , index=[x for x in "abcde"])
print(s)
```
Output:
```
a    1
b    3
c    5
d    7
e    9
dtype: int64
```

Re-ordering indexes reorders data:

```
import pandas as pd
import numpy as np
x = {'a' : 0., 'b' : 1., 'c' : 2.}
s = pd.Series(x, index=['b','c','d','a'])
print(s)
```
Output:
```
b    1.0
c    2.0
d    NaN
a    0.0
dtype: float64
```

> **Note:** *Index order is persisted and the missing element is filled with **NaN** (Not a Number)*

Iteration of Series:

Example1:

```
import pandas as pd
x={'a': 'Argentina', 'b': 'America', 'c': 'Canada', 'd': 'Britain'}
s = pd.Series(x)
print(s)              # Prints with index
print()
for i in s:
    print(i)          # Prints the values, without index
```

Output:

```
a    Argentina
b    America
c    Canada
d    Britain
dtype: object

Argentina
America
Canada
Britain
```

Example2:

```
import pandas as pd
s=pd.Series(['Argentina', 'America', 'Canada', 'Britain'])
print(s)
for i in range(len(s)):
    print(i , ":", s[i])
```

 # To print attributes of Series

```
print(s.shape)
print(s.dtype)
print(s.index)
print(s.values)
```

Output:

```
0    Argentina
1    America
2    Canada
3    Britain
dtype: object
```

0 : Argentina
1 : America
2 : Canada
3 : Britain

(4,)
object
RangeIndex(start=0, stop=4, step=1)
['Argentina' 'America' 'Canada' 'Britain']

 # .items() returns both index and value
```python
import pandas as pd
s = pd.Series([1,2,3,4,5], index = ['a','b','c','d','e'])
for index, value in s.items():
        print(f"{index}: {value}")
```
Output:

a: 1
b: 2
c: 3
d: 4
e: 5

Create a Series from a Scalar value:

If data is a scalar value, an index must be provided. The value will be repeated to match the length of the index.

```python
import pandas as pd
s = pd.Series(15, index=[0, 1, 2, 3, 4])
print(s)
```
Output:
```
0    15
1    15
2    15
3    15
4    15
dtype: int64
```

Accessing Data from its Positional-Index & Label:

Data in a Pandas Series can be accessed like a NumPy array. The first element is at index 0, following zero-based indexing. Data in the series can be accessed similarly to an NdArray, meaning the first element is stored at the zeroth position and so on. For example:

```
# Accessing Data by Index
import pandas as pd
s=pd.Series([1,2,3,4,5], index=['a','b','c','d','e'])
print(s)                    # The series
print (s[0])                # Value of the 0 index
print(s['b'])               # Value of the 'b' label
print (s[0:3])              # Values from 0 index to 2 index (3 −1=>2 index)
print(s[-2:])               # Values from -2 index to last
print(s['a' : 'd'])         # All the values will be printed from 'a' to 'd' label
print(s.loc['a' : 'd'])     # All the values will be printed from 'a' to 'd' label
```

Output:

```
a    1       # s              d    4           # s[-2]
b    2                        e    5
c    3                        dtype: int64
d    4
e    5                        a    1           # s['a' : 'd']
dtype: int64                  b    2
                              c    3
                              d    4
1        # s[0]               dtype: int64

2        # s['b']             a    1           # s.loc['a' : 'd']
a 1      # s[0:3]             b    2
b 2                           c    3
c 3                           d    4
dtype: int64                  dtype: int64

                             Note: loc locates data using label
```

```
# Retrieving the first three elements:
import pandas as pd
s = pd.Series([1,2,3,4,5], index = ['a','b','c','d','e'])
print (s[:3])                   # Retrieves the first three element
```
Output:
```
a       1
b       2
c       3
dtype: int64
```

Retrieve a single element using label:

```
import pandas as pd
s = pd.Series([1,2,3,4,5], index = ['a','b','c','d','e'])
print (s['a'])                    # Retrieves a single element
```

Output:
```
1
```

Retrieving the last three elements:

```
import pandas as pd
s = pd.Series([1,2,3,4,5], index = ['a','b','c','d','e'])
print (s[-3:])          # Retrieves the last three element using -ve index
```
Output:
```
c    3
d    4
e    5
dtype: int64
```

Retrieve multiple elements using labels:

```
import pandas as pd
s = pd.Series([1,2,3,4,5], index = ['a','b','c','d','e'])
print (s['b':'d'])        # Retrieves values by label (user index)
```

Output:
```
b    2
c    3
d    4
dtype: int64
```

Retrieve selective elements using labels:

```
import pandas as pd
s = pd.Series([1,2,3,4,5] ,index = ['a','b','c','d','e'])
print (s [ ['a','c','d'] ])  # Retrieves multiple elements with [[]]
```

Output:
```
a    1
c    3
d    4
dtype: int64
```

Error on non-existence of index

```
import pandas as pd
s = pd.Series([1,2,3,4,5], index = ['a','b','c','d','e'])
print(s['f'])              # Index is not existing, gives error
print(s.get('f', 'Index not found'))
```

Output:
Error message: KeyError: 'f'
Index not found

> **Note:** *If a label is not contained, an exception is raised.*

Use of loc[] and iloc[] to access values:

The difference between **loc[]** & **iloc[]** in Pandas is: **loc** is used on row (& column) by the Labels (or user given index), <u>inclusive last Label,</u> and **iloc** is used to get by the integer index (or default position). For loc[], if the label is not present, then it returns a <u>key error,</u> and for iloc[], if the position is not present, it returns an <u>index error</u>.

- **loc** returns the values of the user-given index (label/name)
- **iloc** returns the values of the default index (i.e. 0,1,2,3…)

 # Display using iloc & loc on user-given character-index (label)
```
import pandas as pd
s=pd.Series([1, 2, 3, 4, 5] , index=['a' , 'b', 'c', 'd', 'e'])
print("Series::\n", s)
print(s[3])      # Though labels are different, it reads on the default index
print(s.iloc[3])         # Works for positional indexing, iloc[] is preferred
print(s['c'])
print("s.iloc[1 : 4]::\n", s.iloc[1 : 4])      # Prints based on position
print("s.loc['b':'e'] \n::", s.loc['b':'e']) # Prints values of labels 'b' to 'e'
```

Output:

Series::
```
a    1
b    2
c    3
d    4
e    5
dtype: int64
4                # Output of s[3]
4                # Output of s.iloc[3]
3                # Output of s['c']
```

> **Note:** *It is always the best choice to use iloc[] for position-based index, rather object[], viz.* ***s.iloc[3]***, *instead of s[3] as it may mislead.*

s.iloc[1 : 4]::	s.loc['b' : 'e']::
b 2	b 2
c 3	c 3
d 4	d 4
dtype: int64	e 5
	dtype: int64

Display element(s) using loc & iloc on user-given numeric-index:

```python
import pandas as pd
s = pd.Series([11, 22, 33, 44, 55, 66, 77, 88, 99, 100],
              index=[49, 48, 47, 46, 45, 1, 2, 3, 4, 5])
print('s::>\n', s)                      # Prints the whole series
print('s.loc[:3]::>\n', s.loc[:3])  # Prints the values of 0-3 user's index
print('s.loc[1:3];:>\n', s.loc[1:3]) # Prints the values of given indexes
print('s[:3]::>\n', s[:3])          # Prints the values of 0-2 indexes
print('s[1:3]::>\n', s[1:3])        # Prints the values from 1 to last index-1
print('s.iloc[:3]::>\n', s.iloc[:3])    # Prints the values of 0-2 indexes
print('s.iloc[1:3]::>\n', s.iloc[1:3])# Prints the values of 1-2 indexes like slicing rules
print('s[1:9:3]::>\n',s[1:9:3] ) # Prints values from 1 to 9-1 index incremented by 3
```

Output:

```
s::>
49    11
48    22
47    33
46    44
45    55
1     66
2     77
3     88
4     99
5     100
dtype: int64
```

> **Note:** If the user index (label) is numeric and we access the <u>range of values using : (not iloc)</u>, then it works on the <u>default index</u> or positions. But accessing a single value by numeric label (user index), then it works on the label only, not on positions (default index). So, here it prints the values of labels from the start up to last label (inclusive).

s.loc[:3]::>	s[1:3]::>
49 11	48 22
48 22	47 33
47 33	dtype: int64
46 44	**s.iloc[:3]::>**
45 55	49 11
1 66	48 22
2 77	47 33
3 88	dtype: int64
dtype: int64	

<table>
<tr><td>

s.loc[1:3];:>

1   66

2   77

3   88

dtype: int64

s[:3]::>

49   11

48   22

47   33

dtype: int64

</td><td>

s.iloc[1:3]::>

48   22

47   33

dtype: int64

s.iloc[1:3]::>

48   22

47   33

dtype: int64

s[1:9:3]::>

48   22

45   55

3   88

dtype: int64

</td></tr>
</table>

Retrieve data using index and label

```
import pandas as pd
s = pd.Series(data=[10,20,30,40,50], index=[1,2,3,4,5])
print(s)                 # Prints values based on label
print(s[4])              # Prints value(s) based on label, Val-1
print(s.loc[4])          # Prints value(s) based on label, val-2
print(s.iloc[4])         # Prints value(s) based on index/position, Val-3
print(s[1:4])            # Prints values based on index
print(s.loc[1:4])        # Prints values based on labels
print(s.iloc[1:4])       # Prints values based on index/position
```

Output:

```
1   10
2   20
3   30
4   40
5   50
dtype: int64

40                       # Val-1

40                       # Val-2

50                       # Val-3
```

```
2    20
3    30
4    40
dtype: int64

1    10
2    20
3    30
4    40
dtype: int64

0    20
1    30
2    40
dtype: int64
```

> **Note:** *Taking a range of values on a Series of Labels (user index) without using loc/iloc, then values are read based on an index, with last-1 rule. Here in above example s[4] works like loc or level while the index is numeric, but for string or non-sequential indexes, s[4] could raise an error or behave unexpectedly.*

Head and Tail functions:

head(n) function returns the first n rows by default. The number of elements to display is five, but we can pass a custom number. Similarly, **tail(n)** function returns the last n rows.

 # Display top 5 data using head():

```
import pandas as pd
s = pd.Series([10,20,30,40,50], index=[1,2,3,4,5])
print(s)
print(s.head())          # top 5 rows by default
print(s.head(2))         # top 2 rows
print(s.head(-2))        # All from top except bottom 2 rows
```

Output:

```
1    10              # print(s)
2    20
3    30
4    40
5    50
dtype: int64

1    10              # Top 5 elements by head()
2    20
3    30
4    40
5    50
dtype: int64
```

```
1    10                          # Top 2 elements by head(2)
2    20
dtype: int64

1    10                          # Except bottom 2 rows by head(-2)
2    20
3    30
dtype: int64
```

 # Display top 2 elements using head():
```
import pandas as pd
import numpy as np
s = pd.Series(np.random.randn(4))      # Series with 4 random numbers
print ('The original series is:')
print (s)
print("")
print ('The first two rows of the data series=>')
print (s.head(2))
```

Output:
The original series is:
```
0   -1.031682
1    0.166210
2    0.276048
3   -0.250155
dtype: float64
```

The first two rows of the data series=>
```
0   -1.031682
1    0.166210
dtype: float64
```

tail(n) function returns the last n rows (observe the indexes). The default number of elements to display is five, but you may pass a custom number.

 # Display the bottom-most 5 elements using tail():
```
import pandas as pd
s = pd.Series([10,20,30,40,50], index=[1,2,3,4,5])
print(s)
print(s.tail())              # By default print 5 lowermost rows
print(s.tail(2))             # Bottommost 2 rows
print(s.tail(-2))            # All from bottom except top 2 rows
```

Output:

```
1    10                          # print(s)
2    20
3    30
4    40
5    50
dtype: int64

1    10                          # Last 5 elements by tail()
2    20
3    30
4    40
5    50
dtype: int64

4    40                          # Last 2 elements by tail(2)
5    50
dtype: int64

3   30                           # Except top 2 elements by tail(-2)
4   40
5   50
dtype: int64
```

 # Display bottom-most 2 elements using tail():
```
import pandas as pd
import numpy as np
# Create a series with 4 random numbers using random.randn() function
s = pd.Series(np.random.randn(4))
print("The original series is=> ")
print(s)
print("The last two rows of the data series=> ")
print(s.tail(2))
```

Output:

```
The original series is=>
0    0.172709
1   -0.298694
2    0.202988
3    0.728251
dtype: float64
```

The last two rows of the data series=>
2   0.202988
3   0.728251
dtype: float64

Adding/Updating value to Series:

```
import pandas as pd
s = pd.Series(data=[10,20,30,40,50], index=[ 'a','b','c','d','e'])
print(s)
s[2]=333              # Adds value on index-based position (index i:s 2)
s['b']=222            # Adds value on label (default index is: 1)
s.iloc[4]=555         # Adds value on index (default index is: 4)
s.loc['d']=444        # Adds value on label 'd' (default index is: 3)
print(s)
```

Output:
```
a    10               # Output of s, before updation
b    20
c    30
d    40
e    50
dtype: int64

a    10               # Output of s, after updation
b    222
c    333
d    444
e    555
dtype: int64
```

Re-Indexing of Series:

It is a fundamental operation over pandas series (or DataFrame). It is a process that makes the data in a Series/Data-Frame conform to a set of labels. Reindexing in Python pandas changes the order of data of a series object, which is possible with the help of the **reindex()** function.

For example, given the series below, the first column is a label (as an index) and the second column is for the value.

A	54	←--After Re-indexing--→	e	34
b	76		d	99
c	88		c	88
d	99		b	76
e	34		a	54

The program given below creates a pandas series with some numeric values, then indexes it with a,b,c,d,e labels, then after the index is changed to e, d, c, b, a with the help of the **reindex()** function.

 # Re-indexing the existing user-given indexes
```
import pandas as pd
data = [54,76,88,99,34]
s1 = pd.Series(data, index=['a','b','c','d','e'])
s2=s1.reindex(['e','d','c','b','a']) # reindex() is assigned to a new object
print(s1)
print(s2)                  # reindex() output comes to s2
```
Output:
```
a    54           # Output of s1
b    76
c    88
d    99
e    34
dtype: int64
```

> **Note:** _NaN_ => Not a Number, or unknown/missing/undefined data

```
e    34           # Output of s2
d    99
c    88
b    76
a    54
dtype: int64
```

 # Re-indexing pandas series without label:
Reindex inserts NaN markers where no data exists for a label. In the program below, f & g are not available as labels, so return NaN.

```
import pandas as pd
data = [54,76,88,99,34]
s1 = pd.Series(data, index=['a', 'b', 'c', 'd', 'e'])
print (s1)
s2=s1.reindex(['f', 'g', 'c', 'b', 'a'])
print(s1)
print(s2)       # When reindexing with non-existent labels, NaN appears.
```
Output:
```
a   54
b   76
c   88
d   99
e   34
dtype: int64
```

```
a    54
b    76
c    88
d    99
e    34
dtype: int64
```

```
f    NaN        # Reindexed with non-existent labels 'f' so NaN appeared.
g    NaN        # Reindexed with non-existent labels 'g' so NaN appeared.
c    88.0
b    76.0
a    54.0
dtype: float64
```

Renaming index/labels by Labels:

```
import pandas as pd
import numpy as np
data = np.array([54,76,88,99,34])
s = pd.Series(data, index=[1,2,3,4,5])
print(s)
s1=s.rename(index={1:'a', 2:'b', 3:'c', 4:'d', 5:'e'}, inplace=True)
print("Inplace=True \n", s)     # s prints update values, as inplace=True
print("Inplace=True \n", s1)    # s1 prints None, as inplace=True
```

Output:

```
1    54              # Output of s
2    76
3    88
4    99
5    34
dtype: int64
```

```
Inplace=True     # inplace=True, the updates take place in the object s, itself
a    54
b    76
c    88
d    99
e    34
dtype: int64

Inplace=True
None             # inplace=True, makes NO effect on the assigned object: s1
```

Boolean-Indexing of Series:

```python
import pandas as pd
import numpy as np
data = np.array([54,76,88,99,34])
s = pd.Series(data, index=[True, False, False, True, True])
print(s)
print(s[s.index==True])          # Access those indexes are True
s.name="Boolean Index"           # Naming of Series
print(s)
```

Output:

```
True    54
False   76
False   88
True    99
True    34
dtype: int32
```
Output of s

```
True    54
True    99
True    34
dtype: int32
```
Output of s[s.index==True]

```
True    54
False   76
False   88
True    99
True    34
```
Output of s
```
Name: Boolean Index, dtype: int32
```

Access values with Conditions (Filtering):

```python
# Filter the values with 3 different conditions
import pandas as pd
s = pd.Series(range(2,10,2))
print(s)
# Shows Boolean value True for those who meet the condition & rest as False
print(s>3)
# Shows all of those values that meet the condition
print(s[s>3])
print(s[s<=3])
```

Output:

# print(s):	# print(s[s>3]):
0 2 1 4 2 6 3 8 dtype: int64	1 4 2 6 3 8 dtype: int64
# print(s>3):	# print(s[s<=3]):
0 False 1 True 2 True 3 True dtype: bool	0 2 dtype: int64

Series.where():

In Pandas Series, the ***where()*** function replaces values where the input condition is False for the given Series object. It takes another object as an input, which is used to replace the value from the original object.

Syntax: *Series.where(cond, other=NaN, inplace=False, axis=None, level=None, errors='raise', try_cast=False, raise_on_error=None)*

 # Print the series of more than 50 using where()
```
import pandas as pd
s = pd.Series([10,20,30,40,50,60])
a=s.where(s>40)
print(a)
```

Output:

```
0    NaN
1    NaN
2    NaN
3    NaN
4    50.0
5    60.0
dtype: float64
```

> **Note:** *Use Series.where() function to replace values in the given Series object with some other value when the condition is not satisfied.*

 # Print the series has a value of 50
```
import pandas as pd
s = pd.Series([10,20,30,40,50])
a=s.where(s == 30)
print(a)
```

Output:
```
0    NaN
1    NaN
2    30
3    NaN
4    NaN
dtype: float64
```

 # Print the series 50 & less
```python
import pandas as pd
s = pd.Series([10,20,30,40,50,60,70,80,90])
a=s.where(s <= 50)
print(a)
```

Output:
```
0    10.0
1    20.0
2    30.0
3    40.0
4    50.0
5    NaN
6    NaN
7    NaN
8    NaN
dtype: float64
```

> **Note:**
> - ***s>3*** -> *Output: Prints only Boolean, True those meet the cond., and False those don't*
> - ***[s[s>3]]*** -> *Output: Prints exact values that only meet the condition.*
> - ***where(s>3)*** -> *Output: Those meet the cond. print the values, rest print NaN*

 # Use Series.where() function to replace values in the given Series.
```python
import pandas as pd
sr1=pd.Series([22, 18, 19, 20, 21],
index = ['Student 1', 'Student 2', 'Student 3', 'Student 4', 'Student 5'])
print(sr1)                    # Printing the Series-1
sr2=pd.Series([19, 16, 22, 20, 18] ,
index = ['Student 1', 'Student 2', 'Student 3', 'Student 4', 'Student 5'])
print(sr2)                    # Printing the second Series-2
b=sr1.where(sr1 >20, sr2) # Replacing values of sr2 by sr1 where sr1>20
print(b)
```

Output:
```
Student 1   22      # Output of sr1
Student 2   18
Student 3   19
Student 4   20
Student 5   21
dtype: int64
```

```
Student 1    19        # Output of sr2
Student 2    16
Student 3    22
Student 4    20
Student 5    18
dtype: int64

Student 1    22        # Output of b
Student 2    16
Student 3    22
Student 4    20
Student 5    21
dtype: int64
```

> **Note:**
>
> ***where(sr1>20, sr2)*** *means:*
>
> *if sr1>20:*
>
> *sr2=sr1*
>
> *It means, if the indices are the same for sr1 & sr2, then the values of sr1, which match according to its condition to sr2, will replace the values of sr2.*

Mathematical Operations:

```
+       add()
-       sub(), subtract()
*       mul(), multiply()
/       div(), divide()
//      floordiv()
%       mod()
**      pow()
```

 # Application of mathematical functions:

```
import pandas as pd
s1 = pd.Series([1,2,3,4], index=[0,1,2,3])
s2 = pd.Series([10,20,30,40] , index=[0,1,2,3])
s3 = pd.Series([101,202,303,404], index=[2,3,4,5]) #Different index
print (s1 , "\n", s2, "\n", s3)
print("ADD: \n", (s2+s1))          # or print(s2.add(s1))
print("MUL: \n", s2*s1)            # or print(s2.multiply(s1))
print("DIV: \n", s2/s1)            # or print(s2.div(s1))
print("FLOORDIV: \n", s2//s1) # or print(s2.floordiv(s1))
print("MOD: \n", s2%s1 )           # or print(s2.mod(s1))
print("POW: \n", s2**s1)           # or print(s2.pow(s1))
print("SUB: \n", s3-s1)            # or print(s3.sub(s1))
```

Output:

# S1=>		MUL:	
0	1	0	10
1	2	1	40
2	3	2	90
3	4	3	160
dtype: int64		dtype: int64	

# S2=> 0 10 1 20 2 30 3 40 dtype: int64	**DIV:** 0 10.0 1 10.0 2 10.0 3 10.0 dtype: float64
# S3=> 2 101 3 202 4 303 5 404 dtype: int64	**FLOORDIV:** 0 10 1 10 2 10 3 10 dtype: int64
ADD: 0 11 1 22 2 33 3 44 dtype: int64	**MOD:** 0 0 1 0 2 0 3 0 dtype: int64
SUB: 0 ***NaN*** 1 ***NaN*** 2 98.0 3 198.0 4 ***NaN*** 5 ***NaN*** dtype: float64	

 # A Series is multiplied by a no, then the values also get multiplied

```python
import pandas as pd
s=pd.Series([30,10,50,30,90])
print(s*2)          # Series is getting multiplied by 2
```

Output:

```
0      60
1      20
2      100
3      60
4      180
dtype: int64
```

Update Series:

```
import pandas as pd
s=pd.Series([1,2,3,4,5], index=[10,20,30,40,50])
print(s)
s.update(pd.Series([1,22,3,44,5], index=[10,20,30,40,50]))
print(s)                        # Update is done on the same/original index
```

Output:

```
10   1                          # Output of s before updation
20   2
30   3
40   4
50   5
dtype: int64

10   1                          # Output of s after updation
20   22
30   3
40   44
50   5
dtype: int64
```

Delete Data of a Series using *del*:

```
import pandas as pd
s1=pd.Series([10,20,30,40,50])
s2 = pd.Series([1,2,3,4,5], index=[10,20,30,40,50])
s3 = pd.Series([11,12,13,14,15], index=['a', 'b', 'c', 'd', 'e'])
print(s1 , "\n" , s2 , "\n" , s3)   # 1st , 2nd , 3rd output
del s1[2]        # Use default index, as there is no label (user index)
print(s1)        # 4th  output
del s2[20]       # Use numeric label (user index) only
print(s2)        # 5th output
del s3['b']      # If label is assigned, then default index will not work
print(s3)        # 6th output
```

Output:

# 1st output:	# 4th output:
0 10	0 10
1 20	1 20
2 30	3 40
3 40	4 50
4 50	dtype: int64
dtype: int64	

<table>
<tr><td>

 # 2nd output:

```
10   1
20   2
30   3
40   4
50   5
dtype: int64
```

</td><td>

 # 5th output:

```
10   1
30   3
40   4
50   5
dtype: int64
```

</td></tr>
<tr><td>

 # 3rd output:

```
a     11
b     12
c     13
d     14
e     15
dtype: int64
```

</td><td>

 # 6th output:

```
a     11
c     13
d     14
e     15
dtype: int64
```

</td></tr>
</table>

Delete Data of a Series using *drop()*:

 # Drop returns updated Series after deleting & retains the Original

```python
import pandas as pd
s1=pd.Series([10,20,30,40,50])
s2 = pd.Series([1,2,3,4,5], index=[10,20,30,40,50])
s3 = pd.Series([11,12,13,14,15], index=['a', 'b', 'c', 'd', 'e'])
print(s1)        # 1st output
print(s2)        # 2nd output
print(s3)        # 3rd output
x1=s1.drop([1])        # After drop s1 retains the same values
print(x1)        # 4th  output,  updated values)
x2=s1.drop([0,3])        # Deletes the values
of 0 & 3 index
print(x2)        # 5th output
# To delete a range of values using index[]
y1=s2.drop(s2.index[1: 3])
print(y1)        # 6th output, updated
print(s2)        # 7th output, no change
# Deletes multiple values of 30, 40 labels
y2=s2.drop([30,40])
print(y2)        # 8th output
z1=s3.drop(['a'])
print(z1)        # 9th output
z2=s3.drop(['c', 'e'])
print(z2)        # 10th output
```

> **NOTE:** *drop()* *function works on index & returns the action (after delete) to the assigned object, & original object retains the original values, because by default* ***inplace=False*** *in drop() function.*

Output:

<table>
<tr><td>

 # 1st output:

```
0   10
1   20
2   30
3   40
4   50
dtype: int64
```

</td><td>

 # 6th output: *Updated*

```
10   1
40   4
50   5
dtype: int64
```

</td></tr>
<tr><td>

 # 2nd output:

```
10   1
20   2
30   3
40   4
50   5
dtype: int64
```

</td><td>

 # 7th output: *No change*

```
10   1
20   2
30   3
40   4
50   5
dtype: int64
```

</td></tr>
<tr><td>

 # 3rd output:

```
a   11
b   12
c   13
d   14
e   15
dtype: int64
```

</td><td>

 # 8th output:

```
10   1
20   2
50   5
dtype: int64
```

</td></tr>
<tr><td>

 # 4th output:

```
0   10
2   30
3   40
4   50
dtype: int64
```

</td><td>

 # 9th output:

```
b   12
c   13
d   14
e   15
dtype: int64
```

</td></tr>
<tr><td>

 # 5th output:

```
1   20
2   30
4   50
dtype: int64
```

</td><td>

 # 10th output:

```
a   11
b   12
d   14
dtype: int64
```

</td></tr>
</table>

Delete Data of a Series using *pop()*:

```
import pandas as pd
s1=pd.Series([10,20,30,40,50])
s2 = pd.Series([1,2,3,4,5], index=[10,20,30,40,50])
s3 = pd.Series([11,12,13,14,15], index=['a', 'b', 'c', 'd', 'e'])
print(s1)        # 1st output
print(s2)        # 2nd output
print(s3)        # 3rd output
print("")
s1.pop(1)                   # Deleting on default index
print(s1)        # 4th output
print("")
s2.pop(20)                  # Deleting on label (index)
print(s2)        # 5th output
print("")
s3.pop('b')                 # Deleting on label
print(s3)        # 6th output
```

Output:

# 1st output:	# 4th output:
0 10 1 20 2 30 3 40 4 50 dtype: int64	0 10 2 30 3 40 4 50 dtype: int64
# 2nd output:	# 5th output:
10 1 20 2 30 3 40 4 50 5 dtype: int64	10 1 30 3 40 4 50 5 dtype: int64
# 3rd output:	# 6th output:
a 11 b 12 c 13 d 14 e 15 dtype: int64	a 11 c 13 d 14 e 15 dtype: int64

Concatenation of two Series:

```python
import pandas as pd
x=[1,2,3,4]
y=[11,12,13,14]
s1 = pd.Series(x)
s2 = pd.Series(y)
con=pd.concat([s1,s2], axis=0)      # axis=0 is by default
print(con)                          # 1st output
con1=pd.concat([s1,s2], axis=1)
print(con1)                         # 2nd output
print(con[2:4])                     # 3rd output on default index
print(con[3])                       # 4th output on label
print(con.iloc[3])                  # 5th output on default index
print(con1.iloc[3])                 # 6th output
```

Output:

# 1st output:		# 2nd output:		# 4th output:
0	1	0 1		3 4 # Value of 3 index from s1
1	2	0 1 11		3 14 # Value of 3 index from s2
2	3	1 2 12		dtype: int64
3	4	2 3 13		
0	11	3 4 14		# 5th output:
1	12	# 3rd output:		4 # Value of 3 index from s1
2	13	2 3		# 6th output:
3	14	3 4		0 4 # Value of 0th column of df
dtype: int64		dtype: int64		1 14 # Value of 1st column of df
				Name: 3, dtype: int64

Note:

- *Hereafter, joining the two series, their individual indices are repeatedly visible as Labels, as 1st output*
- *axis=0 is by default, concatenates, row-wise, from down*
- *While axis=1, concatenates on column, across in the common index*
- *While slicing the concatenated series, the default indexes work as a single series made out of two.*
- *But when printing one value, then it works as the label, so it prints two values (see the 4th output), with label 3 twice.*
- *iloc[] can be used to access a single value by the default index.*
- *Con1 behaves like a DataFrame (df), so row of index 3 has 0 & 1 col.*

Sorting on Series:

```python
import pandas as pd
s = pd.Series(['p', 'q', 'r', 's'], index=[3, 2, 4, 5])
```

 # Sort values in ascending order on the index while inplace=True
```python
s.sort_index(ascending=True, inplace=True)
print(s)
```

 # Sort in descending order on Values while inplace=True
```python
x=s.sort_values(ascending=False, inplace=True)
print(s)
print(x)
```

Output:

```
2   q
3   p
4   r
5   s
dtype: object

5   s
4   r
2   q
3   p
dtype: object

None        # Due to inplace=True, there is no (None) reflection in x obj
```

> **Note:**
> - *When inplace=**False**, sorted values get returned to the assigned object(s1) & the original object (s) remains as it is.*
> - *When inplace=**True**, action (sorting) takes place in the same (object s) & returns **None***
> - *During **sorting values**, corresponding **indexes** also get rearranged with their values.*

 # Sort alphabetically in descending order while inplace=False
```python
import pandas as pd
s = pd.Series(['p', 'q', 'r', 's'], index=[3, 2, 4,1])
s1=s.sort_values(ascending=True, inplace=False)
print(s1)        # Output1
print(s)         # Output2
```

 # Sort alphabetically in ascending order while inplace=False
```python
s2=s.sort_values(ascending=False, inplace=False)
print(s2)        # Output3
```

Output:

# Output1:	# Output2:	# Output3:
3 p	3 p	1 s
2 q	2 q	4 r
4 r	4 r	2 q
1 s	1 s	3 p
dtype: object	dtype: object	dtype: object

Vector operation on Series:

```
import pandas as pd
s=pd.Series([10,20,30,40,50])
print(s)         # Values of s
print(s*2)       # Values of s*2
print(s+2)       # Values of s+2
print(s**2)      # Values of s**2
```

Output:

# Values of s:	# Values of s*2:
0 10	0 20
1 20	1 40
2 30	2 60
3 40	3 80
4 50	4 100
dtype: int64	dtype: int64
# Values of s+2:	# Values of s**2:
0 12	0 100
1 22	1 400
2 32	2 900
3 42	3 1600
4 52	4 2500
dtype: int64	dtype: int64

Chapter 11

Python Pandas:

DataFrame

Chapter Objective:

- DataFrame as Defined
- Data Sources and Key Points of DF
- Creating DataFrame (df)
- Creating df from Dictionary
- Creating DF from NumPy
- Creating DF by Series
- Creating DF using another DF
- Renaming column name
- Sorting of Data
- Print the Values of a Column & Row, Maximum value
- Application of loc[ ] & iloc[ ]
- Application of at[] & iat[]
- Application of head() & tail() funciton
- Update value(s) of row & column
- Adding a new column
- Adding & Replacing Rows
- Adding columns
- Selecting columns
- Selecting rows
- Handling CSV file with DF
- Concept of Axis (0 & 1)
- Deleting Rows
- Deleting Columns
- Joining DF
- Boolean Indexing
- Records with conditions
- Itiration on DF
- Conversion of DF into other data sources
- Binary operations
- Re-indexing Rows & Columns of DF
- Re-naming index/labels by Labels
- Functions of DF
- Pivot & Pivot Table

DataFrame as Defined:

A DataFrame is a **two-dimensional data structure** with **heterogeneous** data, similar to a table with rows and columns, and it is **mutable**.

Many inputs create a Pandas DataFrame, viz.:

- List
- Dictionary
- Series
- NumPy nd-arrays
- Another DataFrame
- .csv files or remote sources
- Databases

Key Points of DataFrame:

- Heterogeneous data (all datatypes)
- Size is mutable (changeable)
- Data is mutable (changeable)
- Supports Arithmetic operations on rows and columns

Example of a Table (Data Structure):

Name	Age	Gender	Rating
Raman	32	Male	3.45
Jayati	28	Female	4.6
Saurav	45	Male	3.9
Subhra	32	Female	3.6

The table displays team data with individual ratings, where columns are headings, and each row contains a person's information corresponding to those headings.

Example of Data Type of the Columns of the Table:

The data types of the four columns are as follows –

Column	Type
Name	String
Age	Integer
Gender	String
Rating	Float

Creating DataFrame:

 # Create an Empty DataFrame:

import pandas as pd   *# import the pandas library and alias it as pd*
df= pd.DataFrame()   *# pd is an alias of Pandas, which works as an object*
print (df)

Output:
Empty DataFrame Columns: [] Index: []

 # Create a DataFrame from a single List:

import pandas as pd
df= pd.DataFrame([10, 20, 30, 40, 50])
print (df)

Output:

```
     0
0   10
1   20
2   30
3   40
4   50
```

 # Create a DataFrame from Nested Lists:

import pandas as pd
df = pd.DataFrame(*[* [1, 2, 3, 4, 5] , [10, 20, 30, 40, 50] *]*)
print (df)

Output:

```
   0   1   2   3   4
0  1   2   3   4   5        # Comes from 1st List
1  10  20  30  40  50       # Comes from 2nd List
```

 # Create a DataFrame with user-given Column Names:

import pandas as pd
x = [['XII',101] , ['XI',201] , ['X',301]]
df = pd.DataFrame(x , columns=['Class' , '90% Score'])
print (df)

Output:

```
     Class      90% Score
0     XII         101
1     XI          201
2      X          301
```

 # Create a DataFrame from Lists of heterogeneous values:
```python
import pandas as pd
L1=[11,'A', 12]
L2=[12, 'B', 15]
L3=[10, 'C', 14]
a=[L2, L2, L3]
idx=[101,102,103]
col=['Class', 'Section', 'Roll No']
df=pd.DataFrame(data=a, index=idx, columns=col)
print(df)
```

Output:

	Class	Section	Roll No
101	11	A	12
102	12	B	15
103	10	C	14

 # Create DataFrame with specific datatype:
```python
import pandas as pd
data = [['Anil',10], ['Bikas',12], ['Rohit',13]]
df = pd.DataFrame(data , columns=['Name' , 'Age'] , dtype=float)
print (df)
```

Output:

	Name	Age
0	Anil	10.0
1	Bikas	12.0
2	Rohit	13.0

Creating DataFrame (df) from Dictionary:

While creating a DF from a Dictionary - created by lists, NumPy arrays, or Series - must have the same length. If an index is provided, its length must match the number of data points. If no index is provided, it assigns a default index using range(n), i.e., 0, 1, 2, ..., n-1

 # Create a DataFrame from a dictionary of numeric values:
```python
import pandas as pd
d = {'col1': [1, 2], 'col2': [3, 4]}
df = pd.DataFrame(d)
print (df)
```

> **Note:** *If DataFrame is made by a dictionary, then **Keys** of the Dictionary become **columns** of the DataFrame*

Output:
```
      col1    col2
0     1       3
1     2       4
```

 # DataFrame from a dictionary of lists of heterogeneous values:
```
import pandas as pd
data = {'Name':['Anil', 'Bikas', 'Rohit', 'Ricky'] , 'Age':[28,34,29,42]}
df = pd.DataFrame(data)
print(df)
```
Output:
```
      Name   Age
0     Anil   28
1     Bikas  34
2     Rohit  29
3     Ricky  42
```

 # DataFrame from Dictionary-of-Lists:
```
import pandas as pd
nme = ["Arpita", "Pankaj", "Sudhir", "Gita"]
deg = ["MBA ", "BCA", "M.Tech", "MBA "]
scr = [90, 40, 80, 98]
dict = {'Name': nme, 'Degree': deg, 'Score': scr}
df = pd.DataFrame(dict)
print(df)
```
Output:
```
      Name    Degree    Score
0     Arpita  MBA       90
1     Pankaj  BCA       40
2     Sudhir  M.Tech    80
3     Gita    MBA       98
```

 # DataFrame with List-of-Dictionaries:
```
import pandas as pd
data = [    {'Name': 'Amit', 'Age': 25, 'City': 'Kolkata'},
            {'Name': 'Sumit', 'Age': 30, 'City': 'Mumbai'},
            {'Name': 'Rohit', 'Age': 35, 'City': 'Chennai'}    ]
df = pd.DataFrame(data)
print(df)
```

Output:

```
     Name   Age   City
0    Amit   25    Kolkata
1    Sumit  30    Mumbai
2    Rohit  35    Chennai
```

 # DataFrame with List of Dictionaries having NaN values:

```
import pandas as pd
d1={'A':100 , 'B': 400, 'C': 300}
d2={'A':111 , 'D': 444, 'C': 555}
d3={'A':123 , 'B': 400, 'E': 356}
df = pd.DataFrame([d1, d2, d3])
print(df)
```

> **Note:** *Missing values are filled by **NaN** & rest of the numeric values become decimal, if one value is NaN*

Output:

```
     A      B      C      D      E
0    100    400.0  300.0  NaN    NaN
1    111    NaN    555.0  444.0  NaN
2    123    400.0  NaN    NaN    356.0
```

Creating DataFrame (df) from NumPy:

 # DF from List of np-Array

```
import pandas as pd
import numpy as np
ar1=np.array([10,20,30,40])
ar2=np.array([11,22,33,44])
df = pd.DataFrame( data=[ar1, ar2],
             columns=['P', 'Q', 'R', 'S'], index=['a', 'b'] )
print(ar1)
print(ar2)
print(df)
```

Output:

[10 20 30 40]	[11 22 33 44]	P Q R S a 10 20 30 40 b 11 22 33 44

 # DF from Dictionary of np-Array

```
import pandas as pd
import numpy as np
a1=np.array([10,20,30,40])
a2=np.array([11,22,33,44])
d={'A':a1 , 'B':a2}
df1=pd.DataFrame(d)
print(df1)
```

Output:
```
   A  B
0  10 11
1  20 22
2  30 33
3  40 44
```

Creating a DataFrame (df) from a Series:

 # Creating DF from list of Series:
```
import pandas as pd
s1=pd.Series([10,20,30,40], index=['P', 'Q', 'R', 'S'])
s2=pd.Series([11,22,33,44], index=['P', 'Q', 'R', 'S'])
print(s1)              # 1st Output
print(s2)              # 2nd Output
df=pd.DataFrame([s1,s2])
print(df)              # 3rd Output
df1=pd.DataFrame([s1,s2], index=['a' , 'b'])
print(df1)             # 4th Output
```

Note:
- *Creating DF with a list of Series, the index (i.e. P, Q, R, S) of the Series becomes the Columns of the DF*
- *'dtype' specifies the data type of the Series elements.*

Output:

# 1st Output:	# 2nd Output:
P 10 Q 20 R 30 S 40 dtype: int64	P 11 Q 22 R 33 S 44 dtype: int64

# 3rd Output: 	
   P Q R S
0 10 20 30 40
1 11 22 33 44
	# 4th Output:
	   P Q R S
	a 10 20 30 40
	b 11 22 33 44

Creating DF from the Dictionary of Series

```
import pandas as pd
cls=pd.Series([10,12,11,19])
std_no=pd.Series([90, 95, 88, 98])
avg=pd.Series([60, 67, 71,58])
dict={'Class':cls , 'Stud_No':std_no , 'Average':avg}
df=pd.DataFrame(dict)
print(df)
```

Output:

	Class	Stud_No	Average
0	10	90	60
1	12	95	67
2	11	88	71
3	19	98	58

 # Creating DF from another Dictionary of Series:

```python
import pandas as pd
dict={'first': pd.Series([10,20,30], index=['a', 'b', 'c'] ) ,
      'second': pd.Series([10,20,30,40], index=['a', 'b', 'c', 'd'])}
df1=pd.DataFrame(dict)
df2=pd.DataFrame(dict, index=['b', 'd', 'a'])
df3=pd.DataFrame(dict, index=['d', 'a'], columns=['second', 'third'])
print(df1)      # 1st Output
print(df2)      # 2nd Output
print(df3)      # 3rd Output
```

Output:

```
# 1st Output:              # 2nd Output:
     first  second              first  second
a    10.0    10          b    20.0    20
b    20.0    20          d    NaN     40
c    30.0    30          a    10.0    10
d    NaN     40

# 3rd Output:
     second  third
d     40     NaN
a     10     NaN
```

Creating DF using & copying another DF:

```python
import pandas as pd
s1=pd.Series([10,20,30,40], index=['P', 'Q', 'R', 'S'])
s2=pd.Series([11,22,33,44], index=['P', 'Q', 'R', 'S'])
print(s1)                    # 1st Output
print(s2)                    # 2nd Output
df=pd.DataFrame([s1, s2], index=['a', 'b'])
print(df)                    # 3rd Output
df1=pd.DataFrame(df)         # Creates a DA df1, using a DF df
df1.index=['A' , 'B']        # Changing index of df1
print(df1)                   # 4th Output
df2=pd.DataFrame(df, copy=True)    # Copies df into df2
print(df2)                   # 5th Output
```

Output:

# 1st Output:	# 2nd Output:	# 5th Output: copy of 3rd output
P 10 Q 20 R 30 S 40 dtype: int64	P 11 Q 22 R 33 S 44 dtype: int64	P Q R S A 10 20 30 40 B 11 22 33 44

# 3rd Output: 	
   P Q R S
a 10 20 30 40
b 11 22 33 44
	# 4th Output:
	   P Q R S
	A 10 20 30 40
	B 11 22 33 44
		Note: *It creates a DF df2 as a True-copy of df, because of **copy=True**. So, now df and df2 are two separate entities, and changes in df will not affect.*

Changing row-indexes *(User-given indexes work as labels):*

```
import pandas as pd
data = { 'Name': ['Jaya', 'Prince', 'Gaurav'] , 'Height': [5.1 , 6.2, 5.5] ,
         'Quali': ['MSc' , 'MA' , 'MSc'] }
df = pd.DataFrame(data)
print(df)                          # Prints dataframe
df1 = pd.DataFrame(data, index=['one', 'two', 'three'])
print(df1)                         # Prints with new index
df1.rename(index={'one':'ONE', 'two':'TWO', 'three':'THREE'},
                                        inplace=True)
print(df1)
```

Output:

```
   Height  Name    Quali
0  5.1     Jaya    MSc
1  6.2     Prince  MA
2  5.5     Gaurav  MSc

      Height  Name    Quali
one   5.1     Jaya    MSc
two   6.2     Prince  MA
three 5.5     Gaurav  MSc

       Height Name    Quali
ONE    5.1    Jaya    MSc
TWO    6.2    Prince  MA
THREE  5.5    Gaurav  MSc
```

> **Note:** *Row index is changed by:*
> - ***Df.DataFrame([data], index=[<indices>])***
> - ***df.index=[<indices>]***
> - ***df.rename(index={<index>:<new index>})***

Renaming column name(label):

```
import pandas as pd
L1=[10,30,50,70,90]
```

```
print(L1)                           # Prints List
df=pd.DataFrame(L1)
print(df)                           # Prints DataFrame
df.columns=['Code']                 # Renaming column
print(df)
```

Output:

```
[10 , 30 , 50 , 70 , 90]            # Output of L1
        0                           # Output of df before replacement
0       10
1       30
2       50
3       70
4       90
        Code                        # Column index 0 is replaced by the label 'Code'
0       10
1       30
2       50
3       70
4       90
```

 # Assigning new column names, replacing existing multiple columns

```
import pandas as pd
data = {        'Name': ['Jaya', 'Prince', 'Gaurav', 'Anu'] ,
                'Height': [5.1 , 6.2 , 5.1 , 5.2] ,
                'Qualification': ['MSc' , 'MA' , 'MSc' , 'MSc']   }
print(df)
df = pd.DataFrame(data, index=['One', 'Two', 'Three', 'Four'])
print(df)
df.columns=['N.Height', 'N.Name', 'N.Qualification'] # New column
print(df)
```

Output:

```
        Name    Height  Qualification
0       Jaya    5.1     MSc
1       Prince  6.2     MA
2       Gaurav  5.1     MSc
3       Anu     5.2     MSc
        Name    Height  Qualification
One     Jaya    5.1     MSc
Two     Princ   6.2     MA
Three   Gaurav  5.1     MSc
Four    Anu     5.2     MSc
```

> **Note:**
> *Two ways we can assing new names to columns:*
> - *df.columns=[]*
> - *df.rename(col={old:new,..}, inplace =True)*

	N. Name	N. Height	N. Qualification
One	Jaya	5.1	MSc
Two	Prince	6.2	MA
Three	Gaurav	5.1	MSc
Four	Anu	5.2	MSc

 # Renaming column names using rename() function*:*

```python
import pandas as pd
df = pd.DataFrame({"A": [1, 2, 3], "B": [4, 5, 6]})
print(df)
df.rename(columns={"A": "a", "B": "b"}, inplace=True)
print(df)
```

Output:

```
     A  B
0    1  4
1    2  5
2    3  6
```

 # df after rename=>

```
     a  b
0    1  4
1    2  5
2    3  6
```

> **Note:**
> - If *inplace=True*, then data is modified in place, which means this will return nothing and the very DataFrame is getting updated.
> - If *inplace=False*, which is the default, then the operation is performed and it returns a copy of the object which is needed to save.

 # Replacing a specific column name:

```python
import pandas as pd
data = { 'Name': ['Jaya', 'Prince', 'Gaurav'] ,
        'Height': [5.1 , 6.2 , 5.1] , 'Qualification': ['MSc' , 'MA' , 'MSc']  }
df = pd.DataFrame(data)
print(df)
# Replacing column
df.rename(columns={'Qualification' : 'Degree'} , inplace=True)
print(df)        # Column 'Qualification' is replaced by 'Degree'
```

Output:

	Name	Height	Degree
0	Jaya	5.1	MSc
1	Prince	6.2	MA
2	Gaurav	5.1	MSc

Re-Ordring index by reindex() function:

```python
import pandas as pd
data = { "Name": ['Jaya', 'Prince', 'Gaurav'] ,
```

```
'Height': [5.1 , 6.2 , 5.1] , 'Quali': ['MSc' , 'MA' , 'MSc']  }
df = pd.DataFrame(data)
print(df)
df1=df.reindex([0,2,1])          # Reorders index, but become labels
print(df1)
print(df1.iloc[1])          # Default value
```

Output:

```
    Name        Height  Quali
0  Jaya         5.1     MSc
1  Prince       6.2     MA
2  Gaurav       5.1     MSc
       Name   Height  Quali
0      Jaya   5.1     MSc
2      Gaurav 5.1     MSc
1      Prince 6.2     MA
```

> **Note:**
> **reindex()** function re-orders the index along with its corresponding values, and new indices become labels.
> By default, here **inplace=False**

```
Name            Gaurav          # df1.iloc[1] prints the value of default index
Height          5.1
Qualification   MSc
Name: 2, dtype: object
```

Setting Column as Index and Printing Column Names:

```
import pandas as pd
data = { 'Name': ['Jaya', 'Prince', 'Gaurav', 'Anuj'] ,
'Height':[5.1, 6.2, 5.1, 5.2] , 'Quali':['MSc', 'MA', 'MSc', 'MSc']  }
df = pd.DataFrame(data)
print(df)
df1=df.set_index('Name')   # 'Name' col. becomes index to new object df1
print(df1)
print(df)                         # df remains unchanged
```

 # Printing Column Names and Row Indices

```
print(df.columns)           # Prints Columns of the DF
print(df.index)             # Prints Row index of the DF
```

Output: # Output of df & df1

	Name	Height	Quali			Height	Quali
0	Jaya	5.1	MSc	**Name**	# It becomes col. name		
1	Prince	6.2	MA	**Jaya**		5.1	MSc
2	Gaurav	5.1	MSc	**Prince**		6.2	MA
3	Anuj	5.2	MSc	**Gaurav**		5.1	MSc
				Anuj		5.2	MSc

```
     Name     Height   Quali
0  Jaya        5.1      MSc          # Output of final df
1  Prince      6.2      MA
2  Gaurav      5.1      MSc
3  Anuj        5.2      MSc
```

Index(['**Name**', '**Height**', '**Quali**'], dtype='object') *# Columns of DF*

RangeIndex(start=**0**, stop=**4**, step=**1**)   *# Index of DF*

Transpose (T) in DF *(Interchange of Row & Column)*:

```
import pandas as pd
L=[ [1, 1, 1], [2, 4, 8], [3, 9, 27], [4, 16, 64], [5, 25, 125],
    [6, 36, 216], [7, 49, 343] ]
idx = [ '1st', '2nd', '3rd', '4th', '5th', '6th', '7th' ]
col = [ 'Number', 'Squares', 'Cubes' ]
df = pd.DataFrame(L, index = idx, columns = col)
print(df)
print(df.T)        # Transpose
```

Output:

> **Note:**
> *Transpose **df.T** makes the Columns and Rows interchanged, i.e. Columns become Rows and Rows become Columns of the same DF.*

```
      Number   Squares   Cubes
1st   1        1         1
2nd   2        4         8
3rd   3        9         27
4th   4        16        64
5th   5        25        125
6th   6        36        216
7th   7        49        343

          1st    2nd    3rd    4th    5th    6th    7th
Number    1      2      3      4      5      6      7
Squares   1      4      9      16     25     36     49
Cubes     1      8      27     64     125    216    343
```

Sorting of Data (in Ascending & Descending order):

```
import pandas as pd
cars = { 'Brand': ['Honda','Tata ','Ford','Maruti'],
'Price': [22000,25000,27000,35000],  'Year': [2015,2013,2018,2018] }
df = pd.DataFrame(cars, columns= ['Brand', 'Price', 'Year'])
```

 # To Print in Ascending order
```
df1=df.sort_values(by=[ "Year"], ascending=True, inplace=True)
print (df)             # Prints sorted values, as inplace=True
print(df1)             # Prints None, as inplace=True
```

 # To Print in Descending order

df2=df.**sort_values**(by=['Brand'], ascending=False, *inplace=False*)

print (df2)   *# Prints sorted values as inplace=False (by fefault)*

Output:

	Brand	Price	Year
1	Tata	25000	2013
0	Honda	22000	2015
2	Ford	27000	2018
3	Maruti	35000	2018

None

	Brand	Price	Year
1	Tata	25000	2013
3	Maruti	35000	2018
0	Honda	22000	2015
2	Ford	27000	2018

> **Note:**
> - *By default, data are sorted into ascending order & indices also get rearranged accordingly*
> - ***inplace=True*** *Modifies the DataFrame directly (**df**), but the assigned object (**df1**) prints **None**, as of no effect.*
> - ***inplace=False*** *returns a new DataFrame.*
> - *By default, **inplace=False***

Application of loc[ ] & iloc[ ]:

loc is used to access data based on labels (user-defined) of rows and columns, where the upper bound is included, i.e. last-1 is <u>not applied</u>. Whereas iloc is used on the default int indices, and the last-1 rule <u>is applied</u>. So, **loc[]** includes the last index, while **iloc[]** excludes it.

- **loc** returns the values of the user-given index (label/name)
- **iloc** returns the values of the default index (i.e. 0,1,2,3...)

Select Row & Column together using iloc (Location):

Syntax: *DataFrame.iloc[range of rows(x:y) , range of columns(a:b)]*

```python
import pandas as pd
L= [[1, 2] ,[ 3, 4], [5, 6], [7, 8] ]
df=pd.DataFrame(L, index=['a', 'b', 'c', 'd'], columns=['One', 'Two'])
print(df)
print(df.iloc[1:2 , 0: ])          # Prints row 'b'
print(df.iloc[1:3 , 0:2])          # Prints rows 'b' & 'c' & 2 columns
```

Output:

```
   One  Two
a  1    2
b  3    4
c  5    6
d  7    8
```
 # Output of df

```
   One  Two           # Output of df.iloc[1:2 , 0: ]
B  3    4
   One  Two           # Output of df.iloc[1:3 , 0:2 ]
B  3    4
C  5    6
```

 # DataFrame.iloc [x: y , a: b]

```
import pandas as pd
data = { 'Name': ['Jay', 'Prince', 'Gaurav', 'Anu'], 'Age': [27, 24, 22, 32],
'Address': ['Delhi', 'Kanpur', 'Allahabad', 'Kannauj'],
'Qualification': ['MSc', 'MA', 'MCA', 'PhD']  }
df = pd.DataFrame(data)
```

 # First part is the range of rows, Second part is the range of columns

x1=df.iloc[: , 1 : 4]   *# Values of all rows and 2nd to 3rd columns*

print(x1)

x2=df.iloc[1:2 , 1:4]   *# Values of 2nd row and 2nd to 3rd columns*

print(x2)

x3=df.iloc[1: , 1:]   *# All values excluding values of 0th row & 0th column*

print(x3)

x4=df.iloc[: , :]   *# All values of df are assigned to x4 object*

print(x4)

Output:

```
   Age       Address      Qualification       # Output of x1
0  27        Delhi        MSc
1  24        Kanpur       MA
2  22        Allahabad    MCA
3  32        Kannauj      PhD

   Age       Address      Qualification       # Output of x2
1  24        Kanpur       MA

   Age       Address      Qualification       # Output of x3
1  24        Kanpur       MA
2  22        Allahabad    MCA
3  32        Kannauj      PhD

   Name    Age  Address      Qualification   # Output of x4
0  Jay     27   Delhi        MSc
1  Prince  24   Kanpur       MA
2  Gaurav  22   Allahabad    MCA
3  Anu     32   Kannauj      PhD
```

Printing selective Rows/Columns using loc[], iloc[]

```
import pandas as pd
data = { 'Name': ['Jay', 'Prince', 'Gaurav', 'Anu'], 'Age': [27, 24, 22, 32],
'Address': ['Delhi', 'Kanpur', 'Allahabad', 'Kannauj'],
'Qualification': ['MSc', 'MA', 'MCA', 'PhD']  }
df = pd.DataFrame(data, index=[10,20,30,40])
print(df)
print(df.iloc[ [1,3] ])            # List of index prints it's values
print(df.loc[ [20,40] ])           # List of label prints it's values

print(df.loc[ [20,40] , ['Name', 'Address'] ])
print(df.iloc[ [1,3] , [0,2] ])
```

Output:

	Name	Age	Address	Qualification
10	Jay	27	Delhi	MSc
20	Prince	24	Kanpur	MA
30	Gaurav	22	Allahabad	MCA
40	Anu	32	Kannauj	PhD

 # Output of df

	Name	Age	Address	Qualification
20	Prince	24	Kanpur	MA
40	Anu	32	Kannauj	PhD

 # Output of df.iloc[[1,3]]

	Name	Age	Address	Qualification
20	Prince	24	Kanpur	MA
40	Anu	32	Kannauj	PhD

 # Output of df.loc[[20,40]]

	Name	Address
20	Prince	Kanpur
40	Anu	Kannauj

 # Output with ['Name', 'Address']

	Name	Address
20	Princ	Kanpur
40	Anu	Kannauj

> **Note:** *To get the values of selective rows/columns, its index/labels must be kept under double brackets [[ ]]*

Application of at[] & iat[]:

Pandas **.at[]** and **.iat[]** are both methods used to return only a single element, whereas **.at[]** uses labels and **.iat[]** uses integer location in DF. The passed location is in the format [**row position, column position**].

Syntax: *DataFrame.**iat**[row, column] & DF.**at**[row-label, col-label]*

Parameters:
- *Row index:* Integer position & Label of the row.
- *Column index:* Integer position & Label of the column.

Return Type:
The method returns the single element present at the specified integer location.

Example:
```
import pandas as pd
df=pd.DataFrame( { "Roll":[10,12,14,16,18] , "Class":[8,9,10,11,12],
                  "Sec":['A', 'B', 'C', 'D', 'E'] } )
print(df)
col = 2
row = 3
res = df.iat[row, col]                    # Row & Column index
print("Element at row", row, "and column", col, "of .iat:", res)
```

Output:

	Roll	Class	Sec
0	10	8	A
1	12	9	B
2	14	10	C
3	16	11	D
4	18	12	E

> **Note:** *.iat[] is integer-based indexing, so the last-1 rule is applied here, and it works faster.*
> *.at[] is label-based indexing, so last-1 rule is not applied here, functions slower. And both of these return only a single value.*

Element at row 3 and column 2 of **.iat**: D

Example:
```
import pandas as pd
df=pd.DataFrame({"Roll" :[10,12,14,16,18] ,
                "Class":[8,9,10,11,12],  "Sec":['A', 'B', 'C', 'D', 'E'] })
print(df)
pos = 2
label = 'Sec'

# Using .at[] method gets the value of pos/row-index of the column-label
res = df.at[pos, label]          # Here pos is treated as label, not index
print(res)

df.index=['a', 'b', 'c', 'd', 'e']     # Assigned labels on rows
print(df.at['c' , 'Sec'])              # Accessing value using labels in .at[]
```

Output:

	Roll	Class	Sec	
0	10	8	A	# Output of df
1	12	9	B	
2	14	10	C	
3	16	11	D	
4	18	12	E	
C				# Output of df.at[pos, label]
C				# Output of df.at['c' , 'Sec']

Print the Filtered values of DF:

- **Reading data with Condition**
- **Values of Column & Row-wise**
- **Maximum value of a Column**
- **Details: who has the maximum value**
- **Records with a condition**

 # Filteration with loc[]

```
import pandas as pd
L= [[1, 2] ,[ 3, 4], [5, 6], [7, 8],  ]
df=pd.DataFrame(L, index=['a', 'b','c','d'], columns=['One', 'Two'])
print(df)
print(df.loc['a':'d' , 'One':'Two']>2)
print(df[df.loc['a':'d' , 'One':'Two']>2]) # If Values don't satisfy, give NaN
```

Output:

	One	Two	
a	1	2	# Output of df
b	3	4	
c	5	6	
d	7	8	

> **Note:** *NaN* comes on the *False* values with *df[df.loc[]]* cond.

	One	Two	
a	False	False	
b	True	True	
c	True	True	# Output of df.loc['a':'d' , 'One':'Two']>2
d	True	True	

	One	Two	
a	NaN	NaN	
b	3.0	4.0	# Output of df[df.loc['a':'d' , 'One':'Two']>2]
c	5.0	6.0	
d	7.0	8.0	

Reading Column & Row-wise values:

```python
import pandas as pd
data = {'Name': ['Jaya', 'Prince', 'Gaurav', 'Anuj'] ,
 'Height': [5.1, 6.2, 5.1, 5.2], 'Qualification': ['MSc', 'MA', 'MSc', 'MSc']}
df = pd.DataFrame(data, index=['A', 'B', 'C', 'D'])
print(df)
print("The values of the column 'Height'-> ")
print(df['Height'])
print("The highest value of column 'Height'-> ")
print(df['Height'].max())
print("The details of Prince present in the 2nd row (label 'B')-> ")
print(df.loc['B'])          # To get Max. value of 'B' row use: df.loc['B'].max()
print(df.iloc[1])           # To get same output of 'B' row with iloc[]
print("The details that has the highest value of column 'Height'-> ")
print(df[df['Height']==df['Height'].max()])
print(df)
```

Output:

```
    Name        Height  Qualification   ┐
A   Jaya          5.1   MSc             │
B   Prince        6.2   MA              ├─  # Output of DF
C   Gaurav        5.1   MSc             │
D   Anuj          5.2   MSc             ┘

The values of the column 'Height'->     ┐
A   5.1                                  │
B   6.2                                  ├─  # Output of df['Height']
C   5.1                                  │
D   5.2                                  │
Name: Height, dtype: float64            ┘

The highest value of Height->
6.2                                         # Output of df['Height'].max()
The details of Prince present in the 2nd row (label 'B')->
Name           Prince                   ┐
Height         6.2                      ├─  # Output of df.loc['B']
Qualification  MA                       │
Name: B, dtype: object                  ┘

Name           Prince                   ┐
Height         6.2                      ├─  # Output of df.iloc[1]
Qualification  MA                       │
Name: B, dtype: object                  ┘
```

 # Output of df.iloc[1] df[df['Height']==df['Height'].max()]
The details, who have the highest Height->

	Name	Height	Qualification
B	Prince	6.2	MA

	Name	Height	Degree
0	Jaya	5.1	MSc
1	Princ	6.2	MA
2	Gaurav	5.1	MSc
3	Anu	5.2	MSc

 # Output of df

 # Row-wise finding Maximum value->

```python
import pandas as pd
data = {        'A': [10,40,30,90,50] ,      'C': [101,505,303,404,707],
            'B': [33,99,55,88,44]      }
df = pd.DataFrame(data, index=['a', 'b', 'c','d','e'])
print(df)
print(df.loc['d'].max())          # Finds maximum value of 'd' row label
print(df.iloc[3].max())           # Finds maximum value of 3 row index
```

Output:

```
   A   C    B                     # Output of df
a 10 101  33
b 40 505  99
c 30 303  55
d 90 404  88
e 50 707  44
404                               # Output of df.loc['d'].max()

404                               # Output of df.iloc[3].max()
```

 # Row and Column-wise conditional values:

```python
4   Trueimport pandas as pd
data = {        'Name': ['Rohan', 'Ashim', 'Chitra', 'Mohan', 'Nandita'],
            'Age': [25, 30, 35, 40, 28],
            'Salary': [50000, 70000, 60000, 80000, 65000]  }
df = pd.DataFrame(data)
print("Original DataFrame:")
print(df)
print("\nTo print Ture/False of Salary>60000")
print(df['Salary']>60000)
print("\nRows where Age > 30:")
print(df.loc[df['Age'] > 30]
print("\nRows where Age > 30 AND Salary > 60000:")
```

```python
print(df[(df['Age'] > 30) & (df['Salary'] > 60000)])
print("\n Mohan's details if his Salary>60000")
print(df[(df['Salary']>60000) & (df['Name']=='Mohan')])
print("\nRows where Age > 30 OR Salary > 60000:")
print(df[(df['Age'] > 30) | (df['Salary'] > 60000)])
print("\nFiltered columns (Name and Salary) where Age > 30:")
print( df.loc[df['Age'] > 30, ['Name', 'Salary']] )          # Line18
print( df[df['Age'] > 30] [ ['Name', 'Salary'] ] )          # Line19
print("\nUsing .where(): Keep Age > 30, NaN otherwise")
print(df.where(df['Age'] > 30))
```

Output:
Original DataFrame:

	Name	Age	Salary
0	Rohan	25	50000
1	Ashim	30	70000
2	Chitra	35	60000
3	Mohan	40	80000
4	Nandita	28	65000

> **Note:** *Statements of Line18 & Line19 give the same output*

To print True/False of Salary>60000

```
0    False
1    True
2    False
3    True
Name: Salary, dtype: bool
```

Rows where Age > 30:

	Name	Age	Salary
2	Chitra	35	60000
3	Mohan	40	80000

Rows where Age > 30 AND Salary > 60000:

	Name	Age	Salary
3	Mohan	40	80000

Mohan's details if his Salary>60000

	Name	Age	Salary
3	Mohan	40	80000

Rows where Age > 30 OR Salary > 60000:

	Name	Age	Salary
1	Ashim	30	70000
2	Chitra	35	60000
3	Mohan	40	80000
4	Nandita	28	65000

Filtered columns (Name and Salary) where Age > 30:

	Name	Salary
2	Chitra	60000
3	Mohan	80000

	Name	Salary
2	Chitra	60000
3	Mohan	80000

Using .where(): Keep Age > 30, NaN otherwise

	Name	Age	Salary
0	NaN	NaN	NaN
1	NaN	NaN	NaN
2	Chitra	35.0	60000.0
3	Mohan	40.0	80000.0
4	NaN	NaN	NaN

Use of head() and tail() functions:

```python
import pandas as pd
data = {        'Name': ['Jaya', 'Prince', 'Gaurav', 'Anu'],
                'Age':[27,24,22,32],
                'Address':['Delhi', 'Kanpur', 'Allahabad', 'Kannauj'],
                'Qualification': ['MSc', 'MA', 'MCA', 'PhD']          }
df = pd.DataFrame(data)
print(df)                   # Prints the DF
print('Uses of head()...')
print(df.head())            # Prints top 5 rec. of DF
print(df.head(2))           # Prints top 2 rec. of DF
print(df.head(-2))          # Prints all excluding bottom 2 rec. of DF
print('Uses of tail()...')
print(df.tail())            # Prints last 5 rec. of DF
print(df.tail(2))           # Prints last 2 rec. of DF
print(df.tail(-2))          # Prints all excluding top 2 rec. of DF
```

Output:

	Name	Age	Address	Qualification	
0	Jaya	27	Delhi	MSc	*# Prints df*
1	Prince	24	Kanpur	MA	
2	Gaurav	22	Allahabad	MCA	
3	Anu	32	Kannauj	PhD	

Uses of head()...

	Name	Age	Address	Qualification	
0	Jaya	27	Delhi	MSc	*# Prints df.head()*
1	Prince	24	Kanpur	MA	
2	Gaurav	22	Allahabad	MCA	
3	Anu	32	Kannauj	PhD	

	Name	Age	Address	Qualification	
0	Jaya	27	Delhi	MSc	*# Prints df.head(2)*
1	Prince	24	Kanpur	MA	

	Name	Age	Address	Qualification	
0	Jaya	27	Delhi	MSc	*# Prints df.head(-2)*
1	Prince	24	Kanpur	MA	

Uses of tail()...

	Name	Age	Address	Qualification	
0	Jaya	27	Delhi	MSc	*# Prints df.tail()*
1	Prince	24	Kanpur	MA	
2	Gaurav	22	Allahabad	MCA	
3	Anu	32	Kannauj	PhD	

	Name	Age	Address	Qualification	
2	Gaurav	22	Allahabad	MCA	*# Prints df.tail(2)*
3	Anu	32	Kannauj	PhD	

	Name	Age	Address	Qualification	
2	Gaurav	22	Allahabad	MCA	*# Prints df.tail(-2)*
3	Anu	32	Kannauj	PhD	

Update value(s) of row(s):

```python
import pandas as pd
data = {       'Name': ['Jaya', 'Prince', 'Gaurav', 'Anu'],
            'Age': [27, 24, 22, 32],
            'Address': ['Delhi', 'Kanpur', 'Allahabad', 'Kannauj'],
            'Qualification': ['MSc', 'MA', 'MCA', 'PhD']          }
df = pd.DataFrame(data)
print(df)
df.at[0 , 'Age']=60                     # To change/update a value using df.at
print(df)
```

```
df.iloc[[0,1,2],[1,3]] = [30, 'MSc']          # Update col. by index
print(df)
df.loc[[0,1,2],['Age', 'Address']] = [50, 'India']   # Update col. by label
print(df)
```

Output:

```
      Name    Age    Address    Qualification    # Output of df
0     Jaya    27     Delhi      MSc
1     Prince  24     Kanpur     MA
2     Gaurav  22     Allahabad  MCA
3     Anu     32     Kannauj    PhD

      Name    Age    Address    Qualification    # Output: df.at[0,'Age']=60
0     Jaya    60     Delhi      MSc
1     Prince  24     Kanpur     MA
2     Gaurav  22     Allahabad  MCA
3     Anu     32     Kannauj    PhD
```

 # Output: *df.iloc[[0,1,2],[1,3]]=[30, 'MSc']*

```
      Name    Age    Address    Qualification
0     Jaya    30     Delhi      MSc
1     Prince  30     Kanpur     MSc
2     Gaurav  30     Allahabad  MSc
3     Anu     60     Kannauj    PhD
```

 # Output: *df.loc[[0,1,2],['Age', 'Address']]=[50, 'India']*

```
      Name    Age    Address    Qualification
0     Jaya    50     India      MSc
1     Prince  50     India      MSc
2     Gaurav  50     India      MSc
3     Anu     60     Kannauj    PhD
```

Adding a new column to an existing DataFrame:

```
import pandas as pd
data ={ 'Name': ['Jaya', 'Prince', 'Gaurav', 'Anu'] , 'Height': [5.1, 6.2, 5.1,
5.2] , 'Qualification': ['MSc' , 'MA' , 'MSc' , 'MSc'] }
df = pd.DataFrame(data)
print(df)                          # Prints the DataFrame
addr = ['Delhi', 'Bangalore', 'Chennai', 'Patna']          # Declare a list
df['New Address']=addr          # A new column added to DataFrame
print(df)                          # Prints the DataFrame with a new column
df[4]=[10,20,30,40]                # A new column added with Col. label 4
print(df)
```

Output:

 # Output of df:

	Name	Height	Qualification
0	Jaya	5.1	MSc
1	Prince	6.2	MA
2	Gaurav	5.1	MSc
3	Anu	5.2	MSc

 # df with a new column label 'New Address':

	Name	Height	Qualification	*New Address*
0	Jaya	5.1	MSc	**Delhi**
1	Prince	6.2	MA	**Bangalore**
2	Gaurav	5.1	MSc	**Chennai**
3	Anu	5.2	MSc	**Patna**

 # df with a new numeric column label 4:

	Name	Height	Qualification	New Address	4
0	Jaya	5.1	MSc	Delhi	*10*
1	Prince	6.2	MA	Bangalore	*20*
2	Gaurav	5.1	MSc	Chennai	*30*
3	Anu	5.2	MSc	Patna	*40*

Adding & Replacing Rows (using loc) in DF:

```python
import pandas as pd
data = {  'Name': ['Jaya', 'Prince', 'Gaurav', 'Anu'],
        'Age': [27, 24, 22, 32],
        'Address': ['Delhi', 'Kanpur', 'Allahabad', 'Kannauj'],
        'Qualification': ['MSc', 'MA', 'MCA', 'PhD']            }
df = pd.DataFrame(data)
print(df)
df.loc[4] = ['Amit', 28, 'Ranchi', 'Mtech']      # Adding a new row
print(df)
df.loc[3] = ['Sumit', 29, 'Patna', 'MA']   # Row-3 is replaced by new values
print(df)
```

Output:

	Name	Age	Address	Qualification
0	Jaya	27	Delhi	MSc
1	Prince	24	Kanpur	MA
2	Gaurav	22	Allahabad	MCA
3	Anu	32	Kannauj	PhD

 # Output of df

	Name	Age	Address	Qualification	
0	Jaya	27	Delhi	MSc	
1	Prince	24	Kanpur	MA	
2	Gaurav	22	Allahabad	MCA	
3	Anu	32	Kannauj	PhD	
4	**Amit**	**28**	**Ranchi**	**Mtech**	*# New row added*
	Name	Age	Address	Qualification	
0	Jaya	27	Delhi	MSc	
1	Prince	24	Kanpur	MA	
2	Gaurav	22	Allahabad	MCA	
3	**Sumit**	**29**	**Patna**	**MA**	*# New row replaced*
4	Amit	28	Ranchi	Mtech	

Adding columns to the DF made of Series:

```
import pandas as pd
d={ 'one' : pd.Series([1, 2, 3], index=['a', 'b', 'c']),
'two' : pd.Series([1, 2, 3, 4], index=['a', 'b', 'c', 'd']) }
df=pd.DataFrame(d)
print(df)
df['three']=pd.Series([10,20,30], index=['a','b','c'])  # Adding a new column
print(df)
```

 # A new column of the sum of 1st & 3rd columns

```
df['four'] = df['one'] + df['three']
print(df)
df['five'] = df['one'] + df['two'] # A new column from sum of 1st & 2nd columns
print(df)
df['five'] = df['four'] - df['two'] # A subtraction of 4th & 2nd columns to a new
print(df)
print (df['one'])
```

Output:

	one	two	
			# Output of df
a	1.0	1	
b	2.0	2	
c	3.0	3	
d	NaN	4	

> **Note:** *If in a column of DF **NaN** exists, then the rest of the numeric values become decimal values.*

	one	two	three	
				# A new column 'three' added
a	1.0	1	10.0	
b	2.0	2	20.0	
c	3.0	3	30.0	
d	NaN	4	NaN	

```
     one    two    three    four    # A new column 'four' added
a    1.0    1      10.0     11.0
b    2.0    2      20.0     22.0
c    3.0    3      30.0     33.0
d    NaN    4      NaN      NaN
     one    two    three    four    five  # A new column 'five' added
a    1.0    1      10.0     11.0    10.0
b    2.0    2      20.0     22.0    20.0
c    3.0    3      30.0     33.0    30.0
d    NaN    4      NaN      NaN     NaN
a    1.0                                  # Output of df['one']
b    2.0
c    3.0
d    NaN
Name: one, dtype: float64
```

Selecting by Columns:

```python
import pandas as pd
data = {  'Name': ['Jaya', 'Prince', 'Gaurav', 'Anu'],
          'Age': [27, 24, 22, 32],
          'Address':    ['Delhi',  'Kanpur',  'Allahabad',  'Kannauj'],
          'Qualification': ['MSc', 'MA', 'MCA', 'PhD']  }
df = pd.DataFrame(data)
x1=df[df.columns[1 : 4]]        # From 2nd col to 4th col
print(x1)
x2=df[df.columns[1:3] ]         # From 2nd col to 3rd col
print(x2)
x3=df[df.columns[:]]            # All columns
print(x3)
x4=df[df.columns[:2]]           # First 1st col to 2nd col
print(x4)
```

Output:

```
   Age        Address       Qualification    # df[df.columns[1:4]]
0  27         Delhi         MSc
1  24         Kanpur        MA
2  22         Allahabad     MCA
3  32         Kannauj       PhD
   Age        Address                        # df[df.columns[1:3]]
0  27         Delhi
1  24         Kanpur
2  22         Allahabad
3  32         Kannauj
```

```
     Name      Age      Address     Qualification
0    Jaya      27       Delhi           MSc
1    Princ     24       Kanpur          MA          # df[df.columns[:]]
2    Gaurav    22       Allahabad       MCA
3    Anu   32  Kannauj           PhD

     Name      Age
0    Jaya      27
1    Princ     24          # df[df.columns[:2]]
2    Gaurav    22
3    Anu       32
```

Selecting by Rows and Printing Total Elements:

```python
import pandas as pd
data = {        'Name': ['Jaya', 'Prince', 'Gaurav', 'Anu'],
                'Age': [27, 24, 22, 32],
                'Address': ['Delhi', 'Kanpur', 'Allahabad', 'Kannauj'],
                'Qualification': ['MSc', 'MA', 'MCA', 'PhD']          }
df = pd.DataFrame(data)
print(df.iloc[ : ])          # Prints all rows
print(df.iloc[1:3])          # Prints 2nd & 3rd rows
print(df.iloc[ :3])          # Prints up-to 3rd row i.e. 0th, 1st & 2nd rows
print(df.size)               # Prints the total number of elements of the DF
```

Output:

```
     Name      Age      Address         Qualification
0    Jaya      27       Delhi           MSc      # Output of all rows
1    Prince    24       Kanpur          MA
2    Gaurav    22       Allahabad       MCA
3    Anu       32       Kannauj         PhD
     Name      Age      Address         Qualification
1    Prince    24       Kanpur          MA       # Output of df.iloc[1:3]
2    Gaurav    22       Allahabad       MCA
     Name      Age      Address         Qualification
0    Jaya      27       Delhi           MSc      # Output of df.iloc[:3]
1    Prince    24       Kanpur          MA
2    Gaurav    22       Allahabad       MCA
16                               # Output of the no. of elements of DF, i.e. 4X4=16
```

Handling CSV File in DF:

A CSV, i.e. Comma Separated Values file, is a plain text file that stores tabular data in spreadsheets, with values separated by a comma on each line. For example, create an Excel file, then go to FILE-> SAVE AS, from the dropdown menu, select a CSV, then "OK" to save it as a **.csv** file. Here, the **emp1.xlsx file** has been changed into **emp1.csv**:

emp1.csv

Emp ID,Emp Name,Emp Role
1,Pankaj Kumar,Admin
2,David Lee,Editor
3,Lisa Ray,Author

emp1.xlsx			
	A	B	C
1	Emp ID	Emp Name	Emp Role
2	1	Pankaj Kumar	Admin
3	2	David Lee	Editor
4	3	Lisa Ray	Author

Import Data in DataFrame from .csv file:

```
import pandas as pd
df = pd.read_csv('emp1.csv')   # Access data of .csv file to DataFrame
print(df)                      # Print DataFrame
```

Output:

```
   Emp ID   Emp Name       Emp Role
0     1     Pankaj Kumar   Admin
1     2     David Lee      Editor
2     3     Lisa Ray       Author
```

Note: *Here after importing data of **.csv** to DF by default index are assigned.*

Accessing .csv file in DataFrame from Google Drive:

Converting the Excel file into .csv file

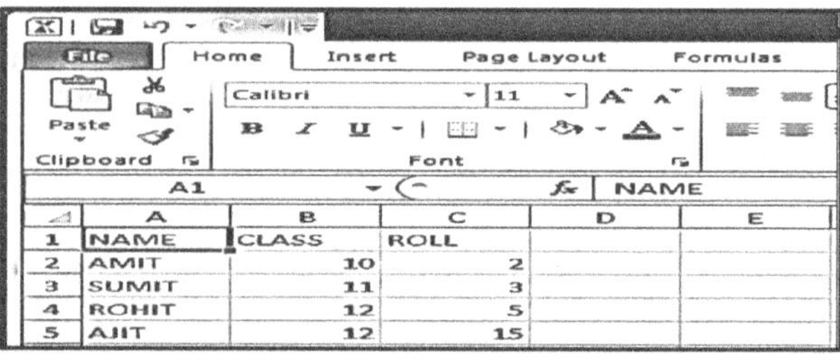

- Upload the .csv file to Google Drive
- Get/copy the accessible link of the .csv file
- Paste the link into a variable (URL)

```
# Derive the ID from the Google Drive shareable link
url = 'https://drive.google.com/file/d/1CSY---------------/view?usp=sharing'
import pandas as pd
path = 'https://drive.google.com/uc?export=download&id='+url.split('/')[-2]
df=pd.read_csv(path) # Here, the file in GDrive must have global permission
print(df)
```

Output:

	NAME	CLASS	ROLL
0	AMIT	10	2
1	SUMIT	11	3
2	ROHIT	12	5
3	AJIT	12	15

 # Update the DataFrame *(on imported .csv file)*
```
import pandas as pd
df = pd.read_csv('emp1.csv')              # Importing to DF from .csv
df['Salary'] = [50000 , 55000, 60000]   # Adding one column to DF
print(df)
```

Output:

	Emp ID	Emp Name	Emp Role	**Salary**
0	1	Pankaj Kumar	Admin	**50000**
1	2	David Lee	Editor	**55000**
2	3	Lisa Ray	Author	**60000**

Export updated DataFrame to .csv file:

```
import pandas as pd
df = pd.read_csv('emp1.csv')
x=[50000 , 55000, 60000]
df['Salary'] = x
df.to_csv('emp2.csv', index=True)      # With index values in .csv
df.to_csv('emp3.csv', index=False)     # Without indexing in .csv
```

Output: *if index=True*:

emp2.csv

	EmpID,	Emp Name,	Emp Role,	Salary
0,	1,	Pankaj Kumar,	Admin,	50000
1,	2,	David Lee,	Editor,	55000
2,	3,	Lisa Ray,	Author,	60000

Output: *if index=False*:

emp3.csv

Emp ID,	Emp Name,	Emp Role,	Salary
1,	Pankaj Kumar,	Admin,	50000
2,	David Lee,	Editor,	55000
3,	Lisa Ray,	Author,	60000

 # Create a .csv file from a DataFrame and export:

import pandas as pd

df = pd.DataFrame([[1,2,3], [4,5,6], [7,8,9]], columns = ['a','b','c'])

print(df)

df.**to_csv**("data.csv", index = False)   *# Without indexing*

Output:

```
     a     b     c
0    1     2     3
1    4     5     6
2    7     8     9
```

data.csv

	A	B	C
1	a	b	c
2	1	2	3
3	4	5	6
4	7	8	9

Concept of Axis (0 & 1):

In a DataFrame, the concept of axis refers to the directions along which operations are performed. It helps to specify whether to work with rows or columns. So, in a DataFrame as a table with rows and columns:

When operating on axis 0, it affects the entire column. For example, df.sum(**axis=0**) Adds up values **row-wise** (i.e., sums through rows on each column). However, when operating on axis 1, it affects the entire row. For example, df.sum(**axis=1**) Adds up values **column-wise** (i.e., sums through column across each row).

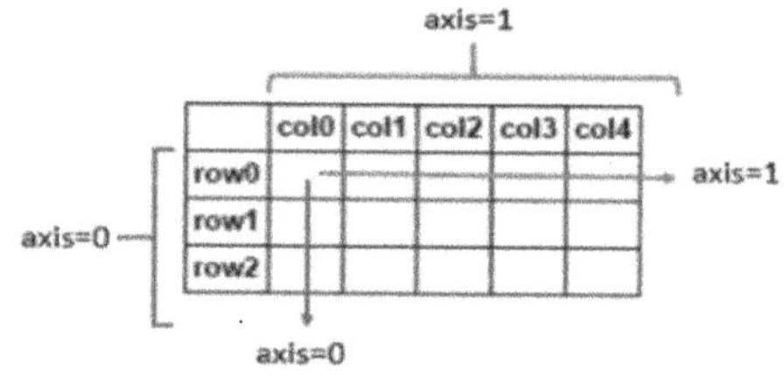

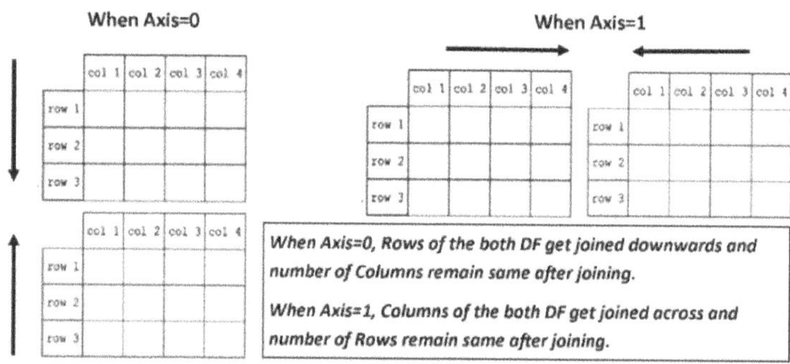

> **Note:** *In a 2D array of DF:*
> - *If **axis=0,** then it operates **on rows**, downwards (effects on columns)*
> - *if **axis=1** operates **on columns**, across (effects on rows)*

Sum of Rows and Columns:

```
import pandas as pd
df = pd.DataFrame( { 'A': [10, 20, 30,40,50],
                     'B': [100, 200, 300,400,500] } )
print(df)                    # Prints DataFrame
d1=df.sum(axis=0)            # Sum of DF through rows
d2=df.sum(axis=1)            # Sum of DF across columns
print(d1)
print(d2)
```

Output:

```
    A   B
0  10  100
1  20  200
2  30  300          # Output of df
3  40  400
4  50  500

A    150
B    1500           # Output of d1
dtype: int64

0    110
1    220
2    330
3    440            # Output of d2
4    550
dtype: int64
```

Deleting Rows:

```
import pandas as pd
data = { 'Name': ['Jaya', 'Prince', 'Gaurav', 'Anu'],
'Age': [27, 24, 22, 32],
'Address': ['Delhi', 'Kanpur', 'Allahabad', 'Kannauj'],
'Qualification': ['MSc', 'MA', 'MCA', 'PhD']  }
```

```
df = pd.DataFrame(data)
df1 = pd.DataFrame(data, index=['A', 'B', 'C', 'D'])
df1.drop(['B','C'], axis=0, inplace=True)
df2= df.drop([1,2], axis=0, inplace=False)     # Axis=0 is On col. Row-wise
print(df1)
print(df2)
```

> **Note:** *For deleting **row** in df only **drop()** fn. works but **pop()** and **del** don't work*

Output:

	Name	Age	Address	Qualification
A	Jaya	27	Delhi	MSc
D	Anu	32	Kannauj	PhD

	Name	Age	Address	Qualification
0	Jaya	27	Delhi	MSc
3	Anu	32	Kannauj	PhD

Deleting Columns:

Deleting a column using del:

```
import pandas as pd
data = {  'Name': ['Jaya', 'Prince', 'Gaurav', 'Anu'], 'Age': [27, 24, 22, 32],
'Address': ['Delhi', 'Kanpur', 'Allahabad', 'Kannauj'],
'Qualification': ['MSc', 'MA', 'MCA', 'PhD']  }
df = pd.DataFrame(data)
print(df)                    # Prints DataFrame
del df['Name']               # Removes / deletes field using del
print(df)                    # Print new format of DataFrame
```

Output:

	Name	Age	Address	Qualification
0	Jay	27	Delhi	MSc
1	Prince	24	Kanpur	MA
2	Gaurav	22	Allahabad	MCA
3	Anu	32	Kannauj	PhD

Output of df

	Age	Address	Qualification
0	27	Delhi	MSc
1	24	Kanpur	MA
2	22	Allahabad	MCA
3	32	Kannauj	PhD

After del df['Name']

Deleting columns using drop() function.:

```
import pandas as pd
data = { 'Name': ['Jaya', 'Prince', 'Gaurav', 'Anu'],
'Age': [27, 24, 22, 32],
'Address': ['Delhi', 'Kanpur', 'Allahabad', 'Kannauj'],
```

```
'Qualification': ['MSc', 'MA', 'MCA', 'PhD']  }
df = pd.DataFrame(data)
df1= df.drop('Address',  axis=1, inplace=False)
print(df)
print(df1)
df1= df.drop(df.columns[[1,3]], axis=1, inplace=True)
print(df)                 # Deleted columns of 1 & 3 index.
```

Output:

 # Output of df:

```
      Name   Age   Address        Qualification
0     Jaya   27    Delhi          MSc
1     Prince 24    Kanpur         MA
2     Gaurav 22    Allahabad      MCA
3     Anu    32    Kannauj        PhD
```

 # Output of df1:

```
      Name   Age   Qualification
0     Jaya   27    MSc
1     Prince 24    MA
2     Gaurav 22    MCA
3     Anu    32    PhD
      Name         Address
0     Jaya         Delhi
1     Prince       Kanpur
2     Gaurav       Allahabad
3     Anu          Kannauj
```

> **Note:** To use *inplace=**True**,* here updated values will not be returned to new object df1, rather df would have it.
>
> *df.columns[[]] works on positions.*

 # Deleting a column using pop() function:

```
import pandas as pd
data = {        'Name': ['Jaya', 'Prince', 'Gaurav', 'Anu'],
                'Age': [27, 24, 22, 32],
                'Address': ['Delhi', 'Kanpur', 'Allahabad', 'Kannauj'],
                'Qualification': ['MSc', 'MA', 'MCA', 'PhD']   }
df = pd.DataFrame(data)
print(df)
df.pop('Age')
print(df)
```

Output:

```
      Name   Age   Address        Qualification
0     Jaya   27    Delhi          MSc
1     Prince 24    Kanpur         MA              # Output of df
2     Gaurav 22    Allahabad      MCA
3     Anu    32    Kannauj        PhD
```

```
      Name        Address      Qualification
0  Jaya         Delhi         MSc
1  Prince       Kanpur        MA          # Output after df.pop('Age')
2  Gaurav       Allahabad     MCA
3  Anu          Kannauj       PhD
```

Joining DF:

 # Joining DataFrames with append() function*(for common columns):*

```
import pandas as pd
df1 = pd.DataFrame([[1, 2], [3, 4]], columns = ['a','b'])
df2 = pd.DataFrame([[5, 6], [7, 8]], columns = ['a','b'])
df3 = df1.append(df2)
print (df3)
```

Output:

```
   a b
0  1 2
1  3 4
0  5 6
1  7 8
```

> **Note:** *To join, **pd.concat()** function is more dynamic than append(), since append() is deprecated in Pandas v1.4+.*

 # Joining DataFrames by concat() function:

```
import pandas as pd
data1={ 'Name':['Jaya', 'Prince', 'Gaurav', 'Anu'], 'Age':[27, 24, 22, 32],
          'Address':['Nagpur', 'Kanpur', 'Allahabad', 'Kannuaj'],
          'Qualification':['MSc', 'MA', 'MCA', 'PhD']          }
data2={ 'Name':['Avi', 'Ayush', 'Dhiraj', 'Hitesh'], 'Age':[17, 14, 12, 52],
          'Address':['Nagpur', 'Kanpur', 'Allahabad', 'Kannuaj'],
          'Qualification':['Btech', 'B.A', 'Bcom', 'B.hons']   }
df1=pd.DataFrame(data1)
df2=pd.DataFrame(data2)
res1=pd.concat( [df1,df2], axis=1)     # Joins Columns on common Rows
print(res1)
res2 = pd.concat([df1,df2], axis=0)    # Joins Rows, on common Columns
print(res2)
```

Output:

```
       Name    Age   Address     ...  Age  Address     Qualification
0      Jaya    27    Nagpur      ...  17   Nagpur      Btech
1      Prince  24    Kanpur      ...  14   Kanpur      B.A
2      Gaurav  22    Allahabad   ...  12   Allahabad   Bcom      # axis=1
3      Anu     32    Kannuaj     ...  52   Kannuaj     B.hons
[4 rows x 8 columns]
```

	Name	Age	Address	Qualification
0	Jaya	27	Nagpur	MSc
1	Prince	24	Kanpur	MA
2	Gaurav	22	Allahabad	MCA
3	Anu	32	Kannuaj	PhD
0	Avi	17	Nagpur	Btech
1	Ayush	14	Kanpur	B.A
2	Dhiraj	12	Allahabad	Bcom
3	Hitesh	52	Kannuaj	B.hons

 # axis=0

[8 rows x 4 columns]

> **Note:**
> - *axis=0 Joins Row-wise and number of Columns remain same.*
> - *axis=1 Colum-wise and number of Rows remain same.*
> - *by default, axis=0*
> - *For Concatenation **pd.concat()** fnc. of Python library is used*

 # Merging data within DataFrames using merge():
```
import pandas as pd
x=pd.DataFrame(
{'id':[1,2],'Name': ['Anil', 'Vishal'], 'subject_id':['Sub1','Sub2']} )
y=pd.DataFrame(
{'id':[1,2],'Name': ['Sumer', 'Salil'], 'subject_id':['Sub2','Sub4']} )
print(pd.merge(x , y , on='id'))
```

> **Note:** *Gets merged only on a common column, i.e. **id** column,*

Output:

	id	Name_x	subject_id_x	Name_y	subject_id_y
0	1	Anil	Sub1	Sumer	Sub2
1	2	Vishal	Sub2	Salil	Sub4

Boolean Indexing:

Boolean indexing helps to select the data from the DataFrames using a Boolean vector (T/F). We need a DataFrame with a boolean index to use the boolean indexing. Let's see how to get Boolean indexing.

- Create a dictionary of data.
- Convert it into a DataFrame object with a boolean index
- Now, access the data using Boolean indexing.

 # Displaying data with Boolean indexing:

```
import pandas as pd
dt = {          'Name':['Mani', "Sreya", "Rupsa", "Udita"],
                'Degree': ["MBA", "BCA", "M.Tech", "B.Tech"],
                'Score':[90, 40, 80,75]        }
# creating a DataFrame with a Boolean index
df = pd.DataFrame(dt, index = [True, False, True, False])
print(df)
# accessing a dataframe using .loc[] function
# it will return rows of Mani and Rupsa only (matching true only)
print("")
print(df.loc[True])        #True/False is a keyword, so it shouldn't be put in " "
print(df.loc[False])
```

Output:

```
        Name    Degree          Score
True    Mani    MBA             90
False   Sreya   BCA             40            # Output of df
True    Rupsa   M.Tech          80
False   Udita   B.Tech          75

        Name    Degree          Score
True    Mani    MBA             90            # Output of df.loc[True]
True    Rupsa    M.Tech         80
        Name    Degree          Score
False   Sreya   BCA             40            # Output of df.loc[False]
False   Udita   B.Tech          75
```

 # Display the records of True & False index:

```
import pandas as pd
data = { 'Name': ['Hafza', 'Srikanth', 'Rakesh'] , 'Age': [19, 20, 19] }
df = pd.DataFrame(data, index = [True, False, True]) # Boolean index
print(df)
print(df.loc[True])
print(df.loc[False])
print(df.iloc[1])
```

Note:
- *True/False is a keyword, not a String value, so it shouldn't be put under quotes " "*
- *True/False is also written as 0 / 1 but with iloc{}*

Output:

```
        Name            Age
True    Hafza           19
False   Srikanth        20            # Output of df
True    Rakesh          19
```

	Name	**Age**
True	Hafza	19
True	Rakesh	19

Output of df.loc[True]

Name Srikanth
Age 20
Name: False, dtype: object

Output of df.loc[False]

Name Srikanth
Age 20
Name: False, dtype: object

Output of df.iloc[1]

Iteration on DF:

Iteration means taking items one by one from the source. Here, applying a loop over a DataFrame, we can access Row and Column-wise data by applying the functions **df.iterrows()** and **df.iteritems()** or **df.items()**. The *latest compiler works on df.items()*. The syntax is:

To access from row: **for (r, c) in df.iterrows():**

Here, **r** is the row index, and **c** carries the values of the row

To access from a column: **for (c, r) in df.items():**

Here, **c** is the column index, and **r** carries the values of the column

 # To print row-wise report:

```
import pandas as pd
df=pd.DataFrame( {   'Class':['X', "XII", 'XI'],
                     'Sem1':[87,90,68],   'Sem2':[88,79,90] } )
df.index=['a', 'b', 'c']
print(df)              # r is the row index, and c is the corresponding values
for (r,c) in df.iterrows():
        print(r,c)     # Row-wise values for each column
```

Output:

	Class	**Sem1**	**Sem2**
a	X	87	88
b	XII	90	79
c	XI	68	90

Output of df

a   # Row-wise values for each column

Class X
Sem1 87
Sem2 88
Name: a,
dtype: object

b
Class XII
Sem1 90
Sem2 79
Name: b,
dtype: object

c
Class XI
Sem1 68
Sem2 90
Name: c,
dtype: object

To print Column-wise report-1:

```python
import pandas as pd
df=pd.DataFrame( {     'Class':['X', "XII", 'XI'],  'Sem1':[87,90,68],
                'Sem2':[88,79,90]   } )
df.index=['a', 'b', 'c']
print(df)
for (c,r) in df.items():     # c is the col index and r is corresponding values
        print(c, r)          # Column-wise values for each Row
```

Output:

```
   Class   Sem1  Sem2              # Output of df
a   X      87    88
b   XII    90    79
c   XI     68    90

Class                             # Column-wise values for each Row
a    X
b    XII
c    XI
Name: Class, dtype: object

Sem1
a    87
b    90
c    68
Name: Sem1, dtype: int64

Sem2
a    88
b    79
c    90
Name: Sem2, dtype: int64
```

> **Note:** *df.items() can be replaced by df.iteritems(), but new compiler works on df.items()*

To print column-wise report-2:

```python
import pandas as pd
df = pd.DataFrame(    { 'A': [1, 2, 3], 'B': [4, 5, 6], 'C': [7, 8, 9]    } )
# Iterating over the columns
for (c, r) in df.items():
        print("Column label:", c)
        print("Column values:\n", r)
        print("-" * 20)          # Prints '-' 20 times
```

Output: # column-wise report

```
Column label: A
Column values:
0   1
1   2
2   3
--------------------
Column label: B
Column values:
0   4
1   5
2   6
--------------------
Column label: C
Column values:
0   7
1   8
2   9
--------------------
```

To display the values of an individual index (row index)

```python
import pandas as pd
data = {'Name':['Anil', 'Bikas', 'Rohit', 'Ricky'] , 'Age':[28,34,29,42]}
df = pd.DataFrame(data)
print(df)
column=list(df)
print(column)
for i in column:
        print(i,':',df[i][2])
```

Output:

```
    Name      Age
0  Anil       28
1  Bikas      34
2  Rohit      29
3  Ricky      42
```

```
['Name', 'Age']
```
Name : Rohit
Age : 29

 # To print conditional value(s):
```
import pandas as pd
df=pd.DataFrame( {        'Class':['X', "XII", 'XI'],
                          'Sem1':[87,90,68],  'Sem2':[88,79,90] } )
df.index=['a', 'b', 'c']
print(df)
for (r, c) in df.iterrows():
        if int(c['Sem1']) >= 60 and int(c['Sem2']) <= 80:
                print("Improvement is needed for class", c['Class'])
        else:
                print('Result of class', c['Class'], 'is Excellent')
```

Output:

	Class	Sem1	Sem2
a	X	87	88
b	XII	90	79
c	XI	68	90

> ***Note:*** ***if Sem1 >= 60 and Sem2 <= 80***
> Row a → 87>=60 **True**, 88<=80 **False => False**
> Row b → 90>=60 **True**, 79<=80 **True => True**
> Row c → 68>=60 **True**, 90<=80 **False => False**

```
Result of class X is Excellent
Improvement is needed for class XII
Result of class XI is Excellent
```

Conversion of DF into other Data Sources:

 # Converting Column Age of DF into List:
```
import pandas as pd
data = {'Name':['Jairaj', 'Prince', 'Gaurav', 'Anil'],
  'Age':[27, 24, 22, 32], 'Address':['Delhi', 'Kanpur', 'Allahabad', 'Agra'],
  'Qualification':['MSc', 'MA', 'MCA', 'PhD']}
df = pd.DataFrame(data)
print(df)
l=df['Age'].tolist()
print(l)                  # Values of 'Age' become a list []
```

Output:

	Name	Age	Address	Qualification
0	Jairaj	27	Delhi	MSc
1	Prince	24	Kanpur	MA
2	Gaurav	22	Allahabad	MCA
3	Anil	32	Agra	PhD

```
[27 24 22 32]                  # Values of the list
```

```python
# Converting DF into a Dictionary
import pandas as pd
data = { 'Name':['Jairaj', 'Prince', 'Gaurav', 'Anil'], 'Age':[27, 24, 22, 32],
         'Address':['Delhi', 'Kanpur', 'Allahabad', 'Kannauj'],
         'Qualification':['MSc', 'MA', 'MCA', 'PhD'] }
df = pd.DataFrame(data)
print(df)
d1= df.to_dict()                 # Whole DF into Dict.
d2=df['Age'].to_dict()           # A column of DF into Dict.
print(d1)
print(d2)
```

Output:

```
      Name        Age   Address      Qualification
0     Jairaj      27    Delhi        MSc
1     Prince      24    Kanpur       MA
2     Gaurav      22    Allahabad    MCA
3     Anil        32    Agra         PhD
```

{ 'Name': {0: 'Jairaj', 1: 'Prince', 2: 'Gaurav', 3: 'Anil' },
'Age': { 0: 27, 1: 24, 2: 22, 3: 32 },
'Address': { 0: 'Delhi', 1: 'Kanpur', 2: 'Allahabad', 3: 'Kannauj' },
'Qualification': {0: 'MSc', 1: 'MA', 2: 'MCA', 3: 'PhD' }}
{ 0: 27, 1: 24, 2: 22, 3: 32 }

Binary operations of DF on Row-Column:

Binary operations refer to operations that involve two operands. Here in Pandas, it means applying operations between two DataFrames, or a DataFrame and a Series/scalar, element-wise.

```python
import pandas as pd
x = pd.DataFrame({0: [1,2,3], 1: [4,5,6], 2: [7,8,9] })
print(x)
y = pd.Series([1, 2, 3])
print(y)
print("\nRow-wise Addition:")
x1 = x.add(y, axis=0)  # Add Series row-wise (matches index )
print(x1)
print("\nColumn-wise Addition:")
y1 = x.add(y, axis=1)  # Add Series column-wise (matches column)
print(y1)
print("\nRow-wise Subtraction:")
x1 = x.sub(y, axis=0)  # Subtract Series row-wise
```

```
print(x1)
print("\nColumn-wise Subtraction:")
y1 = x.sub(y, axis=1)  # Subtract Series column-wise
print(y1)
print("\nRow-wise Multiplication:")
x1 = x.mul(y, axis=0)  # Multiply Series row-wise
print(x1)
print("\nColumn-wise Multiplication:")
y1 = x.mul(y, axis=1)  # Multiply Series column-wise
print(y1)
print("\nRow-wise Division:")
x1 = x.div(y, axis=0)  # Divide Series row-wise
print(x1)
print("\nColumn-wise Division:")
y1 = x.div(y, axis=1)  # Divide Series column-wise
print(y1)
```

Output:

```
   0  1  2                        # Prints the DF
0  1  4  7
1  2  5  8
2  3  6  9

0   1                            # Prints the Series
1   2
2   3
dtype: int64
```

Row-wise Addition: # Prints, while axis=0
```
   0  1  2
0  2  5  8
1  4  7  10
2  6  9  12
```

Column-wise Addition: # Prints, while axis=1
```
   0  1  2
0  2  6  10
1  3  7  11
2  4  8  12
```

Row-wise Subtraction: # Prints, while axis=0
```
   0  1  2
0  0  3  6
1  0  3  6
2  0  3  6
```

Column-wise Subtraction: # *Prints, while axis=1*
```
  0 1 2
0 0 2 4
1 1 3 5
2 2 4 6
```

Row-wise Multiplication   # *Prints, while axis=0*
```
   0  1  2
0 1  4  7
1 4 10 16
2 9 18 27
```

Column-wise Multiplication   # *Prints, while axis=1*
```
   0  1  2
0 1  8 21
1 2 10 24
2 3 12 27
```

Row-wise Division   # *Prints, while axis=0*
```
   0   1   2
0 1.0 4.0 7.0
1 1.0 2.5 4.0
2 1.0 2.0 3.0
```

Column-wise Division   # *Prints, while axis=1*
```
   0   1      2
0 1.0 2.0 2.333333
1 2.0 2.5 2.666667
2 3.0 3.0 3.000000
```

 # Binary element-wise mathematical operation:
```python
import pandas as pd
x = pd.DataFrame({0: [1,2,3], 1: [4,5,6], 2: [7,8,9] })
y = pd.DataFrame({0: [1,2,3], 1: [4,5,6], 2: [7,8,9] })
print(x)        # Output1
print(y)        # Output2
print("Addition: \n")
x1 = x.add(y)
print(x1)
print("Subtraction: \n")
x2 = x.sub(y)
print(x2)
print("Multiplication: \n")
x3 = x.mul(y)
print(x3)
print("Division: \n")
x4 = x.div(y)
print(x4)
```

Output:

# Output1: 	
  0 1 2
0 1 4 7
1 2 5 8
2 3 6 9
	Subtraction:
	  0 1 2
	0 0 0 0
	1 0 0 0
	2 0 0 0

# Output2: 	
  0 1 2
0 1 4 7
1 2 5 8
2 3 6 9
	Multiplication:
	  0 1 2
	0 1 16 49
	1 4 25 64
	2 9 36 81

Addition:
  0 1 2
0 2 8 14
1 4 10 16
2 6 12 18
	Division:
	  0 1 2
	0 1.0 1.0 1.0
	1 1.0 1.0 1.0
	2 1.0 1.0 1.0

Re-indexing Rows/Columns in DataFrame:

 # Re-Indexing of Rows in Pandas DataFrame:

```python
import pandas as pd
table = {        'Name': ['Vishal', 'Anil', 'Mayur', 'Viraj', 'Mahesh'],
            'Age':[15, 16, 15, 17,16], 'Weight': [51, 48, 49, 51,48],
            'Height': [5.1, 5.2, 5.1, 5.3,5.1]      }
d = pd.DataFrame(table)
print("DATA OF DATAFRAME:")
print(d)
print("DATA OF DATAFRAME AFTER REINDEX:")
df=d.reindex([2,1, 0,4,3])      # Re-arranging row-indices
print(df)
```

Output:

DATA OF DATAFRAME:

	Name	Age	Weight	Height
0	Vishal	15	51	5.1
1	Anil	16	48	5.2
2	Mayur	15	49	5.1
3	Viraj	17	51	5.3
4	Mahesh	16	48	5.1

DATA OF DATAFRAME AFTER REINDEX:

	Name	Age	Weight	Height
2	Mayur	15	49	5.1
1	Anil	16	48	5.2
0	Vishal	15	51	5.1
4	Mahesh	16	48	5.1
3	Viraj	17	51	5.3

Re-Indexing of Columns in Pandas DataFrame:

```python
import pandas as pd
table = { "Name": ['Vishal', 'Anil', 'Mayur', 'Viraj', 'Mahesh'],
      'Age':[15, 16, 15, 17,16],   'Weight': [51, 48, 49, 51,48],
      'Height': [5.1, 5.2, 5.1, 5.3,5.1]  }
d = pd.DataFrame(table)
print("DATA OF DATAFRAME=>")
print(d)
print("DATA OF DATAFRAME AFTER RE-ARRANGING COLUMNS=>")
df=d.reindex(columns=['Name', 'Weight', 'Age']) #'Height' column dropped
print(df)
```

Output:

DATA OF DATAFRAME=>

	Name	Age	Weight	Height
0	Vishal	15	51	5.1
1	Anil	16	48	5.2
2	Mayur	15	49	5.1
3	Viraj	17	51	5.3
4	Mahesh	16	48	5.1

DATA OF DATAFRAME AFTER RE-ARRANGING COLUMNS =>

	Name	Weight	Age
0	Vishal	51	15
1	Anil	48	16
2	Mayur	49	15
3	Viraj	51	17
4	Mahesh	48	16

Data Frame Functions:

 # Find max(): *Finds the maximum values*
```
import pandas as pd
x = {  'Name': ['Jaya', 'Prince', 'Gaurav', 'Anu'], 'Age': [27, 24, 22, 32],
'Address': ['Delhi', 'Kanpur', 'Allahabad', 'Kannauj'],
'Qualification': ['MSc', 'MA', 'MCA', 'PhD'] }
df = pd.DataFrame(x)
print(df['Age'].max())
```

Output:
32

 # Find min():
```
import pandas as pd
x = { 'Name': ['Jaya', 'Prince', 'Gaurav', 'Anu'], 'Age': [27, 24, 22, 32],
'Address': ['Delhi', 'Kanpur', 'Allahabad', 'Kannauj'],
'Qualification': ['MSc', 'MA', 'MCA', 'PhD'] }
df = pd.DataFrame(x)
print(df['Age'].min())
```

Output:
22

 # Find count(): *It counts the number of values present in the column*
```
import pandas as pd
x = { 'Name': ['Jaya', 'Prince', 'Gaurav', 'Anu'], 'Age': [27, 24, 22, 32],
'Address': ['Delhi', 'Kanpur', 'Allahabad', 'Kannauj'],
'Qualification': ['MSc', 'MA', 'MCA', 'PhD'] }
df = pd.DataFrame(x)
print(df['Age'].count())
```

Output:
4

 # Find sum(): *Finds the total/addition of the values of the column*
```
import pandas as pd
x = { 'Name': ['Jaya', 'Prince', 'Gaurav', 'Anu'], 'Age': [27, 24, 22, 32],
'Address': ['Delhi', 'Kanpur', 'Allahabad', 'Kannauj'],
'Qualification': ['MSc', 'MA', 'MCA', 'PhD'] }
df = pd.DataFrame(x)
print(df['Age'].sum())
```

Output:
105

 # Find mean():   *# Shows (Sum of values)/(Number of values)*

```python
import pandas as pd
x = {'Age': [27, 24, 22, 32, 33, 32], 'Points': [3,5,7, 9, 7, 9] }
df = pd.DataFrame(x)
print(df.mean())
```

Output:

```
Age   28.333333
Points 6.666667
dtype: float64
```

 # Find mode(): *# The most frequently occurring value*

```python
import pandas as pd
x = { 'Age': [2,4,6,8, 8,7,6,8,5,8], 'Points': [3,5,7,8,9,9,7,5,5,7] }
df = pd.DataFrame(x)
print(df.mode())
```

Output:

```
      Age    Points
0     8.0    5
1     NaN    7
```

 # Find median(): *# The middle value when sorted*

```python
import pandas as pd
x = { 'Name': ['Jaya', 'Prince', 'Gaurav', 'Anu', 'Sourav', 'Sachin', 'Virat'],
'Points': [3,5,7, 7, 8, 9, 8]  }
df = pd.DataFrame(x)
print(df.median())
```

Output:

```
Points 7.0
dtype: float64
```

 # Find quantile(): *Quantiles are quartiles, i.e. divided into 4 equal parts; when they divide the distribution into four equal parts. Quantiles are quantiles that divide a distribution into 10 equal parts, and a Percentile is a value that divides a distribution into 100 equal parts.*

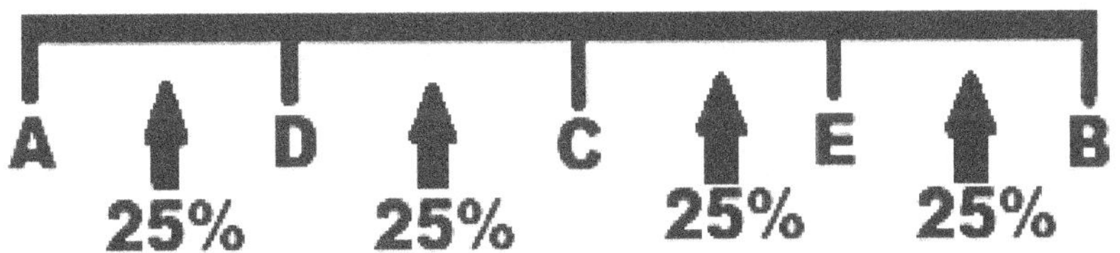

For example, in the above figure, A-B is a line, whose midpoint is C, so C is the Median of the 2-quantiles **A-C** and **C-B**. Again, the midpoint of **A-C** is **D**, and the midpoint of **C-B** is **E**. Now **D, C & E** are 3 Quantiles, i.e. 25th, 50^{th,} and 75th percentile respectively.

```python
import pandas as pd
import numpy as np
x=[[1, 1], [2, 10], [3, 100], [4, 1000], [5, 10000]]
df = pd.DataFrame(np.array(x), columns=['a', 'b'])
print(df)
print(df.quantile())
print(df.quantile(0.1))
print(df.quantile(0.7))
print(df.quantile(axis=0))      # Find quantile row wise (axis=0)
print(df.quantile(axis=1))      # Find quantile column wise (axis=1)
```

Output:

```
       a          b
0      1          1
1      2         10
2      3        100
3      4       1000
4      5      10000

a    3.0
b    100.0
Name: 0.5, dtype: float64
a    1.4
b    4.6
Name: 0.1, dtype: float64

a      3.8
b    820.0
Name: 0.7, dtype: float64

a      3.0
b    100.0
Name: 0.5, dtype: float64

0       1.0
1       6.0
2      51.5
3     502.0
4    5002.5
```

Variance & Standard Deviation:

The variance ($\sigma 2$) is a measure of how far each value in the data set is from the mean. Here is how it is defined:

- *Subtract the mean from each value in the data. This gives you a measure of the distance of each value from the mean.*
- *Square each of these distances (so that they are all positive values), and add all of the squares together.*
- *Divide the sum of the squares by the number of values in the data set.*
- *The Std. deviation (σ) is simply the (+ve) square root of the variance.*
- *Variance = (Sum of squared deviations) / (n - 1)*

Find the mean of each series:

- Subtract the mean from each value in the data. This gives a measure of the distance of each value from the mean.
- Now square each of these distances (they are all positive values).
- Add all of the squares together.
- Divide the sum of the squares by the no. of values in the data set minus 1.

As an example, let's go back to the two distributions as follows:

Data set-1:   10,   20,   30,   40,   50
Data set-2:   3,   5,   7,   9,   11

Mean of Data set-1: (10+20+30+40+50**)/5=30** *# (Sum)/(No of values)*
Mean of Data set-2: (3+5+7+9+11**)/5=7**

New set-1 after subtraction: -20 , -10 , 0 , 10 , 20
New set-2 after subtraction: -4 , -2 , 0 , 2 , 4

Squared set-1: 400 , 100 , 0 , 100 , 400
Squared set-2: 16 , 4 , 0 , 4 , 16

Sum of set-1: 1000 : Variance: 1000/(5-1)=> 250:
Standard deviation: 15.811388300

Sum of set-2: 40: Variance: 40/(5-1)=> 10 :
Standard deviation: 3.162277660

Find variance using var():

```
import pandas as pd
d = {  'Name':['Ravi', 'Rohit', 'Rahul', 'Ramesh', 'Rachna'],
        'Score':[10, 20, 30, 40, 50]   }
df = pd.DataFrame(d)
print(df)
print(df.var(numeric_only=True))   # Print variance (only for numeric columns)
```
Output:

```
      Name         Score    # Output of df
0     Ravi         10
1     Rohit        20
2     Rahul        30
3     Ramesh       40
4     Rachna       50

Score 250.0          # Output of: df.var(numeric_only=True)
dtype: float64
```

Find variance using var():

```
import pandas as pd
x = { 'Name': ['Jaya', 'Prince', 'Gaurav', 'Anu'],
      'Age': [2,4,6,8], 'Points': [3,5,7, 9]          }
df = pd.DataFrame(x)
print(df[['Age', 'Points']].var(axis=1))   # Prints variance
```

Output:

```
0   0.5
1   0.5
2   0.5
3   0.5
dtype: float64
```

Find Standard Deviation using std():

```
import pandas as pd
d =    {      'Name':['Ravi','Rohit','Rahul','Ramesh', 'Rachna'],
          'Score1':[3,5,7,9 ,11],   'Score2':[10, 20,30,40, 50]  }
df = pd.DataFrame(d)
print(df.var())                # Prints variance
print(df.std())                # Prints Standard deviation
```

Output:

```
Score1          10.0        # Output of variance
Score2          250.0
dtype: float64
```

```
Score1          3.162278         # Output of Standard deviation
Score2          15.811388
dtype: float64
```

Pivot and Pivot Table:

Pivot (Reshaping Data**):** Pivot reshapes data by using unique values from specified indexes and columns to structure the resulting DataFrame. The index defines the new row labels, columns set the new column labels, and values specify the data to populate the new frame.

Pivot Table (Aggregation**):** The pivot table takes simple column-wise data as input, and groups the entries with aggregate values into a two-dimensional table that provides a multidimensional summarisation.

So, finally, the difference between pivot and pivot_table is:

pivot() only works if data doesn't contain duplicates for the same index-column pair.

pivot_table() is more flexible because it allows aggregation and handles duplicates with aggfunc.

Let's see the connection between DataFrame, Pivot, and Pivot Table of the same DataFrame, in the following example:

Data Frame: It is a 2D heterogeneous data in a table form.

ITEM	COMPANY	RUPEES	USD
TV	LG	12000	700
TV	VIDEOCON	10000	650
AC	LG	15000	800
AC	SONY	14000	750

Pivot: Summarised data frame, for Example:
df.**pivot(**index="ITEM", columns="COMPANY", values="RUPEES"**)**

COMPANY	LG	SONY	VIDEOCON
ITEM			
AC	15000	14000	NaN
TV	12000	NaN	10000

Pivot Table: Aggregate (mean) of Item-wise costs, for Example:
df.**pivot_table(**index="ITEM", columns="COMPANY", values="RUPEES", aggfunc="mean"**)**

COMPANY	LG	SONY	VIDEOCON
ITEM			
AC	15000	14000	NaN
TV	12000	NaN	10000

Pivot Table and distribution of Index, Column and Values:

```python
import pandas as pd
df = pd.DataFrame( {
'fff':  ['one', 'one', 'one', 'two', 'two', 'two'],
'bbb': ['P',   'Q',   'R',   'P',   'Q',   'R'],
'baa': [ 2,     3,     4,     5,     6,     7],
'zzz': ['h',   'i',   'j',   'k',   'l',   'm'] } )
print(df)
pv1 = df.pivot(index='fff', columns='bbb', values='baa')
print(pv1)
pv2=df.pivot(index='fff', columns='bbb', values=['baa', 'zzz'])
print(pv2)
```

Output:

> **Note:**
> *By default in pivot_table() aggfunc is mean*

```
   fff bbb baa zzz
0  one  P   2   h
1  one  Q   3   i
2  one  R   4   j        # Output of df
3  two  P   5   k
4  two  Q   6   l
5  two  R   7   m


bbb  P  Q  R
fff
                         # Output of pv1
one  2  3  4
two  5  6  7


      baa      zzz
bbb  P Q R   P Q R
fff                      # Output of pv2
one  2 3 4   h i j
two  5 6 7   k l
```

Pivoting: Blank spaces are filled by NaN (non-numeric/unknown)

Now in: df.pivot(index='fff',columns='bbb',values==['baa','zzz'])

	fff	bbb	baa	zzz
0	one	P	2	h
1	one	Q	3	i
2	one	R	4	j
3	two	P	5	k
4	two	Q	6	l
5	two	R	7	m
	Index	Column	Values	Values

	baa			zzz		
	P	Q	R	P	Q	R
One	2	3	4	h	I	J
Two	5	6	7	k	l	m

```
import pandas as pd
table = {  'name': ['Vishal', 'Anil', 'Mayur', 'Viraj','Mahesh'],
        'age':[15, 16, 15, 17,16],  'weight': [51, 48, 49, 51,48],
        'height': [5.1, 5.2, 5.1, 5.3,5.1]    }
df = pd.DataFrame(table)
pv=df.pivot(index='name' , columns='age' , values='height')
print(pv)
```

Output:

```
age     15      16      17
name
Anil        NaN     5.2     NaN
Mahesh      NaN     5.1     NaN
Mayur       5.1     NaN     NaN
Viraj       NaN     NaN     5.3
Vishal      5.1     NaN     NaN
```

*# Pivoting: Replacing NaN values with "**"*

```
import pandas as pd
table = {  'name': ['Vishal', 'Anil', 'Mayur', 'Viraj','Mahesh'],
        'age':[15, 16, 15, 17,16],  'weight': [51, 48, 49, 51,48],
        'height': [5.1, 5.2, 5.1, 5.3,5.1], }
df = pd.DataFrame(table)
pv=df.pivot(index='name' , columns='age' , values='height').fillna('**')
print(pv)
```

Output:

```
age      15    16       17
name
Anil     **    5.2      **
Mahesh **     5.1      **
Mayur  5.1    **       **
Viraj    **    **       5.3
Vishal  5.1   **       **
```

Pivot Table:

```python
import pandas as pd
table = {  'Name': ['Vishal', 'Anil', 'Mayur', 'Viraj','Mahesh'],
        'Age':[15, 16, 15, 17,16],  'Weight': [51, 48, 49, 51,48],
        'Height': [5.1, 5.2, 5.1, 5.3,5.1]  }
df = pd.DataFrame(table)
pt=pd.pivot_table(df, index='name')
print(pt)
```

Output:

Name	Age	Height	Weight
Anil	16	5.2	48
Mahesh	16	5.1	48
Mayur	15	5.1	49
Viraj	17	5.3	51
Vishal	15	5.1	51

<table>
<tr><td>

 # Raw data (rows)

Product	Region	Sales
A	North	100
A	South	150
B	North	200

</td><td>

 # Pivot table result:

Product	North	South
A	100	150
B	200	0

</td></tr>
</table>

> **Note:** *Pivot Table is a data analysis tool that allows taking rows of raw data and transforming/grouping them into a structured summary table. Pivot tables allow for performing common aggregate statistical calculations such as sums, counts, averages, and so on.*

Chapter 12

Data Visualization

Chapter Objective:

- Data Visualisation as Defined

- Histogram in Python

- Difference between a Histogram and Bar Graph

- Creating Histogram

- Creating Frequency Polygon

- Creating Bar Chart

- Creating Line Chart

- Creating Scatter Plot

- Creating Pie Chart

- Creating Box Plot

Data Visualisation as Defined:

Data visualisation is the graphical representation of data from a DataFrame.Here are various types of Data Visualisation techniques:

- Histogram
- Bar chart
- Pie chart
- Line plot
- Scatter plot
- Box plot

Histogram:

A histogram is a graphical representation of the distribution of numerical data, introduced by Karl Pearson. It is a kind of bar graph. To construct a histogram, the first step is to **"bins"**, that is, divide the entire range of values into a series of intervals, and then count how many values fall into each interval (i.e., frequency of values in a bin). The **bins** (intervals) are of equal width, and their height shows the frequency of values within each bin.

Histogram in Python:

To draw a histogram, the following functions must be understood.

Axis: y-axis and x-axis.

title(): To display the heading of the histogram.

xlabel(): Function to display caption at x-axis

ylabel(): Function to display caption at y-axis

xticks(): Function to display scaling on the x-axis

yticks(): Function to display scaling at the y-axis

hist(): Function to generate a histogram

show(): Function to display a histogram

savefig(): Function to save the Graph

color: To show the colour of the bar.

Bins: The width of the bins is calculated by: (Maximum value − Minimum value)/Bin no. Default number/size of bins = 10

edgecolor: Border colour of the bars.

Font (size/color): Captions can be modified

Matplotlib is a whole Python package/library used to create 2D graphs using Python scripts. Pyplot is a module in Matplotlib that supports plots such as histograms, bar charts, line charts, pie charts, box charts, power spectra, error charts, etc.

Pyplot provides the state-machine interface to the plotting library in matplotlib. It means that figures and axes are implicitly and automatically created to achieve the desired plot. For example, calling a plot from pyplot will automatically create the necessary figures and axes to achieve the desired plot. Setting a title will then automatically set that title to the current axes object. The pyplot interface is generally preferred for non-interactive plotting (i.e., scripting).

Difference between a Histogram and a Bar Graph:

A bar chart primarily represents categorical data (data that has some labels associated with it), and it are usually represented using rectangular bars with lengths proportional to the values that they represent. Histograms are used to represent the distribution of numerical data, while bar charts represent categorical data.

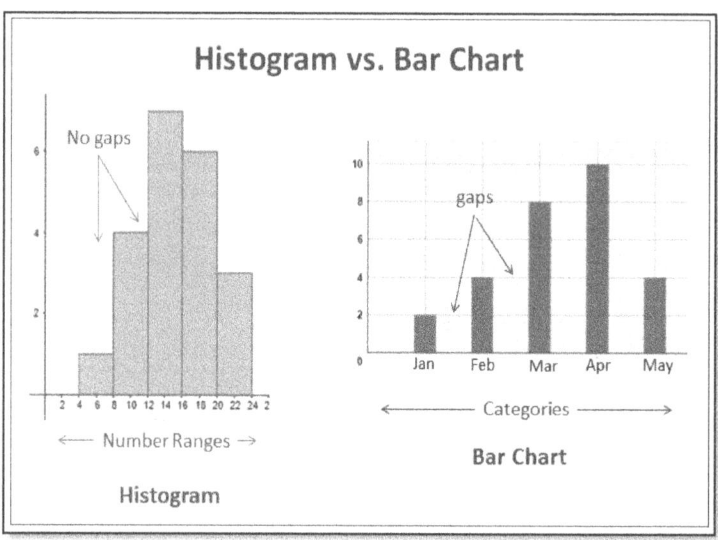

Syntax of Histogram in Python:

import matplotlib.pyplot as plt

x = [value1, value2, value3,...]

plt.hist(x, bins = number_of_bins)

plt.show()

Creating Histogram in Python:

 # Create a histogram (show the frequency of data within each bucket/bin of 10) of average marks scored by the students of a class.

```
import matplotlib.pyplot as plt
x=[50,60,60,60,75,75,80,80,80,85,85,89,89,93,95,95,95,95,100,100,100]
plt.hist(x, bins=10)     # Creates Histogram & default bin=10
plt.show()               # Prints the histogram
```

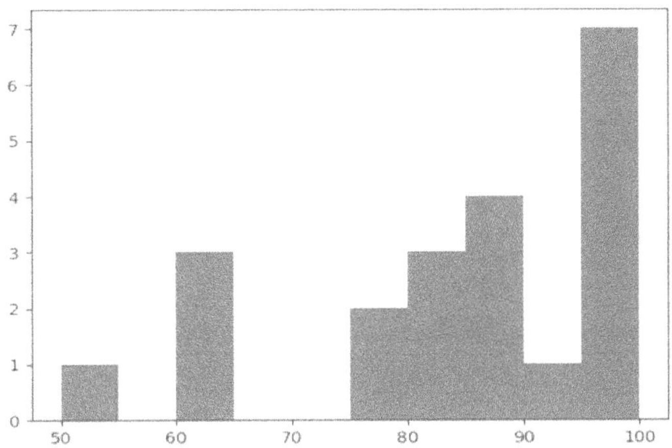

 # Histogram with bins=5
```
import matplotlib.pyplot as plt
x=[50,60,60,60,75,75,80,80,80,85,85,89,89,93,95,95,95,95,100,100,100]
plt.hist(x, bins=5)      # Now bin is 5
plt.show()
```

> **Note:**
> - *The values: [50,60,60,60,75,75,80,80,80,85,85,89,89,93,95,95,95,95, 100,100,100] of the list becomes Histogram by df.hist() function.*
> - *The number of bins is set to 10, meaning the range of values is divided into 10 intervals.*
> - *Each bar shows the frequency (time of occurrence of values within the range of each bin i.e. 50-59, 60-69, 70-79, 80-89, 90-100)*
> - *The width of each bar is: (100-50)/10=5 unit*
> - *Between 50-59: 1, 60-69: 3, 70-79: 2, 80-89: 3+4, 90-100: 1+7*
> - *In the Y-axis values are 0-7 because the maximum frequency is 7*

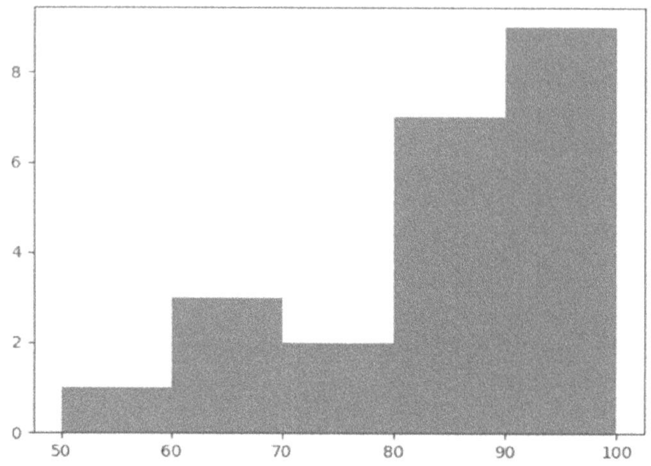

> **Note:**
> - *Each bar shows the frequency (time of occurrence of values within the range of 5)*
> - *Between 50-54: **1**, 55-59: **1**, 60-64: **2**, 65-69: **2**, 70-74: **2**, 75-79: **2**, 80-84: **7**, 85-89: **7**, 90-94: **9**, 95-100: **9***
> - *The width of each bar/bin size is: Width of each bin is = (max value of data − min value of data) / total number of bins. i.e. (100-50)/5=10*

 # Plot a Histogram to show the various frequencies of given marks

```
import matplotlib.pyplot as plt
avmark=[50, 55, 65,76,77,54, 75, 90, 99, 100,100,90, 95,95, 86,88,77, 79, 80]
plt.xlabel("X-AXIS===>>")
plt.ylabel("Y-AXIS===>>", fontsize=12)
plt.title("HISTOGRAM OF STD_AVG MARKS", fontsize=18)
plt.xticks([50,55,60,65,70,75,80,85,90,95,100])
plt.yticks([1,1.5,2,2.5,3,3.5,4,4.5,5])
plt.hist(avmark, bins=10, edgecolor='red', facecolor='yellow')
plt.show()
plt.savefig('abc.jpeg')        # Graph will be saved in picture file
```

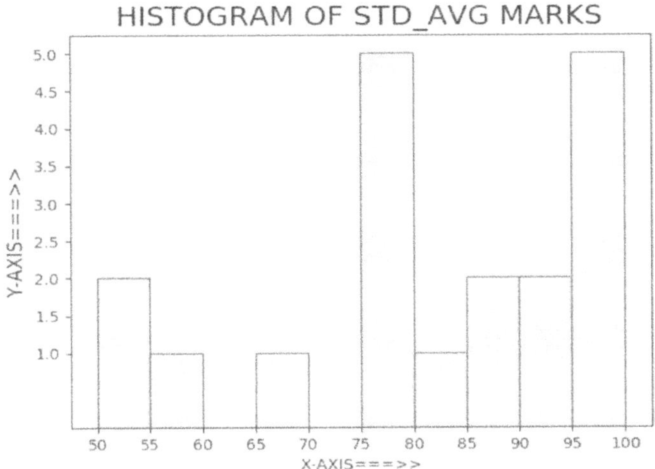

 # Create with values DataFrame taken from a Dictionary
```
import pandas as pd
import matplotlib.pyplot as plt        # MAT-PLOT-LIB <DOT>PY-PLOT
x={"AvMark": [90,95,95,93,94,78,69,85,74,86,75,79,98] }
df=pd.DataFrame(x)
df.hist()                 # hist() Converts the df into Histogram
plt.show()
```

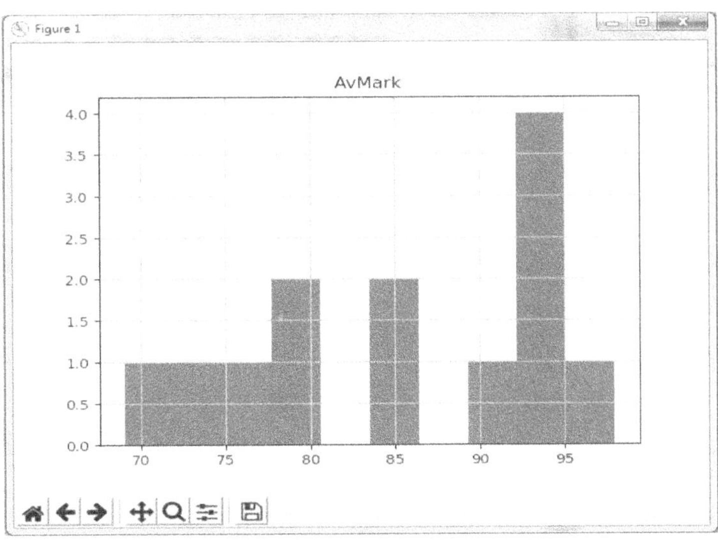

Histogram of 2 sets of values of 'Age' & 'Points'

```python
import pandas as pd
import matplotlib.pyplot as plt
x = {'Age': [27, 24, 22, 32, 33, 32], 'Points': [3,5,7, 9, 7, 9] }
df = pd.DataFrame(x)
print(df)
hist = df.hist()
plt.show()
```

Output:

```
   Age  Points
0  27      3
1  24      5
2  22      7
3  32      9
4  33      7
5  32      9
```

A Case Study on Histogram

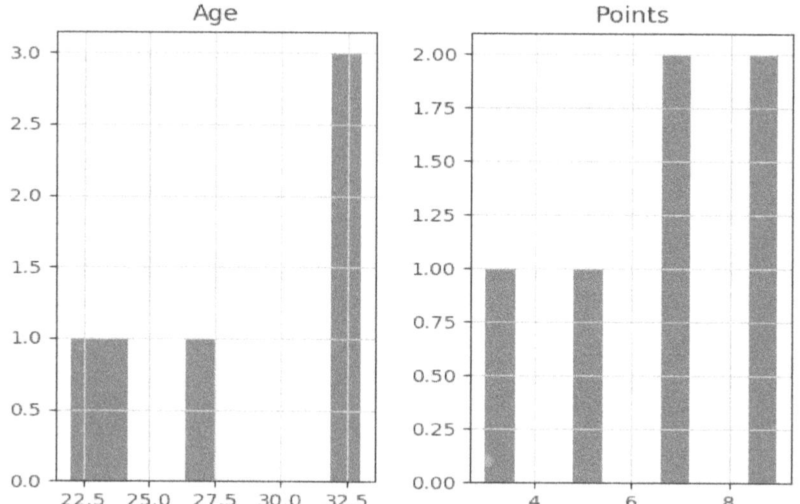

The manager at a local bank recently received customer feedback saying that the wait times for a client to be served by a customer service representative are too long. He decides to observe and write down the time spent by each customer waiting. Here are his findings from observing and writing down the wait times spent by 20 customers:

Histogram Data:

Customer wait time in seconds	
43.1	42.2
36.6	45.5
37.6	30.3
36.5	31.4
45.3	35.6
43.5	45.2
40.3	54.1
50.2	45.6
47.3	36.5
31.2	43.1

The corresponding histogram with 5-second bins (5-second intervals) would look as follows. We can see that:

43.1, 36.6, 37.6, 36.5, 45.3, 43.5, 40.3, 50.2, 47.3, 31.2, 42.2, 45.5, 30.3, 31.4, 35.6, 45.2, 54.1, 45.6, 36.5, 43.1

- 3 customers are waiting between 1 and 35 seconds
- 5 customers are waiting between 36 and 40 seconds
- 5 customers are waiting between 41 and 45 seconds
- 5 customers are waiting between 46 and 50 seconds
- 2 customers are waiting between 51 and 55 seconds

Test-1

```
import matplotlib.pyplot as plt
wt=[43.1 , 36.6, 37.6, 36.5, 45.3, 43.5, 40.3, 50.2, 47.3, 31.2, 42.2,
45.5, 30.3, 31.4, 35.6, 45.2, 54.1, 45.6, 36.5, 43.1]
plt.hist(wt, bins=10)
plt.show()
```

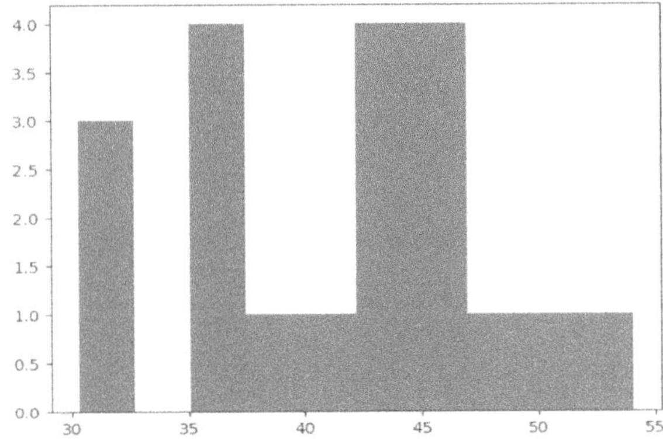

Test-2: With border colour and Horizontal orientation

```
import matplotlib.pyplot as plt
wt=[43.1 , 36.6, 37.6, 36.5, 45.3, 43.5, 40.3, 50.2, 47.3, 31.2, 42.2,
45.5, 30.3, 31.4, 35.6, 45.2, 54.1, 45.6, 36.5, 43.1]
plt.hist(wt, bins=10, edgecolor='red', orientation='horizontal')
plt.show()
```

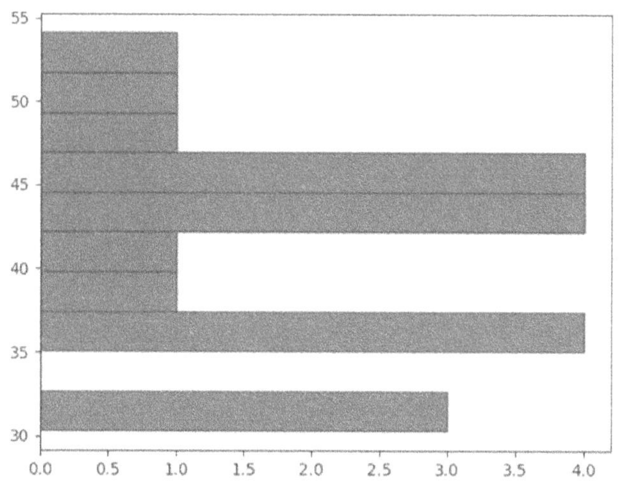

Test-3: With customisation (Label, Title, Font size, colours)

```
import matplotlib.pyplot as plt
wt=[43.1, 36.6, 37.6, 36.5, 45.3, 43.5, 40.3, 50.2, 47.3, 31.2, 42.2, 45.5,
30.3, 31.4, 35.6, 45.2, 54.1, 45.6, 36.5, 43.1]
plt.hist(wt, bins=10, edgecolor='y', facecolor='r')
plt.xticks()
plt.xlabel('Value=> ', fontsize=15)
plt.ylabel('Frequency=>', fontsize=15)
plt.title('Normal Distribution Histogram', fontsize=15)
# savefig() func. Saves the graph in picture format (jpeg, png...)
plt.savefig('Wait_time.jpeg')
plt.show()
```

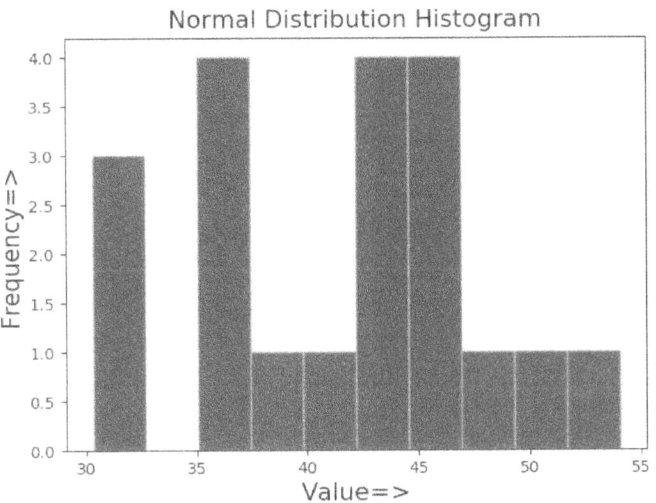

 # Test-4: With Step type

```python
import numpy as np
import matplotlib.pyplot as plt
plt.hist([5,15,25,35,15,44, 55], bins=[0,10,20,30,40,50, 60],
weights=[20,10,45,33,6,10,8], edgecolor="red", histtype='step')
plt.xlabel('Value')
plt.ylabel('Probability')
plt.title('Histogram')
plt.show()
```

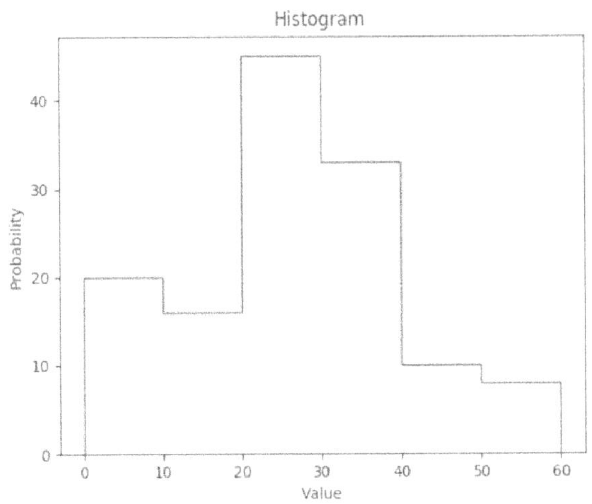

Frequency Polygon (*on step-Histogram*):

A frequency polygon is a line graph of frequency distribution made on a step histogram. The theory of the Frequency Polygon is:

- In a frequency polygon, the number of observations is marked with a single point at the midpoint of an interval (of a step Histogram). A straight line then connects each set of points.
- Pyplot doesn't provide a function for a frequency polygon. For this, one has to follow the following steps:
  - ✓ Plot a histogram from the data.
  - ✓ Mark a single point at the midpoint of an interval/bin.
  - ✓ Draw straight lines to connect the adjacent points.
  - ✓ Connect the first data point to the midpoint of the previous interval on the x-axis.
  - ✓ Connect the last data point to the midpoint of the following interval on the x-axis.

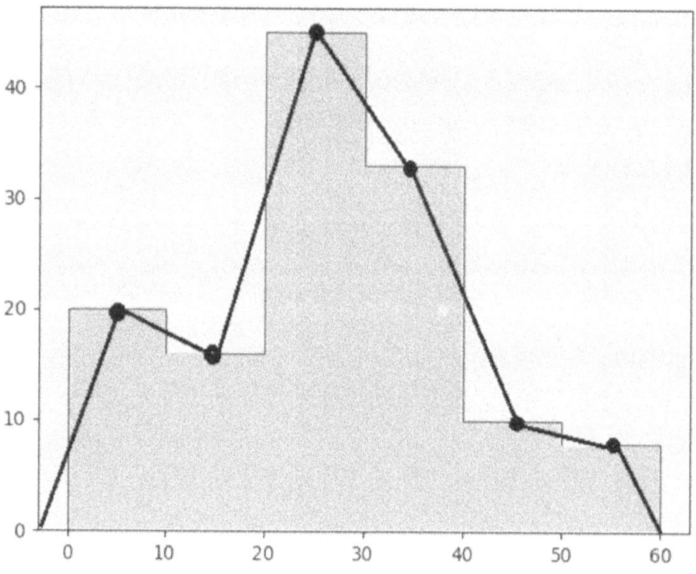

Creating a Bar-Chart in Python *plt.bar()*:

A bar chart or bar plot is a graphical representation of data with rectangular bars with lengths and heights that are proportional to the values that they represent.

A bar graph shows comparisons among discrete categories. One axis of the chart shows the specific categories being compared, and the other axis represents a measured value.

Syntax:
```
import matplotlib.pyplot as plt
plt.bar(x-data, y-data, width=.5, color='g')
plt.show()
```

 # Create a Bar Chart of the class-wise average marks of the students:
```
import matplotlib.pyplot as plt
marks=[85.85, 69.00, 89.90, 75.85, 95.89]
cls=['VIII', 'IX', 'X', 'XI', 'XII']
plt.bar(cls, marks)
plt.show()
```

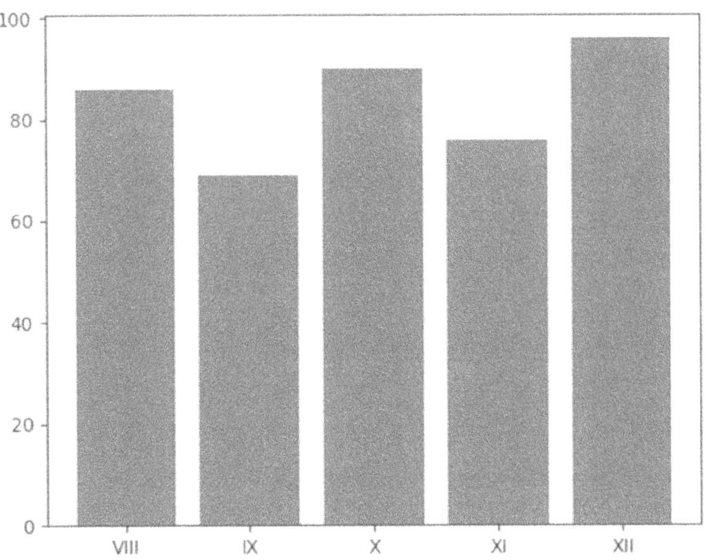

 # Create a Bar Chart of the number of students in different subjects:
```python
import matplotlib.pyplot as plt
langs = ['C', 'C++', 'Java', 'Python', 'PHP']
students = [23,17,35,29,12]
plt.bar(langs , students, width=.5, color='g')
plt.xlabel('X-Axis➜', fontsize=20)
plt.ylabel('Y-Axis➜', fontsize=20)
plt.xticks(langs, fontsize=10, rotation=40)
plt.yticks(students, fontsize=15, rotation=90)
plt.title('Bar Graph of Result=> ', fontsize=20)
plt.show()
```

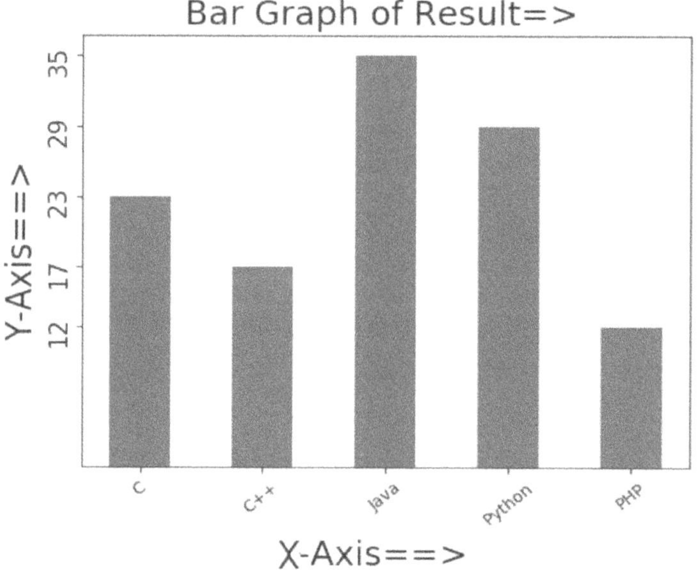

 # Create a comparative Bar Chart of section-wise marks scored in the Mock test and Board exams, as given:

Sections are: 'A', 'B', 'C', 'D', 'E'
Average marks in Mock exam: 65, 77, 78, 69, 67
Average marks in Board exam: 82, 86, 93, 88, 91

> **Note:** *For a comparative graphical study, data have been taken into the Dictionary, where the **index** (A, B, C) of the DF becomes the **values** of the x-axis*

```python
import pandas as pd
import matplotlib.pyplot as plt
data = {"avg_mock":[65,77,78,69,67], "avg_board":[82,86,93, 88, 91] }
index= ["A", "B", "C", "D", "E"]
# data variable has two sets of values as X-axis
df = pd.DataFrame(data=data, index=index)
# rot => Angle of rotation
df.plot.bar(rot=15, title="Comparative Average Marks of Mock & Board Exams")
plt.show()
```

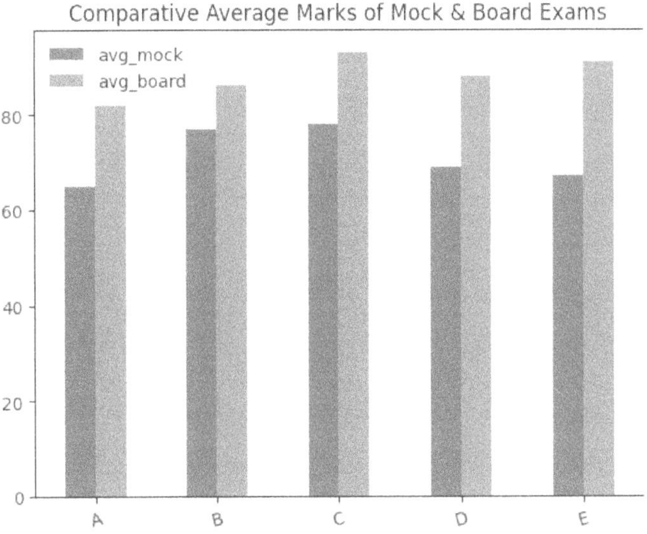

***# Create a comparative Bar Chart of session-wise No. of Students in
different Branches, as given:***
IT=[12, 30, 1, 8, 22]
ECE=[28, 6, 16, 5, 10]
CSE = [29, 3, 24, 25, 17]
Session = [2015, 2016, 2017, 2018, 2019]

```python
import pandas as pd
import matplotlib.pyplot as plt
data=  {       'IT': [12, 30, 1, 8, 22],
               'ECE' : [28, 6, 16, 5, 10],
               'CSE' : [29, 3, 24, 25, 17]           }
idx=[2015, 2016, 2017, 2018, 2019]
df=pd.DataFrame(data, idx)
print(df)
```

```
df.plot.bar(title="Session wise No. of Students in different Branches ")
plt.savefig("exam.jpeg")
plt.show()
```

	IT	ECE	CSE
2015	12	28	29
2016	30	6	3
2017	1	16	24
2018	8	5	25
2019	22	10	17

> **Note:** *Here the index of DF becomes of values of x-axis*

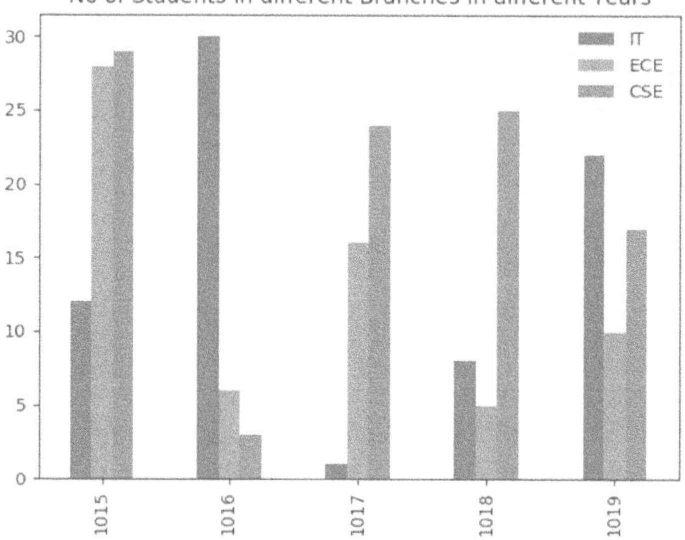

 # Create a comparative Bar Chart of session-wise No. of Students in different Branches, using Stack.

```
import pandas as pd
import matplotlib.pyplot as plt
data=   { 'IT': [12, 30, 1, 8, 22],
'ECE' : [28, 6, 16, 5, 10],
'CSE' : [29, 3, 24, 25, 17] }
idx=[2015,2016,2017,2018,2019]
df=pd.DataFrame(data, idx)
df.plot.bar(stacked=True, title='Session & Branch wise no of Students')
plt.show()
```

> **Note:** *Here in* **Stack,** *the index of DF becomes the values of x-axis, and branch wise numbers for each session comes in stack form i.e. one above the other with its values.*

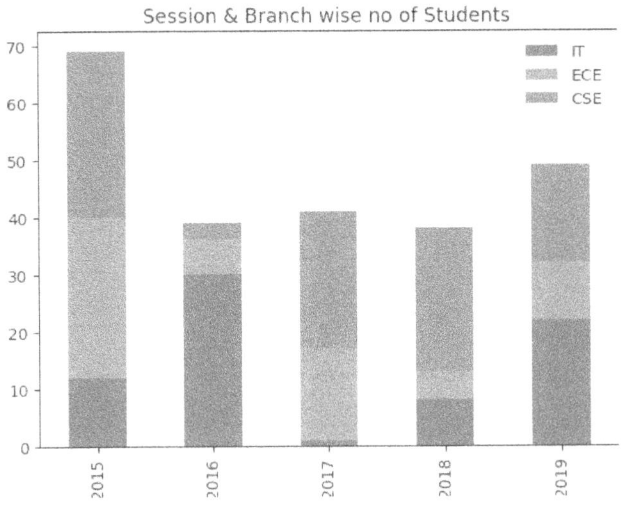

Creating a Line-Chart in Python using *plt.plot()*:

A line graph or line chart is generated to represent the relation between two sets of data, the progress of the X-axis and Y-axis.
import matplotlib.pyplot as plt
*plt.**plot**(x-axis_data , y-axis_data)*
plt.show()

 # Create a line chart of a list of values [1,2,3,4,5] with a grid:
import matplotlib.pyplot as plt
plt.grid()   # *Reformat the layout with grid*
 # Given a single set of values is treated as Y-Axis, X-Axis values are taken by default
plt.**plot**([1,2,3,4,5]**)**
plt.savefig("chartline.jpeg")
plt.show()

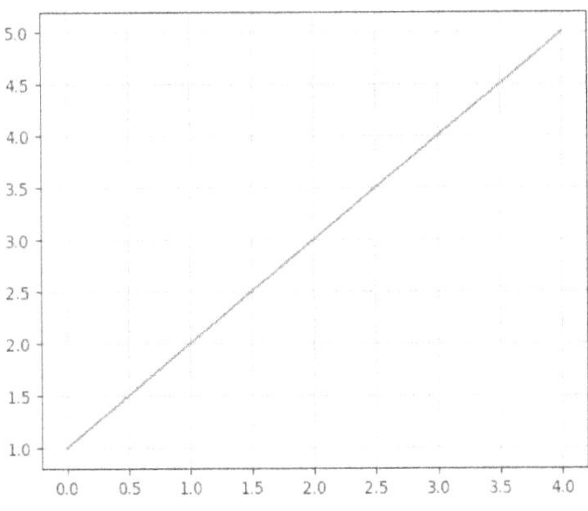

 # Create a line chart of a list of values of X & Y Co-ordinates:

```
import matplotlib.pyplot as plt
plt.grid()        # Reformat the layout with grid
# First set of values works as X-axis & Second set of values works as Y-Axis
plt.plot([1,2,3,4,5] , [2,4,6,8,5])
plt.savefig("chartline.jpeg")
plt.show()
```

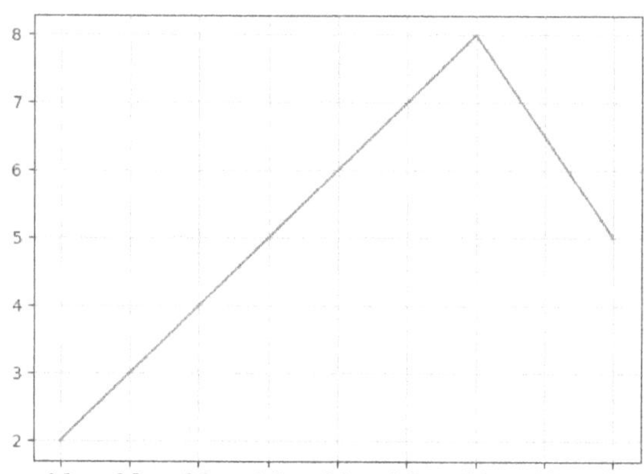

 # Graphically display the paths of the two trains of the data given:

```
import matplotlib.pyplot as plt
# Creates a line in ref to X-Axis & Y-Axis respectability of Green colour('g')
plt.plot([2,4,6,8,10,12], [1, 2, 3, 4, 5, 4], 'g')
plt.plot([1,2,3,4,5,6], [1, 2, 3, 4, 5, 4], 'b')
plt.grid()                        # Reformat the layout with grid
plt.title('My Pyplot')            # Displays title of the layout at the top
plt.ylabel('some numbers')        # Displays label of Y-Axis
plt.xlabel('values')              # Displays label of X-Axis
plt.savefig('abc.jpeg')
plt.show()
```

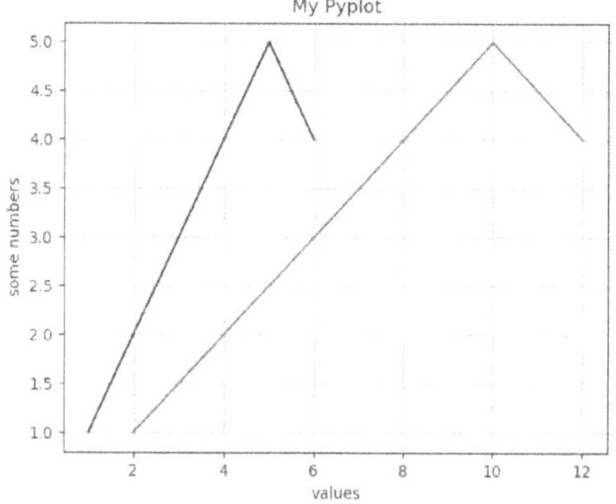

Create a comparative overview of the progress of cricket teams.

```python
import matplotlib.pyplot as plt
over=[10,20,30,40,50]
team_ind=[50,90,145,200,248]
team_sa=[65,130,140,225,240]
plt.plot(over,team_ind, color='b', marker='*', label='India')
plt.plot(over,team_sa, color='g', marker='o', label='South Africa')
plt.title("India v/s South Africa Comparative Score Line",  fontsize=15)
plt.xlabel("Overs=>", fontsize=12)
plt.ylabel("Runs per 10 overs=>", fontsize=12)
plt.legend()
plt.grid()
plt.savefig('abc.jpeg')
plt.show()
```

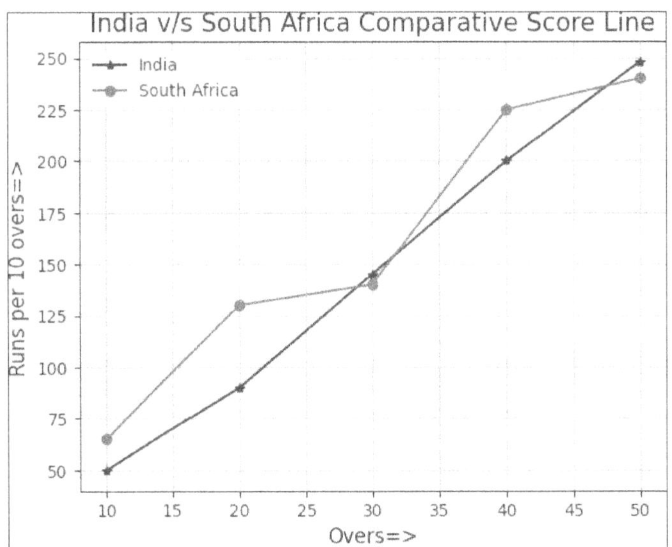

Note:
- **legend()** shows the line indicator according to labels in **plot()** function
- **grid()** shows the graphical grid on the plot
- marker type gets printed at the coordinates of the corresponding lines
- color type makes the color of the lines
- Font size value makes the size of the labels, title, etc.

 # Application of arange() function that creates parallel lines:

```python
import numpy as np
import matplotlib.pyplot as plt
x=np.arange(1,5,1)
# 'r' makes the red colour of the line generated according to the value of x
plt.plot(x, 'r')
# 'y' makes the yellow colour of the line according to the value of x+1
plt.plot(x+1, 'y')
# 'b' makes the blue colour of the line according to the value of x+2
plt.plot(x+2, 'b')
plt.legend([x, x+1, x+2])
plt.show()
```

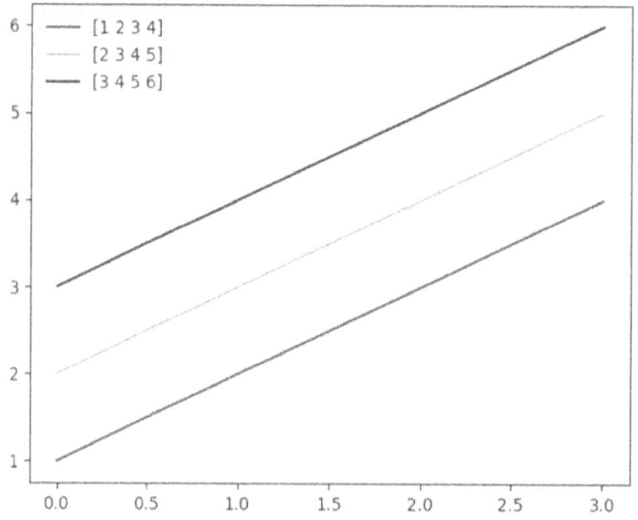

Note:
- *X=[1, 2, 3, 4]*
- *X+1 = [2 , 3, 4, 5]*
- *X+2= [3 , 4, 5, 6]*

Font size value makes the size of the labels, title, etc.

Creating a Scatter-Plot in Python using *plt.scatter()*:

A scatter plot is a two-dimensional data visualisation that uses dots to represent the values obtained for two different variables – one plotted along the x-axis and the other plotted along the y-axis.

Syntax:
import matplotlib.pyplot as plt
*plt.**scatter**(values_of_x-axis, values_of_y-axis)*
plt.show()

 # Creating a scatter chart of a set of values of Weight and Height
```
import matplotlib.pyplot as plt
weight=[11,12,13,14,15]
height=[10,20,30,40,50]
plt.scatter(weight, height, c='b')        # c denotes color
plt.xlabel('Weight', fontsize=16)
plt.ylabel('Height', fontsize=16)
plt.title('Scatter Plot->', fontsize=20)
plt.show()
```

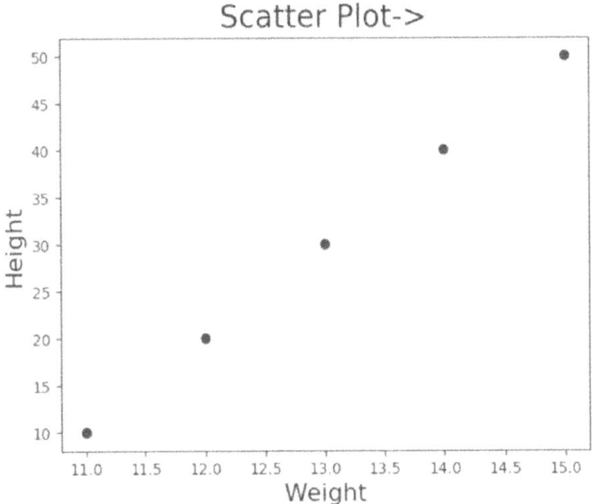

 # Create a scatter graph based on weight and height and save.
```
import matplotlib.pyplot as plt
weight1=[93.3,67,62.3,43,71,71.8]
height1=[116.3,110.7,124.8,176.3,137.1,113.9]
weight2=[90,50,69,90,58,78]
height2=[111.3,130.7,144.8,156.3,177.1,133.9]
```

```
plt.scatter(weight1, height1,  c='b', marker='s', s=150)
plt.scatter(weight2, height2,  c='r', marker='o', s=200)
plt.xlabel('Weight', fontsize=16)
plt.ylabel('Height', fontsize=16)
plt.title('Variations of Height vs Weight', fontsize=20)
plt.savefig('abc.jpeg')
plt.show()
```

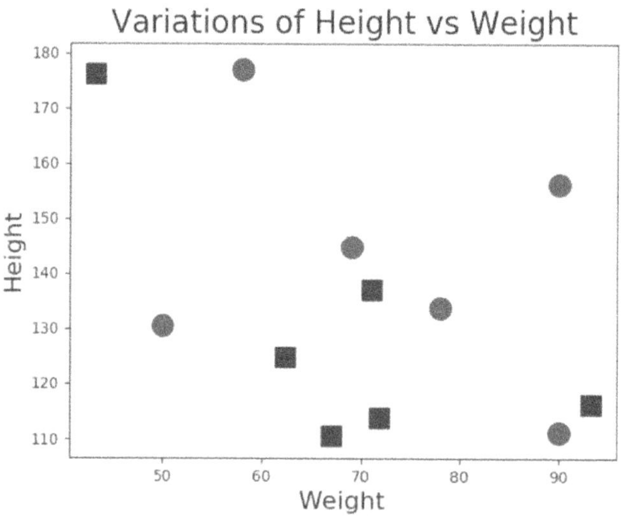

> **Note:**
> - *Here marker='s' means Square & s=150 means Size=150*
> - *Here marker='o' means Circular & 0=200 means its Size*

Combination of Scatter and Line chart

```
import matplotlib.pyplot as plt
weight=[11,12,13,14,15]
height=[10,40,20,30,50]
plt.scatter(weight, height, c='b')
plt.plot(weight, height, c='r')          # Line chart with scatter chart
plt.xlabel('Weight', fontsize=16)
plt.ylabel('Height', fontsize=16)
plt.title('Scatter Plot->', fontsize=20)
plt.show()
```

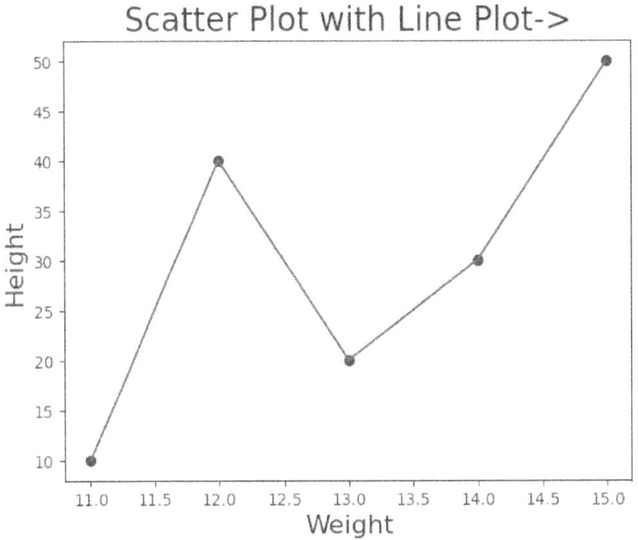

Creating a Pie-Chart in Python using *.pie()*:

Syntax: **plt.pie(data-set,** *[lables=value], [shadow=True]***)**

 # Create a pie chart of the Result analysis out of 100 students as given:

70-75% Scorer	***=> 10/100***
91-100% Scorer	***=> 20/100***
76-80% Scorer	***=> 30/100***
81-90% Scorer	***=> 40/100***

```python
import matplotlib.pyplot as plt
mrk=[10,20,30,40]
x=['70-75% Scorer', '91-100% Scorer', '76-80% Scorer', '81-90% Scorer']
plt.pie(mrk, labels=x, shadow=True)    # Data and Labels
plt.title('Result analysis=>', fontsize=20)
plt.show()
```

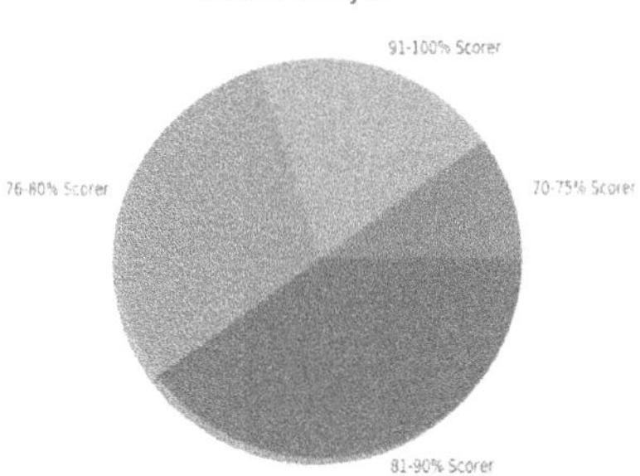

Creating a Box-Plot in Python using *.boxplot()*:

Understanding Box Plot:

A box plot displays a summary of a set of data containing the minimum, first quartile, median, third quartile, and maximum. In a box plot, we draw a box from the first quartile to the third quartile. A vertical line goes through the box at the median.

To understand a Box Plot, we must have a structural understanding of the Box Plot. Consider the following Box Plot:

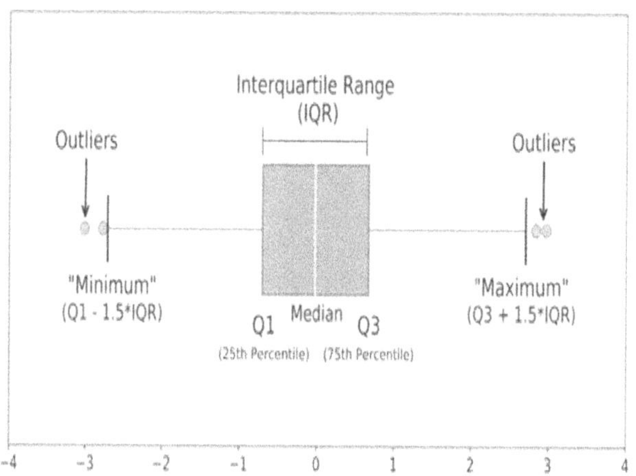

The whole set of data is first distributed into four groups, i.e. four quartiles. Those are four sets of 25% of data, i.e. Minimum, 25th Percentile (1st Quartile), Median (2nd Quartile or 50th Percentile), 75th Percentile (3rd Quartile), and Maximum. So, Q1 = 25th percentile, Q2 = 50th percentile (median), Q3 = 75th percentile.

For example, to find the median of the following list of values:

12, 14, 15, 13, 18, 20, 17, 16, 21

The median is the middle value. There are nine numbers in the list, so the middle one will be the (9 + 1) ÷ 2 = 10 ÷ 2 = 5th number: So, among the arranged values (12,13,14,15,16,17,18,20,21), the median is **16**. The Maximum value is 21, and the minimum is 12

Box Plot graph in programming:

```
import matplotlib.pyplot as plt
data=[12, 14, 15, 13, 18, 20, 17, 16, 21]
plt.boxplot(data)
plt.show()
```

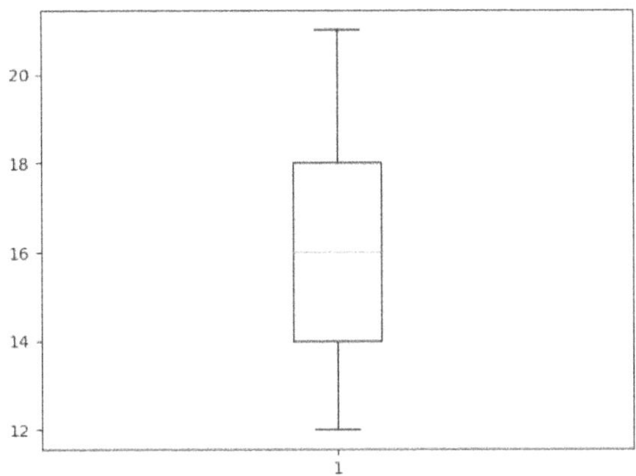

> **Note:**
> Here in the graph, it is visible that:
> 1st quartile is: 14.
> The 3rd quartile is: 18.
> The 2nd quartile or Median is: 16.
> The Minimum is: 12
> The Maximum is: 21

 # Create a Box Plot of the given data of Marks

```
import matplotlib.pyplot as plt
data=[[95,95,78,88,95],[95,76,81,63,55],[90,79,75,67,51],[94,77,76,77,59]]
plt.boxplot(data)
plt.title('Performance Analysis')
plt.xlabel('Subjects')
plt.ylabel('Marks')
plt.show()
```

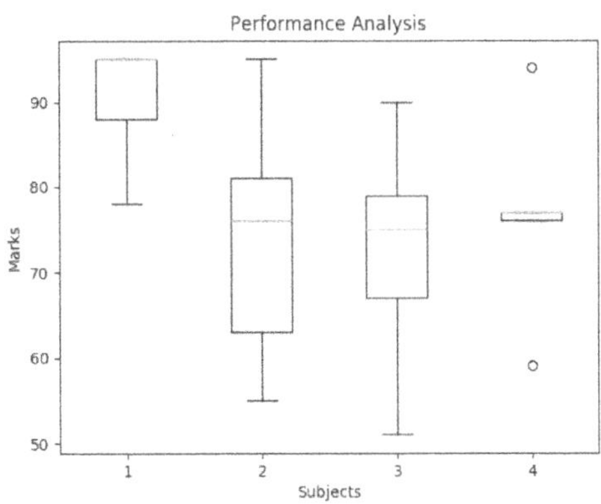

Create a Box Plot of the given data of Marks

```python
import numpy as np
import pandas as pd
import matplotlib.pyplot as plt
data={ 'Name': ['Rishika' , 'Waseem', 'Kulpreet', 'Annie','Shiksha'],
      'English' : [95 , 95 , 78 , 88, 95] ,
      'Maths' : [95, 76, 81, 63, 55 ],
      'Social Sc' : [90, 79, 75, 67, 51 ],
      'Science':[94, 77, 76, 77, 59 ]   }
df= pd.DataFrame(data)
# df.plot(kind='box') or...
df.boxplot()
#set title,xlabel,ylabel
plt.title('Performance')
plt.xlabel('Subjects')
plt.ylabel('Marks')
plt.savefig('result.jpeg')
plt.show()
```

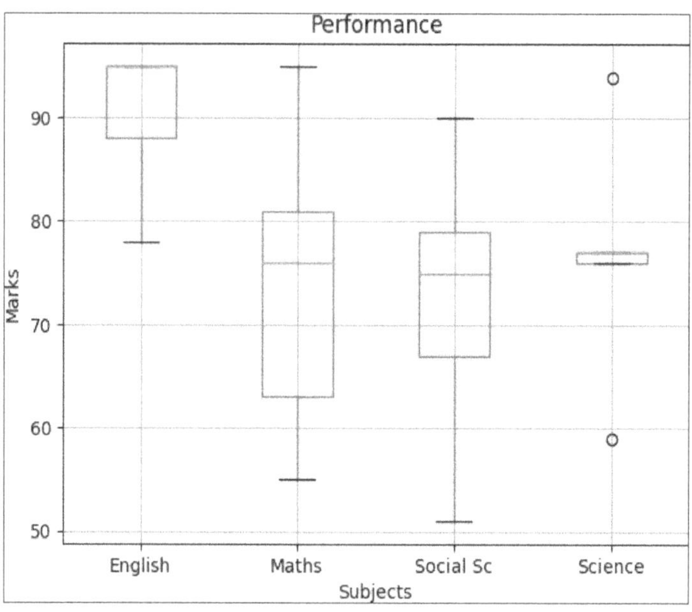

Chapter 13

Database
with
MySQL

Chapter Objective:

- Database as Defined

- Need a Database

- DBMS

- Advantages of Database System

- Relational Database Terms

- Components of a Table

- Types of Keys in DBMS

- Structured Query Language (SQL)

- MySQL Features

- Types of SQL Commands

- MySql DataTypes

- Constraints in Database

- SQL Commands in MySQL

- Procedural Coding in MySQL

Database as Defined:

A database is a structured collection of data stored in a tabulated form, which can be accessed and managed using various mechanisms. When managed with software, it becomes a Database Management System (DBMS).

In a Database, Data is organised into rows, columns, and tables, and it is indexed to make it easier to find relevant information. It works like a container that holds various objects, such as Tables, Queries, Reports, etc., in an organised way.

Why do we need a Database?

- **To manage large chunks of data:** If the size of the data is increased to thousands of records, it will simply create a problem to manage. The database can manage a large amount of data.

- **Accuracy:** Through the validation rule in the database, data accuracy can be maintained.

- **Ease of updating data:** With the database, we can flexibly update the data according to our convenience. Moreover, multiple people can also edit data at the same time.

- **Security of Data:** With a database system, we can use security groups and privileges to restrict access to authorised users.

- **Data Integrity:** In databases, we can be assured of the accuracy and consistency of data due to the built-in integrity checks and access controls.

Database Management System (DBMS):

A DBMS refers to software that is responsible for storing, maintaining, and efficiently utilising the database. A database, when managed by DBMS software, is called a Database System.

Examples of DBMS software are Oracle, MS SQL Server, MS Access, Paradox, DB2, MySQL, etc. MySQL is an open-source and freeware DBMS.

Advantages of Database System:

- **A Database reduces Redundancy:** It removes duplication of data because data is kept in one place, and all the application refers to the centrally maintained database.

- **A Database controls Inconsistency:** When two copies of the same data do not agree with each other, then it is called Inconsistency. By controlling redundancy, the inconsistency is also controlled.

- **A Database facilitates the Sharing of Data:** Data stored in the database can be shared among several users. Access to data can be restricted with authentication and authorisation mechanisms.

- **Data Protection:** Data are protected against accidental or intentional disclosure to unauthorised persons or unauthorised modification.

- **A Database maintains Integrity:** It enforces certain integrity rules to ensure the validity or correctness of data. For exp. A date can't be an invalid format like: 31/31/2000.

Relational Database Terms:

A Relational Database is a collection of tables that are interconnected on key fields. There is at least one Parent table that connects other tables called Child tables, which have Foreign keys.

Components of a Table:

Attribute (column or field), **Tuple** (row or record), **Degree,** i.e., number of attributes present in the table, and **Cardinality,** i.e., number of tuples present in the table.

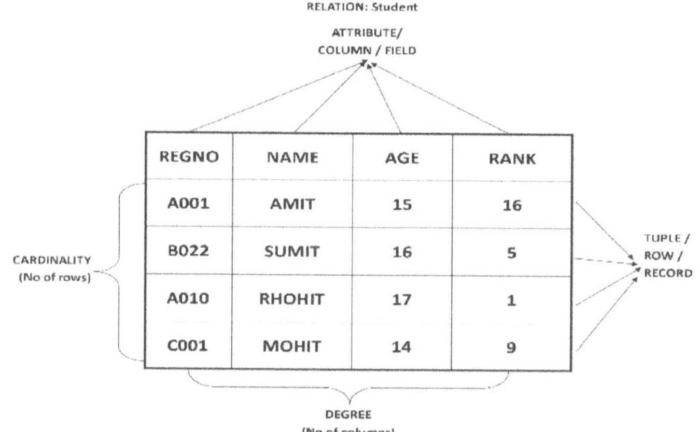

Relation (Table): A Relation or Table is a Matrix-like structure arranged in Rows and Columns. It has the following properties-

- **Atomicity:** Each column is assigned a unique name and must have an atomic (indivisible) value, i.e., a value that cannot be further subdivided.
- **No duplicity:** No two rows of relation will be identical, i.e., in any two rows, the value in at least one column must be different. All items in a column are homogeneous, i.e., the same data type.

Ordering of rows and columns is immaterial:

The rows of a table are called a Tuple or a Record.

The column of a table is called an Attribute or Field.

The number of columns (attributes) in a table is called the Degree. The number of rows (records) in a table is the Cardinality.

Keys in Database:

Key plays an important role in a relational database; it is used for identifying unique rows from the table & establishing relationships among tables as needed.

Types of Keys in DBMS:

- **Primary Key** – A primary key is a column or set of columns in a table that uniquely identifies tuples (rows) in that table.
- **Candidate Key** –It is an attribute or a set of attributes or keys participating in the Primary Key, to uniquely identify each record in that table.
- **Alternate Key** – Out of all the candidate keys, only one is selected as the primary key; the remaining keys are known as alternate or secondary keys.
- **Foreign Key** – A Foreign Key is a column or a set of columns in one table that establishes a relationship by referring to the Primary Key of another table. They act as a cross-reference between tables.
- **Composite Key -** A composite key is a combination of two or more attributes that uniquely identify a row of a table in a database. While each column may not be unique on its own, its combined values must be unique across the table.

Structured Query Language (SQL):

SQL is an acronym for Structured Query Language. It is a standard language developed and used for accessing and modifying relational databases. The SQL language was originally developed at the IBM research laboratory in San José. SQL is being used by many DBMSs. Some of them are:

- MySQL
- PostgreSQL
- Oracle
- SQLite
- Microsoft SQL Server

MySQL is currently the most popular open-source database software. It is a multi-user, multithreaded database management system. MySQL is widely used for web applications and is a key component of the LAMP (Linux, Apache, MySQL, PHP) and WAMP (Windows, Apache, MySQL, PHP) platforms. MySQL AB was founded by Michael Widenius (Monty), David Axmark, and Allan Larsson in Sweden in 1995.

MySQL Features:

- **Open Source & Free of Cost**: It is Open Source and available free of cost.
- **Portability**: Small enough in size to install and run it on any type of Hardware andOS, like Linux, MS Windows or Mac, etc.
- **Security**: Its Databases are secured & protected with a password.
- **Connectivity**: Various APIs are developed to connect it with many programming languages.
- **Query Language**: It supports SQL (Structured Query Language) for handlingdatabases.

Types of SQL Commands:

- **DDL** (Data Definition Language): To create database and table structure commands like CREATE, ALTER, DROP, etc.
- **DML** (Data Manipulation Language): Record/rows-related operations. Commands like SELECT…., INSERT, DELETE, UPDATE, etc.
- **DCL** (Data Control Language): Used to control user access to the database. Commands like GRANT and REVOKE.
- **TCL** (Transactional Control Language): Used to manipulate permissions or access tables, COMMIT, ROLLBACK, SAVEPOINT, etc.

MySql DataTypes:

- **Numeric**
  - ✓ **Decimal** - DECIMAL(precision, scale) [zerofill] For storing floating-point. Example: Avno DECIMAL(5,2), Total of 5 digits, with 2 after decimal, so max value is 999.99.
  - ✓ **Int** – INT(size) [auto_increment] [unsigned] [zerofill]
  - ✓ A whole number, with a maximum range of 4 bytes in size.

  Signed: -2,147,483,648 *to* 2,147,483,647

  Unsigned: 0 *to* 4,294,967,295

- **String**
  - ✓ **Char** (<size>) [binary]
    - ➢ Fixed length – for storing strings that won't vary.
    - ➢ Range of 0 to 255, stores that amount in bytes
  - ✓ **Varchar** (<size>) [binary]
    - ➢ Variable-length – for storing strings that will vary in size. Range of 0 *to* 255, stores that amount in bytes, plus 1 byte. The maximum size is 65535 bytes.

- **Date**
  - ✓ Date-Format: YYYY-MM-DD
  - ✓ Example: 2006-09-23, Range of years 1000 to 9999

Operators:

- Comparison operators are: < ; <= ; = ; != or <> ; >= ; >
- Logical operators are: AND, OR, NOT
- Comparison operator for special value NULL: IS

The common Table Constraints are:

- **NOT NULL** – It ensures that a column cannot have a NULL value.
- **UNIQUE** – It ensures that all values in a column are different
- **PRIMARY KEY** – A combination of NOT NULL and UNIQUE. Uniquely identifies each row in a table
- **FOREIGN KEY** – It uniquely identifies a row/record in another table
- **CHECK** – It ensures that all values in a column satisfy a specific condition
- **DEFAULT** – It sets a default value for a column when no value is specified

The differences between Unique and Primary Key are:

Primary Key	Unique Key
Uniquely identifies each record in a table. A Primary Key inherently enforces uniqueness, so an additional Unique constraint is not mandatory.	Prevents duplication in a field. Unique constraints must be applied in a field where we never want a duplicate value.

- A primary key can constitute one or more fields of a table to identify records in a table. On the other hand, a unique key prevents two rows from having duplicate entries in a column.
- A table cannot have more than one primary key in a relational database, while there can be multiple unique keys per table.
- A primary key column cannot contain NULL values, whereas a unique key can have NULL values, but only one NULL is allowed in a table.
- A primary key should be unique, but a unique key cannot necessarily be the primary key.
- The primary key by default is a clustered index where data is physically organised in a sequential index. In contrast, the unique key is a unique non-clustered index.
- The primary key implements entity integrity, whereas the unique key enforces unique data.

SQL Commands:

 # Creating a database:
CREATE DATABASE myschool;

 # Getting listings of databases and tables:
SHOW Databases;
SHOW TABLES;

 # Deleting a database:
DROP database abc;

 # Remove a table:
DROP TABLE abctable;

 # Open Database:
USE myschool;

Creating a table using – CREATE TABLE:

 # Creating a Parent table (using Primary Key):
CREATE TABLE Student(StdID INT NOT NULL PRIMARY KEY, Name CHAR(20), Class INT CHECK (Class>=5), Perc DECIMAL(6,2), DOB DATE, City VARCHAR(20) DEFAULT 'Ranchi');

 # Creating a Child table(using Foreign Key):
CREATE TABLE Class (AdmID INT NOT NULL PRIMARY KEY, Class INT NOT NULL, Sec CHAR(2), RollNo INT, StdID INT, FOREIGN KEY (StdID) REFERENCES Student (StdID) ON DELETE CASCADE ON UPDATE CASCADE);

> **Note:** *Cascade makes the transaction (Delete/Update) automatically in the child table.*

 # View the structure (Field, Datatype, Size, Constraints) of a table:
DESCRIBE Student;

Entering record(s) in a table using – INSERT INTO:

Syntax: Insert Into <Table Name> Values <Data> ;

 # Insert a new row/record into the table:
INSERT INTO Student **VALUES** (1005 , 'Abhinav Kumar Sinha' , 11, 96.85 , "2004-08-25" , "Mumbai");

 # We can insert multiple records, such as:
INSERT INTO Student (StdID, Name, Class, Perc, DOB, City) **VALUES** (1008, 'Sumitra Upadhyay', 12, 95.95, "2003-11-18", "Varanasi");
INSERT INTO Student (StdID, Class, City)
VALUES (1008, 12, "Varanasi"), (1009, 11, "Delhi");

Printing/Showing/Displaying records using – SELECT:

 # Display details of the table:
SELECT * FROM student;

 # Display Name, DOB & Perc of the table:
SELECT Name, DOB, Perc FROM Student;

 # Display Name, DOB & Perc of the students of class 10 & above:
SELECT Name, DOB, Perc FROM Student WHERE Class>=10;

 # Display records of classes 8 to 11:
SELECT * FROM Student WHERE Class>=8 AND Class<=11;
SELECT * FROM Student WHERE Class BETWEEN 8 AND 11;

 # Display records of classes 6, 7, 10 & 12:
SELECT * FROM Student WHERE Class IN (6,7,10,12);

 # Display records whose name is 'Sharat Pandey':
SELECT * FROM Student WHERE Name='Sharat Pandey';

 # Display records whose 3rd character of the name is 'a':
SELECT * FROM Student WHERE Name LIKE '_ _a%';

 # Display records whose 3rd the last character of the name is 'd':
SELECT * FROM Student WHERE Name LIKE '%a_ _';

 # Display records whose name contains the title 'Roy':
SELECT * FROM Student WHERE Name LIKE '%Roy%';

 # Display records of class 11 and names beginning with 'S':
SELECT * FROM Student WHERE Class=8 AND Name LIKE 'A%';

> **Note:** *The symbols % and _ are called wildcards, and each has a specific role. '%' means any type and any number of characters. And '_' any single character.*

 # Display the records where the percentage is a Null value:
SELECT * FROM Student WHERE Perc IS NULL;

 # Display the records of different sections (no duplicates) ***of class 10***
SELECT DISTINCT (Sec) FROM Student WHERE Class=10;

 # Deleting specific rows from a table using the DELETE command
DELETE FROM student WHERE Name="Amit Mishra";

Ordering Query Result – ORDER BY Clause:

A query result can be ordered in ascending (A-Z) or descending (Z-A) order as per any column. The default is ascending order.

 # Display records in ascending order in class:
SELECT * FROM Student ORDER BY Class ASC;

> **Note:** *Order By comes after the condition **Where***

 # Display records in descending order in class:
SELECT * FROM Student ORDER BY Class DESC;

 # Display records in descending order on a class of 10 & above:
SELECT * FROM Student WHERE Class>=10 ORDER BY Class DESC;

 # Display in descending order on percentage & ascending on class:
SELECT * FROM Student ORDER BY Perc DESC, Class ASC;

Grouping of data – GROUP BY Clause:

To collect similar types of values together, the **Group By** clause is used. Let's understand:

Class	Perc	Group of Class	Average
11	88	Class-11	88+93+90+89=360
10	91		90
11	93		
12	92	Class-10	91+95+94=280
10	95		93.33
11	90		
11	89	Class-12	92+91=183
10	94		91.5
12	91		

Here, two attributes of the table are taken to understand the functions of Group By. There are multiple sections of each of the three classes (10,11,12), and every section has a unique percentage of marks. Now, the average of all sections in each group has been calculated. There are three averages for three classes. This operation is Group By.

Syntax: **SELECT <FieldName> FROM <TableName> WHERE <cond.> GROUP BY <FieldName> HAVING <cond.>;**
 # Find the average marks of each of the different classes:
SELECT Class, AVG(Perc) FROM Student GROUP BY Class;

Output:
Class   AVG(Perc)
10   93.33
11   90.00
12   91.50

 # Display class-wise numbers which are 8 & above:

SELECT Class, COUNT(*) FROM Student **GROUP BY** Class **HAVING** Class>=8;

Output:
Class COUNT(*)
10   3
11   4
12   2

 # Display the number of students of each class that have more than 10 students, and the percentage of 80 and above:

SELECT Class, COUNT(*) FROM Student **WHERE** Perc>=80 **GROUP BY** Class **HAVING** Count(*)>10;

> **Note:** *While using the Group By clause to apply a condition on the **Group By** field, we use **Having** instead of <u>where</u>.*

 # Display Min, Max, and salary of those who have a salary of more than 60000, of the Department-wise Sum of salary in 50000 & above.

Mysql> Select Min(Salary), Max(Salary), Avg(Salary) from EMP **WHERE** Salary > 60000 **GROUP BY** Dept **HAVING** Sum(Salary)>=50000;

> **Note:**
> **WHERE** *clause works in respect of the whole table, but **HAVING** clause works on **Group By** column only. If **Where** and **Having** both are used, then **Where** will be executed first, just after <FROM TABLE_NAME>*

Aggregate (multiple-row) Functions & NULL:

Function	Purpose
SUM()	*Returns the sum of a given column.*
MIN()	Returns the minimum value in the given column.
MAX()	Returns the maximum value in the given column.
AVG()	Returns the Average value of the given column.
COUNT()	Returns the total number of values/ records as per the given column.

> **Note:**
> - *In the Aggregate function, **Null** values are excluded (not taken into acc.)*
> - ***Multiple or Aggregate row function:** Work on multiple records on a column and returns a single value, viz. max(), min(), sum(), avg()...*
> - ***Single row function:** Work on single value & returns single value, viz. substr(), right(), instr()...*

Library Functions:

Function	Examples	Output
# Math functions:		
POWER()	SELECT POWER(5,2);	25
ROUND()	SELECT ROUND(123.58);	124
	SELECT ROUND(123.58,0);	124
	SELECT ROUND(123.58,1);	123.6
	SELECT ROUND(123.58,-1);	120
	SELECT ROUND(123.58,-2);	100
	SELECT ROUND(163.58,-2);	200
MOD()	SELECT MOD(173,3);	2
TRUNCATE()	SELECT TRUNCATE(135.375, 2);	135.37
	SELECT TRUNCATE(135.375, -2);	100
# String (Single-row / Scalar) functions :		
UCASE()	SELECT UCASE("IndoAryan");	INDOARYAN
UPPER()	SELECT UPPER("IndoAryan");	
LCASE()	SELECT LCASE("IndoAryan");	indoaryan
LOWER()	SELECT LOWER("IndoAryan");	
SUBSTRING()	SELECT SUBSTRING("IndoAryan",5,5);	Aryan
SUBSTR()	SELECT SUBSTR("IndoAryan" -5);	
MID()	SELECT MID("IndoAryan",5,5);	
INSTR()	SELECT INSTR("IndoAryan Existence",'n');	2
LENGTH()	SELECT LENGTH("IndoAryan");	9
LEFT()	SELECT LEFT('IndoAryan', 4);	Indo
RIGHT()	SELECT RIGHT('IndoAryan', 5);	Aryan
TRIM()	SELECT TRIM(' IndoAryan ');	IndoAryan
LTRIM()	SELECT LTRIM(' IndoAryan ');	IndoAryan
RTRIM()	SELECT RTRIM(' IndoAryan ');	IndoAryan
# Date functions:		
NOW()	SELECT NOW();	2021-05-14 03:50:40
DATE()	SELECT DATE(NOW());	2021-05-14
TIME()	SELECT TIME(NOW());	03:50:40
MONTH()	SELECT MONTH(NOW());	5
MONTHNAME()	SELECT MONTHNAME(NOW());	May
YEAR()	SELECT YEAR(NOW());	2021
DAY()	SELECT DAY(NOW());	14
DAYNAME()	SELECT DAYNAME(NOW());	Friday

Query with a Sub-query / Nested-query:
 # Find details of the student who got the highest percentage:
SELECT * FROM Student WHERE Perc=**(SELECT MAX(Perc) FROM STUDENT)**;

UPDATE Records/Data – UPDATE …. SET:
Syntax: **UPDATE <TableName> SET <FieldName> = <Value> <Cond.>**;
 # Replace class with 10 of the student name 'Sazid Ahmed':
UPDATE student SET Class=10 WHERE Name="Sazid Ahmed";
 # Increase the Perc by 5 for those whose percentage is less than 40:
UPDATE Student SET Perc=Perc+5 WHERE Perc<=40;
 # To find the Sum, Minimum, Maximum, Average, and total no of records, consider the following table EMP:

EmpId	Dept	Salary
A001	HR	60000
B010	Production	76000
A100	Finance	65000
CA01	Admin	NULL
D101	Admin	80000

Select SUM(Salary) from EMP;   *# Ignores Null value*
Select MIN(Salary) from EMP;
Select MAX(Salary) from EMP;
Select AVG(Salary) from EMP;   *# Ignores Null value*
Select COUNT(Salary) from EMP;   *# Ignores Null value*
Select COUNT(*) from EMP;   *# Counts Null value*
Select Dept, Salary from EMP where Salary **IS NULL**;
Select Dept, Salary from EMP where Salary **IS NOT NULL**;

Output:
281000
60000
80000
70250
4
5

> **Note:**
> *In the condition **IS NULL**, it shows those records that are **Null** in the condition Column, and in the condition **IS NOT NULL**, it shows those that have no **Null** values.*

Altering Table *(Makes structural change / DDL)* :
 # Adding attribute:
Syntax: **ALTER TABLE <tablename> ADD COLUMN <column_name> <datatype>**;
ALTER TABLE Student **ADD** COLUMN Address VARCHAR(20) ;
ALTER TABLE Student **ADD** Address VARCHAR(20) **AFTER** Name ;
ALTER TABLE Student **ADD** Address VARCHAR(20) **BEFORE** Name;

 # Deleting attribute:
Syntax: **ALTER TABLE <table_name> DROP COLUMN <columnname>;**
ALTER TABLE Student DROP COLUMN Address;

 # Updating attribute:
Syntax: **ALTER TABLE <tablename> MODIFY COLUMN <columnname>**
<DataType>;
ALTER TABLE Student MODIFY COLUMN Average DECIMAL(6,2);
 # Rename the table from tab1 to tab2:
Syntax: **ALTER TABLE <existing table name> RENAME <new table name>**
ALTER TABLE tab1 RENAME tab2;

 # Rename the column "Address" to "Addr" of the Student table:
Syntax: **ALTER TABLE <table name> CHANGE <present col> <new col.> datatype;**
ALTER TABLE Student CHANGE Address Addr1 Char(50);
ALTER TABLE Student RENAME Addr1 TO Addr2 Char(50);

 # Remove/delete a table:
Syntax: **DROP TABLE <table name>;**
DROP TABLE Student;

Joining Of Tables:

There are different types of MySQL joins, a few of which are:
- Equi Join
- Non-Equi Join
- Natural Join
- Cartesian Join or Cross Join or Cartesian Product

 # Equi Join: When a field is present in both tables that has common values, it combines the tables based on the matching values in the specified common column, such as STUD & CLASS.

STUD				CLASS		
REGNO	NAME	CLASS	DOB	REGNO	ROLL	SUBJ
A001	AMIT	11	2002-05-23	A001	12	PHYSICS
B001	SUMIT	12	2003-03-22	C001	15	MATHS
C001	ROHIT	12	2003-12-30	D001	16	IT
D001	SUJIT	11	2004-10-15	F001	18	CS

SELECT STUD.REGNO, **STUD**.NAME, **CLASS**.ROLL, **CLASS**.SUBJ **FROM** STUD, CLASS **WHERE STUD**.REGNO=**CLASS**.REGNO;

OR

SELECT X.REGNO, **X**.NAME, **Y**.ROLL, **Y**.SUBJ **FROM** STUD **X**, CLASS **Y**
WHERE X.REGNO=**Y**.REGNO;

OR

SELECT REGNO, NAME, ROLL, SUBJ **FROM** STUD **NATURAL JOIN** CLASS;

OR

SELECT X.REGNO, X.NAME, Y.ROLL, Y.SUBJ

FROM STUD X **JOIN** CLASS Y

ON X.REGNO = Y.REGNO;

Output:

REGNO	NAME	ROLL	SUBJ
A001	AMIT	12	PHYSICS
C001	ROHIT	15	MATHS
D001	SUJIT	18	IT

 # To print Class-wise number of subjects in the tables STUD & CLASS:

SELECT X.CLASS, COUNT(**Y**.SUBJ) **FROM** STUD **X**, CLASS **Y WHERE X**.REGNO =**Y**.REGNO GROUP BY **X**.CLASS;

 # Non-Equi-Join: When there is no common field in the tables, but they have similar data in columns, such as AvMark, MaxMark, and MinMark, then it works using the BETWEEN clause. Assume there are two tables **Table-1** & **Table-2** as given:

TABLE1		TABLE2		
Name	AvMark	Class	MaxMarks	MinMarks
Rahim	88.80	11	98.98	65.65
Sudhir	90.00	12	94.99	70.75
Rashi	94.80	12	99.90	66.65

SELECT TABLE1.NAME, TABLE2.CLASS, TABLE1.AVMARK,

TABLE2.MAXMARKS

FROM TABLE1, TABLE2

WHERE

TABLE1.AvMark

BETWEEN

TABLE2.*Min*Marks

AND

TABLE2.*Max*Marks;

> **Note:**
> *The value being checked (TABLE1.AvMark) should be compared between MinMarks (**lower** bound) and MaxMarks (**upper** bound).*

Output:

Name	Class	AvMark	MaxMarks
Rahim	11	88.80	98.98
Sudhir	12	90.00	94.99
Rashi	12	94.80	99.90

Difference between Equi & Non-Equi join:

Equi Join	Non-Equi join
Must be a common field	No common field & must be fields of similar types of values.
Us sign of equality (=)	Apply the BETWEEN clause.

Natural Join (Based on common columns):

When we combine rows of two or more tables based on a common column between them, this operation is called joining. A natural join is a type of join operation that creates an implicit join by combining tables based on common columns (with the same name and data type).

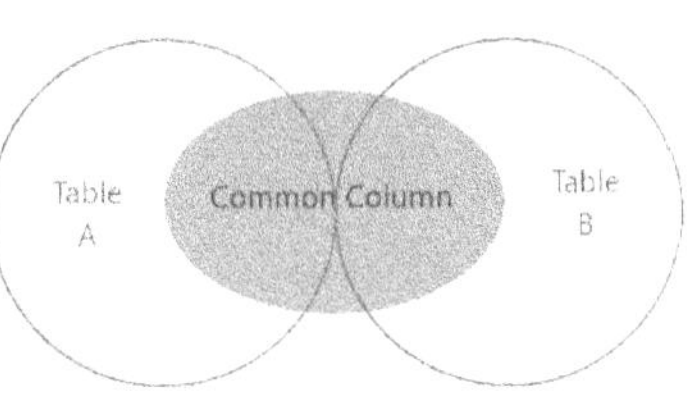

Note:
- *There is no need to specify the column names for Natural join.*
- *The resultant table always contains unique columns.*
- *It is possible to perform a natural join on more than two tables.*
- *Must not use the ON clause like other joins (Left or Inner).*

Syntax:
SELECT [column_names | *] **FROM** table_name1
NATURAL JOIN table_name2;

Find the Natural join of the following tables: Customer & Amount:

Table: **Customer**

Id	Cust_name	Account
1	Stish	1030
2	Julee	2035
3	Madan	5564
4	Sumit	4534
5	Davesh	7648

Table: **Amount**

Id	Account	Balance
1	1030	50000.00
2	2035	230000.00
3	5564	125000.00
4	4534	80000.00
5	7648	45000.00

```
MySQL> SELECT Cust.Cust_name, Amt.Account
          FROM Customer AS Cust
          NATURAL JOIN Amount AS Amt;
```

Output:

Cust_name   Balance

Stish   50000.00
Julee   230000.00
Madan   125000.00
Sumit   80000.00
Davesh   45000.00

Cartesian Join or Cross Join:

The Cartesian Join or Cross Join returns the Cartesian product of the sets of records from two or more joined tables. Thus, it equates to an inner join where the join-condition always

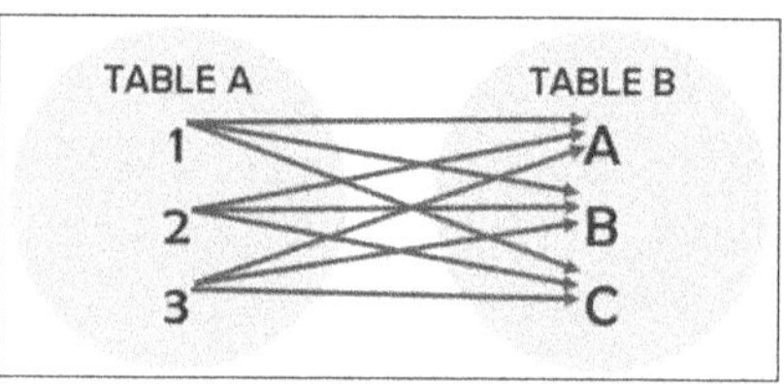

evaluates to either True or where the join-condition is absent from the statement.

The basic syntax of the Cartesian Join or the Cross Join is as follows, which makes the total N rows a product (multiplication) of the number of rows of the first table and the second table.

Syntax:

SELECT table1.column1, table2.column2... FROM table1, table2 [, table3]

OR

SELECT Table1.Col1, Table2.Col2 FROM Table1 CROSS JOIN Table2;

Consider the following two tables: Customers & Orders

Table: **CUSTOMERS**

ID	NAME	AGE	ADDRESS	SALARY
1	Raman	32	Ahmedabad	2000.00
2	Khilan	25	Delhi	1500.00
3	Kaushik	23	Kota	2000.00
4	Chaitali	25	Mumbai	6500.00
5	Hritik	27	Bhopal	8500.00
6	Komal	22	MP	4500.00
7	Mufty	24	Indore	10000.00

Table: ORDERS

ID	DATE	CUSTOMER_ID	AMOUNT
102	2008-10-08	3	3000
100	2008-10-08	3	1500
101	2008-11-20	2	1560
103	2009-05-20	4	2060

Now, let us join these two tables using a **CARTESIAN JOIN** as follows –
SQL> SELECT ID, NAME, AMOUNT, DATE FROM CUSTOMERS, ORDERS;

Output:

ID	NAME	AMOUNT	DATE
1	Raman	3000	2008-10-08
1	Raman	1500	2008-10-08
1	Raman	1560	2008-11-20
1	Raman	2060	2009-05-20
2	Khilan	3000	2008-10-08
2	Khilan	1500	2008-10-08
2	Khilan	1560	2008-11-20
2	Khilan	2060	2009-05-20
3	Kaushik	3000	2008-10-08
3	Kaushik	1500	2008-10-08
3	Kaushik	1560	2008-11-20
3	Kaushik	2060	2009-05-20
4	Chaitali	3000	2008-10-08
4	Chaitali	1500	2008-10-08
4	Chaitali	1560	2008-11-20
4	Chaitali	2060	2009-05-20
5	Hritik	3000	2008-10-08
5	Hritik	1500	2008-10-08
5	Hritik	1560	2008-11-20
5	Hritik	2060	2009-05-20
6	Komal	3000	2008-10-08
6	Komal	1500	2008-10-08
6	Komal	1560	2008-11-20
6	Komal	2060	2009-05-20
7	Mufty	3000	2008-10-08
7	Mufty	1500	2008-10-08
7	Mufty	1560	2008-11-20
7	Mufty	2060	2009-05-20

> **Note:** *The total number of records is: 7X4=28 as a product/output.*

Union:

The Union operator combines the results of two or more queries into a distinct single result set that includes all the rows that belong to all queries in the Union. This operation combines two more queries and removes the duplicates.

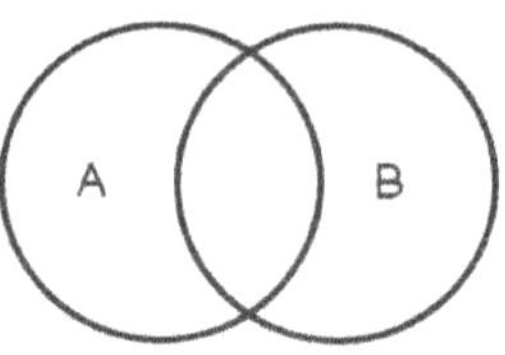

The UNION operator is used to combine the result set of two or more SELECT statements. Unions combine the results from multiple SELECT queries into a consolidated result set and

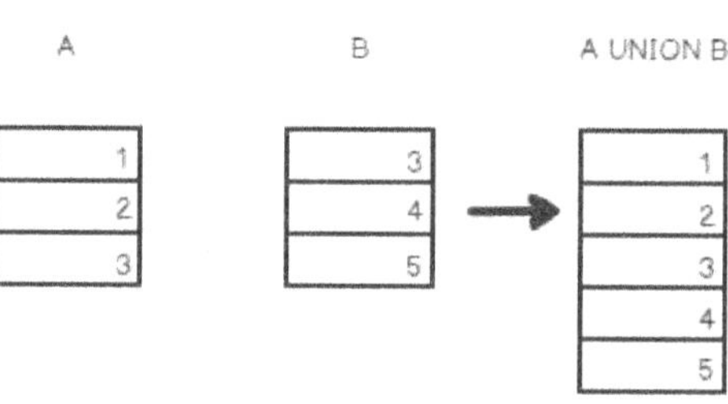

return only the DISTINCT values. Each SELECT statement within a UNION must have the same number of columns. The columns must also have similar data types. The columns in each SELECT statement must also be in the same order.

Syntax:

SELECT column_name(s) **FROM** table1 [WHERE conditions]
UNION [DISTINCT]

Assume the two tables, **Customers** & **Suppliers.**

Table: **Customers**

CustomerID	CustName	Address	City	Country
1	Amit Sharma	21, Park Street	New Delhi	India
2	Anjali Trivedi	112, Ashram Road	Ahmedabad	India
3	Arvind Kumar	56, Saroj Nagar	Bengaluru	India

Table: **Suppliers**

SupplierID	SupplierName	Address	City	Country
1	Surya Traders	14, MG Road	Mumbai	India
2	New Kolkata Foods	78, Circular Road	Kolkata	India
3	Grandma Spices	32, Avinashi Road	Coimbatore	India

Example:

SELECT City FROM Customers **UNION SELECT** City FROM Suppliers
ORDER BY City;
Number of Records: 13

City	Country
Aachen	Germany
Berlin	Germany
Brandenburg	Germany
Cunewalde	Germany
Cuxhaven	Germany
Frankfurt	Germany
Köln	Germany
Leipzig	Germany
Mannheim	Germany
München	Germany
Münster	Germany
Stuttgart	Germany

Note: *The following SQL statement returns the cities (<u>only distinct values</u>) from both the "Customers" and the "Suppliers" table:*

Intersection:

There is no Intersection operator in MySQL. However, an INTERSECT SQL query returns the intersection of 2 or more datasets. If a record exists in both data sets, it will be included in the INTERSECT results.

However, if a record exists in one data set and not in the other, it will be omitted from the INTERSECT results. Suppose we have two queries that return the T1 and T2 result sets. T1 result set includes 1, 2, 3. T2 result set includes 2, 3, 4.

The intersection of T1 and T2 results in 2 and 3. These are distinct values that are output by both queries.

The following picture illustrates the intersection of T1 and T2:

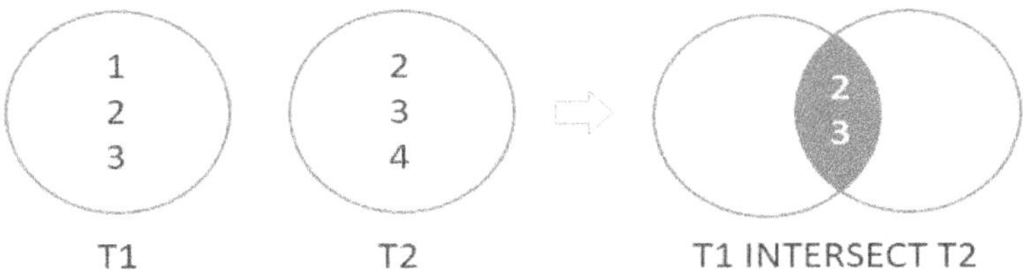

Explanation: The INTERSECT query returns the records in the shaded area. These records exist in both circles (sets) T1 and T2.

Syntax:

SELECT field-1, field-2, ... field-n FROM table-1 [***WHERE*** conditions]
INTERSECT
SELECT field-1, field-2, ... field-n FROM table-2 [***WHERE*** conditions];

> **Note:** *There must be the same number of expressions in both SELECT statements, and they must have similar data.*

Table: **CUSTOMER**

ID	NAME	AGE	ADDRESS	SALARY	DATE	AMOUNT
1	Raman	32	Ahmedabad	2000.00	2008-03-20	3060
2	Khilan	25	Delhi	1500.00	2009-11-20	1560
3	Kaushik	23	Kota	2000.00	2009-10-08	3000
4	Chaitali	25	Mumbai	6500.00	2008-05-20	2060
5	Hritik	27	Bhopal	8500.00	2005-06-22	4060
6	Komal	22	MP	4500.00	2006-03-25	3333
7	Mufty	24	Indore	10000.00	2006-03-20	4560

Table: **ORDER**

ID	NAME	DATE	Age	AMOUNT
3	Kaushik	2009-10-08	23	3000
5	Hritik	2005-05-22	27	4060
2	Khilan	2009-11-20	25	1560
4	Chaitali	2008-05-20	25	2060

SQL> **SELECT** ID, NAME, AMOUNT, DATE **FROM** CUSTOMER
    INTERSECT
    SELECT ID, NAME, AMOUNT, DATE **FROM** ORDER;

Output:

ID	NAME	AMOUNT	DATE
3	Kaushik	3000	2009-10-08
5	Hritik	4060	2005-05-22
2	Khilan	1560	2009-11-20
4	Chaitali	2060	2008-05-20

> **Note:** *Here in INTERSECT, only records of the common values of ID will appear in the output.*

Minus:

There is **no** MINUS operator in MySQL. Compares the results of two queries and returns distinct rows from the result set of the first query that do not appear in the result set of the second query. The following Venn diagram illustrates the MINUS operation:

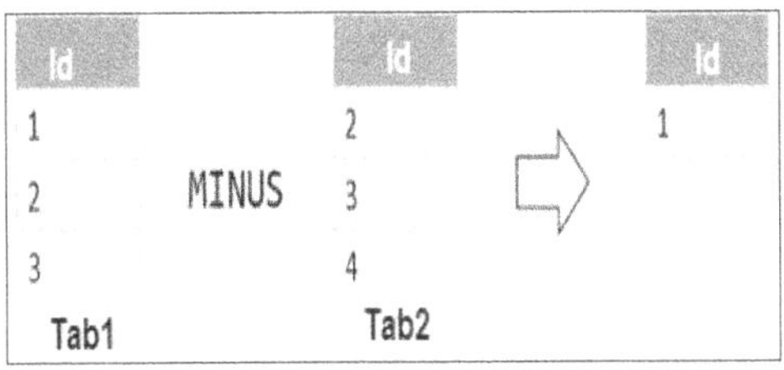
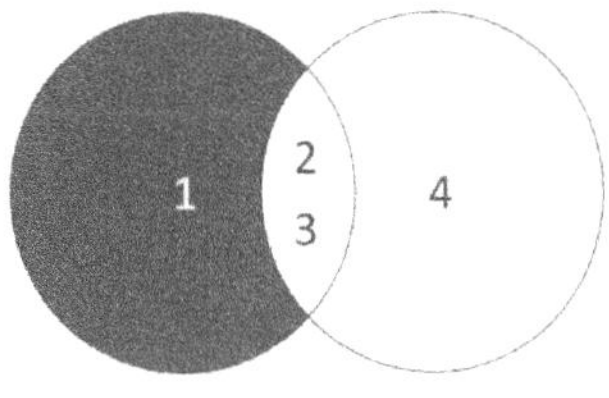

Syntax:
SELECT select_list1 FROM table_name1
MINUS
SELECT select_list2 FROM table_name2;

The basic rules for a query that uses the MINUS operator are:
- The number and order of columns in both select_list1 and select_list2 must be the same.
- The data types of the corresponding columns in both queries must be compatible.
- Suppose that we have two tables, Tab1 and Tab2, with the following structure and data:

CREATE TABLE Tab1 (Id INT PRIMARY KEY);
CREATE TABLE Tab2 (Id INT PRIMARY KEY);

INSERT INTO Tab1 VALUES (1, 2, 3);
INSERT INTO Tab2 VALUES (2, 3, 4);

The following query returns distinct values from the query of the Tab1 table that are not found in the result of the query of the Tab2 table.

MySQL> **SELECT** Id **FROM** Tab1 **MINUS SELECT** Id **FROM** Tab2;

Output:
Id
4

Procedural Coding in MySQL, on the table given:

EMPLOYEE

empId	name	dept	salary
1	Ajit	Sales	50000
2	Amit	Accounting	45000
3	Rohit	Sales	65000
4	Sumit	HR	65000

-- *MySQL Procedure with IF-ELSE condition:*

```
DELIMITER //
CREATE PROCEDURE check_sal(IN salary INT)
BEGIN
  IF salary >= 50000 THEN
    SELECT 'YES';
  ELSE
    SELECT 'NO';
  END IF;
END;
//
DELIMITER ;
```

> **Note:** *Here — in PL-Sql works as comment*

-- fetch/caller method

```
CALL check_sal(55000);
```

-- *MySQL Procedure with WHILE loop:*

```
DELIMITER //
CREATE PROCEDURE show_count()
BEGIN
  DECLARE num INT DEFAULT 1;
  WHILE num <= 3 DO
    SELECT CONCAT('Count: ', num);
    SET num = num + 1;
  END WHILE;
END;
//
DELIMITER ;
```

-- fetch/caller method

```
CALL show_count();
```

-- MySQL Procedure with CASE:

```
DELIMITER //
CREATE PROCEDURE find_grade(IN salary INT)
BEGIN
  CASE
    WHEN salary >= 70000 THEN SELECT 'Grade A';
    WHEN salary >= 60000 THEN SELECT 'Grade B';
    WHEN salary >= 50000 THEN SELECT 'Grade C';
    ELSE SELECT 'Grade F';
  END CASE;
END;
//
DELIMITER ;
```

-- fetch/caller method

```
CALL find_grade(65000);
```

-- MySQL Procedure with WHILE loop and IF condition

```
DELIMITER //
CREATE PROCEDURE count_even()
BEGIN
  DECLARE i INT DEFAULT 1;
  DECLARE result VARCHAR(50);

  WHILE i <= 5 DO
    IF MOD(i, 2) = 0 THEN
       SET result = CONCAT(i, ' is even');
       SELECT result;
    END IF;
    SET i = i + 1;
  END WHILE;
END;
//
DELIMITER ;
```

-- fetch/caller method

```
CALL count_even();
```

Output:

```
+---------+-----------+--------+----------+
|empId | name    | dept  | salary  |
+---------+-----------+--------+----------+
|   1   | Ajit    | Sales |  50000 |
|   3   | Rohit   | Sales |  65000 |
+---------+-----------+--------+----------+
```

```
+------+
| YES |
+------+
```

```
+----------------------+--------+
| CONCAT('Count: ', num) |
+----------------------+--------+
| Count: 1             |        |
+----------------------+--------+
```

```
+----------------------+--------+
| CONCAT('Count: ', num) |
+----------------------+--------+
| Count: 2             |        |
+----------------------+--------+
```

```
+----------------------+--------+
| CONCAT('Count: ', num) |
+----------------------+--------+
| Count: 3             |        |
+----------------------+--------+
```

```
+------------+
| Grade B |
+------------+
```

```
+-------------+
| result    |
+-------------+
| 2 is even |
+-------------+
```

```
+-------------+
| result    |
+-------------+
| 4 is even |
+-------------+
```

Chapter 14

FrontEnd-BackEnd Connectivity

Python-MySQL

Chapter Objective:

- Import/Export between data DataFrame and DataBase

- Installation of mysql-python connector

- Establish connection through coding

- Create Database in MySQL through Python coding

- Create Database into MySQL from Python-application

- Create table into MySQL from Python-application

- Export data to MySQL from Python-application

- Import data from MySQL to Python DataFrame

- Update data in MySQL from Python-application

Import-Export between DataFrame & DataBase (DB):

We know how Python applications like pandas can import and export data from and to other external files (.csv). But the most secure storage of data is a DataBase. Like other programming languages, Python also establishes a connection with a DataBase, but with the easiest technique. Here we shall see how connectivity between a DataFrame (a Python application) and MySQL (RDBMS) would be made:

Installation of the connection between DataFrame and MySQL DB:

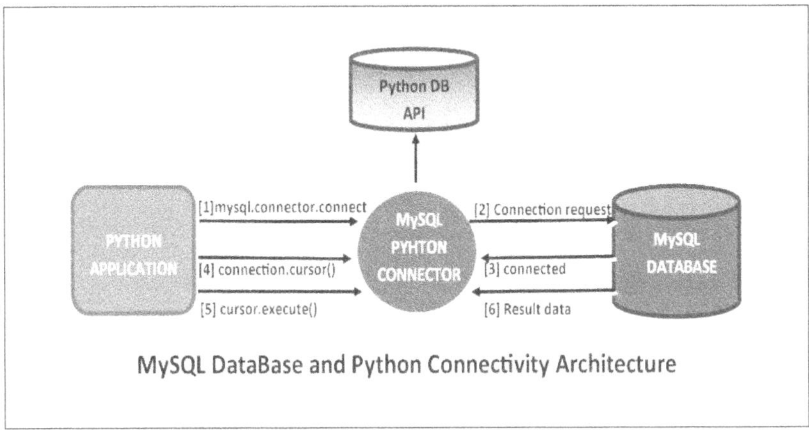

MySQL DataBase and Python Connectivity Architecture

Installation of MySQL-Connector:
Use the following pip command to install MySQL Connector for Python in the command prompt. **Pip** is a package-management system written in Python used to install and configure connections to other package repositories (local or remote).

> `pip install mysql-connector-python`

After running pip command and successfully installing MySQL Connector, the following messages are displayed:

Collecting mysql-connector-python Downloading packages.
Requirement already satisfied: setup tools in *D:python\python37-32\lib\site-packages. Installing collected packages: mysql-connector-python*
Successfully installed mysql-connector-python-8.0.13

Argument	Description
Username	*The username is used to work with the MySQL Server. The default username for the MySQL database is 'root'.*
Password	*The password is given by the user at the time of installing the MySQL server. If it is the root, then a password is not needed.*
Host	*The server's name (or IP address) on which MySQL runs. If it is running on a localhost, i.e., an offline computer, then we use 'localhost' or its IP address, 127.0.0.1*
Database	*The name of the database to which we want to connect is given to establish the connectivity.*

Establish connection through coding:

```python
import mysql.connector as mycon
try:
  con=mycon.connect(user='root', password='mysql', host='localhost',
                    database="School")
  if con.is_connected():
      print("Connected to MySQL database")
except mycon.Error as e:
  print("Error connecting to MySQL:", e)
  con = None
finally:
  if con and con.is_connected():
      con.close()
      print("MySQL connection is closed")
```

Output:

```
Connected to MySQL database
MySQL connection is closed
```

Create a Database in MySQL through Python coding:

```python
import mysql.connector as mycon

try:    # First connect without specifying a database
    con = mycon.connect( user='root',  password='mysql',
                         host='localhost', database="SCHOOL" )
    if con.is_connected():
            print("Connected to MySQL server")
    mycur = con.cursor()     # Create a cursor object
    # Create database if it doesn't exist
    mycur.execute("CREATE DATABASE IF NOT EXISTS SCHOOL")
    print("Database created or already exists")
    mycur.execute("SHOW DATABASES")
    for db in mycur:
            print(db)
except mycon.Error as e:
    print("Error:", e)
finally:                        # Check if the connection was established
    if con and con.is_connected():
            mycur.execute("SHOW DATABASES")  # Execute if connected
    mycur.close()          # Close cursor
    con.close()            # Close connection
    print("Connection closed.")
```

Output:

```
Connected to MySQL server
Database created or already exists
('information_schema',)
('mysql',)
('performance_schema',)
('school',)   # This will appear if it already
existed or was just created
('sys',)
Connection closed.
```

Export data to MySQL from a Python application:

```python
import mysql.connector as mycon
try:    con= mycon.connect(user='root', password='mysql',
        host='localhost', database= 'SCHOOL')
        mycur=con.cursor()
# Create table if it doesn't exist
        mycur.execute(""" CREATE TABLE IF NOT EXISTS CLASS (ID
        VARCHAR(10) PRIMARY KEY, NAME VARCHAR(50), CLASS INT) """)
        sql="INSERT INTO CLASS (ID, NAME, CLASS) VALUES (%s, %s, %s)"
        values = ("I001", "RAJIV SINHA", 12)
        mycur.execute(sql, values)
        con.commit()              # To SAVE all the transactions permanently
        print(mycur.rowcount, "record(s) inserted")
except mycon.Error as e:
        print("Error:", e)
finally:
        if con and con.is_connected():
                mycur.close()
                con.close()
```

Output:

```
1 record(s) inserted
```

Import data from MySQL to Python DataFrame:

```python
import pandas as pd
import mysql.connector as mycon
con=mycon.connect(user='root', password='mysql', host='localhost',
database='SCHOOL')
try:    con = mycon.connect ( user='root', password='mysql',
        host='localhost', database='SCHOOL' )
        mycur=con.cursor()
        mycur.execute("USE SCHOOL")
        mycur.execute("SELECT * FROM CLASS")
        xy = mycur.fetchall()
        # Get column names
        mycur.execute("DESCRIBE CLASS")
        columns = [column[0] for column in mycur.fetchall()]
```

```python
# Create DataFrame with column names
df = pd.DataFrame(xy, columns=columns)
print("Data imported from MySQL:")
print(df)
```
except mycon.Error as e:
```python
print("Error:", e)
```
finally:
```python
if con and con.is_connected():
        mycur.close()
        con.close()
```

Output:

```
Data imported from MySQL:
    ID     NAME          CLASS
0   I001   RAJIV SINHA   12
```

Update data in MySQL from a Python application:

```python
import mysql.connector
try:    con = mysql.connector.connect(user='root', password='mysql',
        host='localhost', database='SCHOOL')
        mycur = con.cursor()
# Use '=' instead of 'LIKE' for pattern matching
        sql = "UPDATE CLASS SET NAME = %s WHERE ID = %s"
        values = ("Sayan Pandey", "I001")
        mycur.execute(sql, values)
        con.commit()
        print(mycur.rowcount, "record(s) updated")
```
except mycon.Error as e:
```python
print("Error:", e)
```
finally:
```python
if con and con.is_connected():
        mycur.close()
        con.close()
```

Output:

```
1 record(s) updated
```

Note:

- *Importing the connecting Python package to connect MySQL*
- *Applying the command to connect i.e. **.connect()** MySQL with the following arguments:*
- *After successfully establishing the connection, the message 'Connected to MySQL database' is returned to ensure.*
- *Close the application by **.close()** function.*
- *Connecting MySQL with mysql.**connector**.connect()*
- *To run SQL command **.cursor()** function is fired.*
- *The **.cursor()** allows iterating through a database using a cursor object (mycur), which executes multiple queries.*
- *The object mycur runs SQL command by **.execute()** function.*
- *Reorganized steps into logical order (connect → cursor → execute → commit/close → check update).*
- *In MySQL, %s is a parameter style that specifies variables in an operation.*
- *If there are any connection issues or errors, we'll see error messages instead of the success messages.*
- *The final DataFrame display would show the updated name "Sayan Pandey" instead of "RAJIV SINHA" if you check the database after the update operation.*

Chapter 15

File Handling

Chapter Objective:

- Text File Handling in Python:
  - ✓ Reading mode
  - ✓ Writing mode
  - ✓ Append mode
  - ✓ Read/Write mode
  - ✓ Writing multiple lines to a Text File

- Binary File Handling in Python:
  - ✓ Reading mode
  - ✓ Writing mode
  - ✓ Append mode
  - ✓ Use Pickle to Read/Write file
  - ✓ Pickling Chunk file
  - ✓ Pickling Image file

- File Handling with CSV File:
  - ✓ Reading csv file
  - ✓ Reading with csv.DictReader
  - ✓ Creating/Overwriting file
  - ✓ Writing with csv.DictWriter
  - ✓ Appending Data to a CSV File

File Handling:

File handling is the process of working with files in Python. It allows creating, reading, writing, updating, and deleting files on the file system. Python provides built-in functions and methods to handle files effectively. File handling is important as it allows interaction with external files for data processing, logging, and configuration management.

Pandas also handles files. Each line of a file is terminated with EOL (End of Line) characters like comma {,}, and it tells the interpreter to initiate a new line. This function returns a file object with two arguments that accept the file name and the mode, whether to read or write.

There are two types of files: **Text** (human-readable) and **Binary** (Non-readable by humans).

Text Files: Human-readable files contain plain text, stored as ASCII or UNICODE values. Common extensions: .txt, .csv, .py.

Common file operations include opening, reading, writing, closing, and handling exceptions. The file modes are as follows:

```
Read Only ('r')            # Opens a text file for reading (default mode)
Read and Write ('r+')      # Opens a file only for both reading and writing
Write Only ('w')           # Opens a file for writing (creates & overwrites)
Write and Read ('w+')      # Opens a file to read and write (create & overwrite)
Append Only ('a')          # Opens a file to append at the end (if it doesn't exist)
Append and Read ('a+')     # Opens a file for both appending and reading
Binary mode ('b')          # Opens in binary mode with 'rb', 'wb', etc. modes
Closing: file_object.close() # Closing a file
```

Read Only ('r'): Open text file for reading. The handle is positioned at the beginning of the file. If the file does not exist, it raises the I/O error. This is also the default mode in which a file is opened.

Read and Write ('r+'): Open the file for reading and writing. The handle is positioned at the beginning. Raises I/O error if the file does not exist.

Write Only ('w'): Open the file for writing. The handle is positioned at the beginning. For the existing files, the data is truncated and overwritten. Creates a new file.

Write and Read ('w+'): Open the file for reading and writing. The handle is positioned at the beginning. For an existing file, data is truncated and overwritten. It is positioned at the beginning of the file.

Append Only ('a'): Open the file for writing. The file is created if it does not exist. Here, the handle is positioned at the end of the file. The data being written will be inserted at the end, after the existing data.

Append and Read ('a+'): Open the file for reading and writing. The handle is positioned at the end of the file. The data being written will be inserted at the end of the existing data.

Closing file: After completing operations, close the file using the **.close()** function

Binary file ('b'): When the 'b' mode is added to text file modes like Read ('r'), Write ('w'), or Append ('a'), the file is treated as binary, such as:
- **rb:** Read binary
- **wb:** Write binary
- **ab:** Append binary

The Syntax is: ***open(<filename>, 'mode')***

In Python, a file operation takes place in the following order:
- Open a file
- Read or write (operation)
- Close the file

 # To create a text file:
- Open a text file (in Notepad) and save it with the name 'myfile.txt'
- Write Python code in a .py file (e.g., myprog.py) to read the text file using appropriate file modes, in the same location where the text file has been saved.

 # Reading a text file *("r" mode):*
 # The 'myfile.txt' contains:

myfile.txt

Hello, Friends!
Hope you are fine.

```
with open("myfile.txt", "r") as file:
    content = file.read()
    print(content)
```

Output:
Hello, Friends!
Hope you are fine.

> **Note:**
> *While writing text file in 'w' mode, then it:*
> * *Overwrites existing file or creates a new one.*
> * *Is to be used when we want to write fresh content.*

Writing to a text file ("w" mode):

```python
with open("myfile.txt", "w") as file:
    file.write("This is a new line!\n")
    file.write("Have a happy life.\n")
```

 # Now 'myfile.txt' contains:

```
                myfile.txt
This is a new line!
Have a happy life.
```

Appending to a text file ("a" mode):

*# Adds content to the **end** of the file without deleting old content.*

```python
with open("myfile.txt", "a") as file: # with open() automatically closes the file
    file.write("This is added at the end.\n")
```

 # After running this, 'myfile.txt' contains:

```
                myfile.txt
This is a new line!
Have a happy life.
This is added at the end.
```

Reading line by line

```python
with open("myfile.txt", "r") as file:
    for line in file:
        print(line.strip())                 # .strip() removes newline
```

Printing File Content

```python
with open("myfile.txt", "r") as file:
    print(file.read())
```

Output:
This is a new line!
Have a happy life.

 # Reading and Writing mode ('r+') of the text file:
```
with open("myfile.txt", "r+") as file:
    print("Original content:")
    print(file.read())          # Read content first
    file.seek(0)                # Moves the pointer to the beginning
    file.write("Good Day")      # Overwrites 1st same no of char. Only
    file.truncate()  # This will truncate the file to the current position
```

> **Note:**
> - *.seek(0) Moves the pointer back to the beginning of the file*
> - *.seek(1) Pointer to begin from the current position*
> - *.seek(2) Moves pointer to the end of the file*
> - *readline() reads a single line*
> - *readlines() reads all lines as a list*
> - *write() writes a single line*
> - *writelines() writes multiple lines*

Handling Binary File:

Binary Files are humans' non-readable files that contain non-text data like images, audio, video, etc. Require specific software to read/write.

Key Binary File Modes:

Mode	Function
"rb"	To Read Binary
"wb"	To Write Binary (overwrite file)
"ab"	To Append Binary
"rb+"	To Read and write Binary

 # Open a binary file for reading using 'rb' mode
```
with open("stud.bin", "rb") as file:
    data = file.read()              # Read all binary content
    print(data)                     # Output the binary content
```

 # Open a binary file for writing, use "wb" mode
```
with open("stud.bin", "wb") as file:
    file.write(b"Hello Binary World!")     # Writing binary by prefix 'b'
```

```python
# Append binary data to a file using "ab" mode
with open("stud.bin", "ab") as file:
    file.write(b"\nNew binary data!")
```

```python
# Read a binary file in chunks to avoid memory issues with large files
with open("stud.bin", "rb") as file:
    while chunk := file.read(1024):     # Read 1024 bytes at a time
        print(chunk)
```

```python
# Copy an image using binary mode
with open("pic1.jpg", "rb") as src, open("pic2.jpg", "wb") as dest:
    dest.write(src.read())      # Copy the entire binary content
```

Use of Pickle in Handling Binary Files:

In Python, the pickle module allows us to convert objects into a byte stream and back into objects. This is useful for saving complex data structures like lists, dictionaries, and objects to a binary file.

Writing (Pickling) & Reading (Unpickling) Objects to BinaryFile

```python
import pickle                    # Importing pickle module
# A dictionary object
data_dict = {"name": "Anil", "age": 35, "city": "New Delhi"}
# Opens 'data.pkl' file to write-binary mode('wb') and closes by with
# Then converts object into binary by dump() in file
with open("data.pkl", "wb") as file:
        pickle.dump(data_dict, file)
print("Data successfully saved!")
```

```python
# Reading (Unpickling) Objects from a Binary File
with open("data.pkl", "rb") as file:     # Read in binary mode by 'rb'
```

```python
# To retrieve the stored object into Python by load()
    x = pickle.load(file)
# Prints data-file
    print("Loaded Data:", x)
```

Output:
Data successfully saved!
Loaded Data: {'name': 'Anil', 'age': 35, 'city': 'New Delhi'}

Pickling Multiple Objects

```python
import pickle
L1 = ["Ranchi", "Kolkata", "Patna"]
D1 = {"Python": "Excellent", "Java": "Great", "C++": "Good"}
```

 # Writes into multiple objects into binary format by 'wb'
```
with open("multi.pkl", "wb") as file:
    pickle.dump(L1, file)
    pickle.dump(D1, file)
```
 # Reading multiple objects
```
with open("multi.pkl", "rb") as file:
    data1 = pickle.load(file)
    data2 = pickle.load(file)
```
 # Prints data-file
```
print("Loaded First Data:", data1)
print("Loaded Second Data:", data2)
```

Output:
Loaded First Data: ['Ranchi', 'Kolkata', 'Patna']
Loaded Second Data: {'Python': 'Excellent', 'Java': 'Great', 'C++': 'Good'}

File Handling with .csv file:

As we have already discussed in DataFrame, **CSV** is a **comma-separated values** file, which allows data to be saved in a tabular format. CSVs look like a garden-variety spreadsheet, but with a **.csv** extension. One can convert such a spreadsheet into .csv, by:

FILE -> SAVE AS (then selecting CSV option). Here is an example of the conversion of **data.xlsx** into **data.csv**:

data.xlsx

	A	B	C
1	**Name**	**Age**	**City**
2	Joy	25	New Delhi
3	Amit	30	Kolkata
4	Bobby	22	Pune

data.csv

```
Name,Age,City
Joy,25,New Delhi
Amit,30,Kolkata
```

 # Reading CSV file with csv.reader() function
```
import csv
with open("data.csv", mode="r") as file:    # Opens CSV file in read mode
    csv_reader = csv.reader(file)            # csv.reader() fn. reads CSV file
    next(csv_reader)                         # Skips header (optional)

    for row in csv_reader:                   # Loop through rows
        print(row)                           # row is a list, e.g., ['Joy', '25', 'New Delhi']
```

Output:
['Joy', '25', ' New Delhi']
['Amit', '30', ' Kolkata']
['Bobby', '22', ' Pune']

 # Reading csv.DictReader() to convert the CSV file into a Dictionary
```python
import csv
with open("data.csv", mode="r") as file:
    csv_reader = csv.DictReader(file)   # This fn. Converts CSV into a Dict.
    for row in csv_reader:
        print(row["Name"], row["Age"], row["City"])
```
Output:
Joy 25 New Delhi
Amit 30 Kolkata
Bobby 22 Pune

 # Creating / Overwriting a CSV file.
```python
import csv
data = [ ["Name", "Age", "City"],
        ["Joy",     25,    "New Delhi"],
        ["Amit",   30,    "Kolkata"],
        ["Bobby", 22,     "Pune"]  ]
with open("output.csv", mode="w", newline="") as file:
        writer = csv.writer(file)
        writer.writerows(data)
print("CSV file written successfully!")
```

Output *(in the csv file)*:

```
Name,Age,City
Joy,25,New Delhi
Amit,30,Kolkata
Bobby,22,Pune
```

Output *(after execution of the program)*:
CSV file written successfully!

 # Using csv.DictWriter() fn. creates a CSV file from a Dictionary
```python
import csv
data = [ {"Name": "Joy", "Age": 25, "City": "New Delhi"},
        {"Name": "Amit", "Age": 30, "City": "Kolkata"},
        {"Name": "Bobby", "Age": 22, "City": "Pune"}  ]
```

```python
with open("output_dict.csv", mode="w", newline="") as file:
        fieldnames = ["Name", "Age", "City"]
        writer = csv.DictWriter(file, fieldnames=fieldnames)
        writer.writeheader()            # Write column names/headers
        writer.writerows(data)          # Write the multiple rows
print("CSV file written successfully!")
```

Output *(in the CSV file)*:

```
Name,Age,City
Joy,25,New Delhi
Amit,30,Kolkata
Bobby,22,Pune
```

Output *(after execution of the program)*:
CSV file written successfully!

 # Appending Data to a CSV File
```python
import csv
new_data = ["Dolly", 28, "Bombay"]
# Fixed newline parameter
with open("output.csv", mode="a", newline="") as file:
        writer = csv.writer(file)
        writer.writerow(new_data)
print("Row appended successfully!")
```

Output *(after appending, in the csv file)*:

```
Name,Age,City
Joy,25,New Delhi
Amit,30,Kolkata
Bobby,22,Pune
```

Output *(After execution of the program)*:
Row appended successfully!

> **Note:** *In the File Handling with CSV, different modes work as follows:*
>
> | Mode | Meaning | File Exists? | Overwrites? | Use Case |
> |------|---------|--------------|-------------|----------|
> | 'r' | Read | Yes | No | Reading existing csv |
> | 'w' | Overwrite | No (creates file) | Yes | Writing/replacing csv |
> | 'a' | Append | No (creates if needed) | No | Adding rows to csv |
>
> ***newline=""*** *adds a new blank line between rows for a better format.*

Chapter 16

Artificial

Intelligence

An Introduction

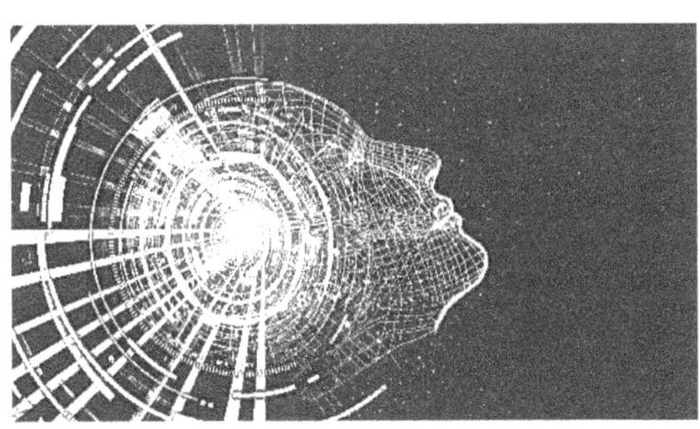

Chapter Objective

- AI - An Introduction
- AI in the Current Context
- Research in AI
- AI & Data Analysis
- Explainable AI
- Machine Learning (ML)
- Deep Learning (DL)
- Natural Language Processing (NLP)
- Generative AI (GAI)
- Large Language Models (LLM)
- Ethics in AI
- Future of AI
- Conclusion

Artificial Intelligence (AI) – an introduction:

Definition: AI refers to human-created intelligence that mimics human cognitive abilities, including decision-making and learning from experience, as a child. The more AI systems interact and process data, the better they become at tasks, similar to human learning.

Background: The concept of AI has been around for decades, with initial work in the 1940s and 50s when pioneers like Alan Turing proposed that machines could simulate human intelligence. The term "Artificial Intelligence" was coined in 1956 during the Dartmouth Conference, marking the field's official birth. AI has advanced from basic rule-based systems to complex algorithms capable of handling sophisticated tasks.

Types of AI:

- **Narrow AI (Weak AI):** AI designed to perform specific tasks (e.g., virtual assistants, facial recognition).

- **General AI (Strong AI):** A theoretical form of AI that can perform any intellectual task a human can.

- **Superintelligent AI:** Hypothetical AI that surpasses human intelligence across all domains.

Key Techniques and Methods of AI:

- **Machine Learning (ML):** Enables machines to learn from data and improve over time without being explicitly programmed.

- **Deep Learning (DL):** A subset of ML based on neural networks, used in image and speech recognition.

- **Natural Language Processing (NLP):** Helps machines understand and generate human language.

- **Generative AI (GAI):** It uses advanced models to create text, images, music, video, and code, revolutionising creative industries and content generation.

- **Robotics:** Combines AI with mechanical and electronic engineering to create robots capable of autonomous decision-making.

Applications:

- **Education:** Personalised learning, automated tutoring systems, and question-answer sessions, 24/7 virtual assistance to students, etc.

- **Healthcare**: AI-driven diagnostics, personalised medicine, and predictive analytics.
- **Finance**: Fraud detection, algorithmic trading, and credit scoring.
- **Transportation**: Self-driving cars and traffic optimisation.
- **Customer Service**: Chatbots and virtual assistants.
- **Manufacturing**: Predictive maintenance and automation.
- **Ethical and Social Implications:** As AI technologies evolve, ethical considerations, such as bias, fairness, job displacement, privacy, and security, are critical topics in the discussion.

Artificial Intelligence (AI) in the Current Context:

It refers to a rapidly advancing field that is reshaping industries, enhancing human capabilities, and posing complex ethical, social, and economic questions. Here's how AI is relevant and impactful today:

Pervasive in Everyday Life:

- **AI-Driven Assistants**: Tools like Siri, Alexa, and Google Assistant have become commonplace, simplifying daily tasks using voice recognition and smart responses.
- **Recommendation Engines**: Online platforms like Netflix, YouTube, and Amazon use AI algorithms to provide personalised recommendations based on user data.
- **Generative AI**: Tools like ChatGPT and DALL-E produce human-like text, images, and even code, democratizing access to creative and problem-solving capabilities.

AI in Industry and Business:

- **Healthcare**: AI assists in medical diagnostics, drug discovery, treatments, and predictive analytics of patient and surgical precision.
- **Finance**: AI detects fraud, automates trading, assesses credit risk, and provides chatbot services for customer support and inventory management.
- **Manufacturing**: AI-driven automation optimises supply chains, predicts equipment failures, and reduces production downtime.

AI Research and Technological Developments:

AI today is a broad set of technologies and capabilities transforming nearly every industry and aspect of life. While it presents vast opportunities, it also raises questions and challenges that societies, governments, and businesses must navigate carefully.

- **Machine Learning (ML) and Deep Learning (DL)**: Recent innovations, especially in deep learning, are pushing boundaries in natural language processing (NLP), computer vision, and other fields.
- **AI Models like GPT (Generative Pre-trained Transformer)**: Language models can generate coherent text, answer questions, summarise documents, and assist in creative tasks, increasing productivity.
- **Edge AI**: AI capabilities are being deployed directly on devices (like phones or IoT devices) to enable real-time processing without relying on cloud connectivity.

AI and Automation:

- **Job Impact**: AI-driven automation is both creating new job opportunities (like AI specialists) and displacing repetitive tasks traditionally done by humans. This shift requires workforce reskilling and presents challenges in employment policies.
- **Robotics**: AI-powered robots are used in logistics, warehousing, and even for delivery drones.

Societal and Ethical Issues:

- **Bias and Fairness**: There is concern that AI systems can perpetuate bias if trained on biased data, impacting decisions like hiring, criminal justice, or lending.
- **Data Privacy**: AI's reliance on large data sets raises questions about privacy, consent, and data security.
- **Accountability**: Determining responsibility for decisions made by AI, especially in critical sectors like healthcare or autonomous vehicles, is complex.
- **Regulation**: Governments and organisations are grappling with creating laws and standards that foster innovation while safeguarding society from AI-related risks.
- **AI and Global Competition:** Countries are investing heavily in AI research and innovation to gain competitive advantages in technology, economics, and military strategy. The AI race is reshaping geopolitics and economic policies worldwide.

- **AI for Social Good:** AI is being used to address climate change, enhance education, predict and mitigate natural disasters, and improve accessibility for people with disabilities.

AI and Data Analysis:

AI is making data analysis, processing, prediction, and decision support by enhancing the efficiency, accuracy, and depth of insights that businesses and researchers can extract from data. A few key points are:

- **Automated Data Processing:** Data Cleaning: AI algorithms can automatically detect and correct errors in data, fill in missing values, and ensure data quality and consistency.

- **Data Integration:** AI can combine data from different sources and formats, making it easier for analysts to gain a holistic view.

Predictive Analytics:

- **Forecasting Trends:** AI models can analyse historical data to predict future outcomes, such as customer behaviour, market trends, or product demand.

- **Risk Assessment:** AI-driven predictive models help in identifying potential risks and opportunities, which are crucial for decision-making in finance, healthcare, and more.

Data Visualisation and Interpretation:

- **Advanced Visualisation:** AI-powered tools can generate interactive and insightful visualisations, making complex data easier to understand.

- **Natural Language Processing (NLP):** AI can analyse textual data, understand trends in unstructured data (e.g., social media), and even generate human-readable summaries and reports.

Pattern Recognition and Anomaly Detection:

- **Fraud Detection**: AI systems analyse vast amounts of transactional data in real-time to spot unusual patterns indicative of fraud.

- **Quality Control:** In manufacturing, AI can detect anomalies in production processes, ensuring products meet specified standards.

Personalisation and Recommendation Systems:

- **Tailored User Experiences:** AI analyses user data to recommend personalised products, services, or content (as seen in platforms like Amazon and Netflix).

- **Behavioural Analysis:** AI can segment audiences based on their behaviours and preferences, enabling targeted marketing efforts.

- **Machine Learning (ML) and Deep Learning:**

- **Data Modelling:** ML algorithms identify relationships and correlations in data without being explicitly programmed for a task.

- **Image and Video Analysis:** AI models analyse visual data to identify objects, patterns, or insights for applications like facial recognition and medical imaging.

Real-Time Data Analysis:

AI-driven systems process large volumes of data in real-time, useful for applications like stock market analysis, IoT monitoring, and dynamic pricing strategies.

AI-Powered Decision Support Systems:

AI can offer recommendations, simulate scenarios, and assist human analysts in making informed decisions based on data.

Explainable AI (XAI):

XAI refers to AI systems that offer transparency, accountability, and comprehensibility of their decision-making processes to humans. It is an important subset of AI aimed at ensuring that humans can understand, trust, and effectively interact with AI models, especially as AI plays a bigger role in critical decision-making areas such as healthcare, finance, criminal justice, and autonomous systems.

Importance of Explainable AI:

- **Trust and Transparency:** In fields like healthcare, users need to trust AI decisions. XAI provides clarity on how an AI model arrives at a diagnosis or treatment recommendation.

- **Accountability:** When AI systems make decisions, especially in regulated industries, it is essential to understand why and how the AI reached a particular outcome for auditing, compliance, or legal reasons.

- **Ethical and Fair AI:** Explainability can help identify and mitigate biases in AI models. It ensures decisions are fair and non-discriminatory, aligning with ethical standards.

- **Debugging and Improvement:** Developers need to understand their AI models' behaviour to fix issues, improve accuracy, and prevent unintended outcomes.

Challenges in Achieving Explainable AI:

- **Complexity of AI Models**: Modern AI models, like deep neural networks, are often treated as "black boxes" because of their intricate inner workings, making it hard to explain their outputs.

- **Trade-offs:** Highly accurate models like deep learning models are often less interpretable, while simpler models (e.g., decision trees) are easier to explain but may perform less effectively.

- **User Requirements:** Different users (e.g., end-users, developers, regulators) have different levels of understanding and need different explanations. Designing XAI systems that cater to various audiences is a challenge.

Methods and Techniques of Explainable AI:

- **Feature Importance:** Identifying and ranking which features or inputs are most significant in making a prediction (e.g., a specific health metric in predicting a disease).

- **Model-Agnostic Methods**: Techniques that explain any AI model, regardless of its inner workings:

- **LIME (Local Interpretable Model-agnostic Explanations):** Generates interpretable approximations of complex models for specific predictions, showing which features led to a decision.

- **SHAP (Shapley Additive Explanations):** A game-theoretic approach that explains the contribution of each feature to the model's output.

- **Visualisation Tools:** Tools such as heatmaps or decision trees make AI decisions more interpretable by displaying where the model "focused" during its decision-making process (e.g., visualising which parts of an image an image-classification model focused on).

- **Interpretable Models:** Using inherently interpretable models, such as linear regression or decision trees, where the relationships between inputs and outputs are easily understood.

Applications and Use Cases:

- **Healthcare:** Physicians need to understand AI-driven diagnosis recommendations. XAI ensures decisions can be justified with relevant clinical factors.

- **Finance:** Banks use XAI to explain why a loan application was approved or denied, ensuring compliance with anti-discrimination laws and transparency.

- **Legal and Criminal Justice:** Decisions like sentencing or parole recommendations made by AI-driven systems must be explainable to ensure fairness and accountability.

- **Autonomous Vehicles:** When self-driving cars make decisions (e.g., stopping or changing lanes), explainability is critical for ensuring safety and regulatory compliance.

Regulatory and Ethical Implications:

- **GDPR (General Data Protection Regulation):** In the EU, regulations require explanations for automated decisions impacting individuals, such as loan rejections, fostering the need for explainable AI.

- **Bias and Fairness:** XAI methods help detect and correct biases by providing insight into the internal workings of AI models, reducing discriminatory outcomes.

- **Future of Explainable AI:**

- **Balancing Interpretability and Complexity:** Efforts are ongoing to make even the most complex models, like neural networks, interpretable.

- **Human-Centred XAI:** Designing explanations tailored to human understanding, making them accessible and actionable for a broad range of users.

- **Ethical Frameworks:** Growing recognition of the need for AI that is explainable and aligns with human values, ethics, and societal norms.

Machine Learning (ML):

Machine Learning (ML) is a subset of AI that allows systems to learn from data and improve over time without explicit programming, making predictions and solving problems by identifying patterns in large datasets. It is used in applications like recommendation engines, fraud detection, and image recognition.

How Machine Learning Works:

Machine learning involves feeding data into algorithms, which analyse it, identify patterns, and make predictions or decisions based on those patterns. The process generally involves the following steps:

- **Data Collection and Preprocessing:** Raw data is gathered, cleaned, and transformed into a format suitable for the ML algorithm.

- **Model Selection:** Choosing the right type of ML model based on the problem (e.g., regression, classification, clustering).

- **Training:** The model is fed with training data so it can learn from input-output mappings or recognise patterns.

- **Evaluation:** The model is tested on new, unseen data (testing data) to assess its performance and accuracy.

- **Optimisation:** The model's parameters are adjusted to improve accuracy and reduce errors.

Types of Machine Learning:

There are three primary types of machine learning-

- **Supervised Learning:** In this type, the algorithm is trained on labelled data, meaning the input-output pairs are known. The algorithm learns the mapping function from the input to the output.
  - ✓ **Example Applications:** Spam detection in an email (classifying emails as spam or not based on labelled examples), predicting house prices.
  - ✓ **Common Algorithms:** Linear regression, decision trees, support vector machines (SVMs), neural networks.

- **Unsupervised Learning:** Here, the algorithm works with unlabelled data and tries to uncover hidden patterns or structures without prior knowledge of output values.
  - ✓ **Example Applications:** Customer segmentation, dimensionality reduction for data visualisation, and market basket analysis.
  - ✓ **Common Algorithms:** K-means clustering, hierarchical clustering, principal component analysis (PCA), and autoencoders.

- **Reinforcement Learning:** In this approach, an agent interacts with an environment to achieve a goal by taking actions and receiving rewards or penalties as feedback. The agent learns through trial and error to maximise cumulative rewards.

- ✓ **Example Applications:** Game-playing AI (like AlphaGo), robotics, and self-driving cars.
- ✓ **Key Concepts:** Reward signals, exploration vs. exploitation trade-off, policy learning.

Key Concepts in Machine Learning:

- **Features:** The input variables or attributes used to make predictions.
- **Labels:** The output variable or target value for supervised learning tasks.
- **Training and Testing Data:** The dataset is usually divided into training data (to train the model) and testing/validation data (to evaluate its performance).
- **Overfitting:** When a model performs well on training data but poorly on unseen data because it learns noise or overly complex patterns.
- **Underfitting:** When a model is too simple and cannot capture the underlying patterns of the data, leading to poor performance.

Common Machine Learning Algorithms:

- **Regression Algorithms:** Predict a continuous output (e.g., linear regression, ridge regression).
- **Classification Algorithms:** Assign inputs into predefined categories (e.g., logistic regression, decision trees, random forests, support vector machines).
- **Clustering Algorithms:** Group similar data points together (e.g., k-means, DBSCAN).
- **Dimensionality Reduction:** Simplifies data while retaining important information (e.g., PCA, t-SNE).
- **Neural Networks and Deep Learning:** Use layers of interconnected nodes (neurons) to model complex patterns, often used in image recognition, NLP, etc.

Applications of Machine Learning:

- **Healthcare:** Diagnosing diseases, predicting patient outcomes, and personalising treatment plans.
- **Finance:** Detecting fraudulent transactions, predicting stock prices, and credit scoring.

- **Retail:** Product recommendations, inventory management, and customer sentiment analysis.

- **Natural Language Processing (NLP):** Chatbots, language translation, and sentiment analysis.

- **Image and Speech Recognition:** Face recognition systems, virtual assistants like Siri, and real-time translation tools.

Challenges in Machine Learning:

- **Data Quality and Quantity:** Good performance often depends on having large, high-quality datasets.

- **Bias and Fairness:** Algorithms can reflect biases present in the data, leading to unfair or discriminatory outcomes.

- **Interpretability:** Complex models (like deep learning) can be hard to understand, leading to issues with transparency and trust.

Deep Learning (DL):

Deep Learning is a subset of machine learning that uses multi-layered neural networks to automatically learn hierarchical representations and patterns from large datasets. Inspired by the human brain, major advancements in AI power are being made in image recognition, language processing, and speech recognition.

Core Concepts of Deep Learning:

Artificial Neural Networks (ANNs): Deep learning models are built from artificial neurons (or nodes), organised into layers. Data passes through these layers, with each layer learning increasingly abstract features.

- **Input Layer:** Receives the raw data (e.g., pixel values in an image).

- **Hidden Layers:** These layers perform intermediate processing; each hidden layer transforms its inputs before passing them on. "Deep" networks have many hidden layers, making them powerful but complex.

- **Output Layer:** Produces the final output, such as a prediction or classification.

- **Activation Functions:** Each neuron in a layer typically applies an activation function to its output. This introduces non-linearities, enabling the model to learn complex mappings from inputs to outputs. Common activation functions include:

- **ReLU (Rectified Linear Unit):** Outputs the input directly if positive; otherwise, it outputs zero. It is widely used because it helps prevent issues like vanishing gradients.

- **Sigmoid and Tanh:** These functions squash the output between 0–1 and -1–1, respectively.

- **Learning Process (Training):** Deep learning models learn by adjusting weights (parameters) through a process called backpropagation, which uses optimisation algorithms (e.g., gradient descent) to minimise a loss (error) function that quantifies the difference between predicted and actual outputs.

Popular Deep Learning Models:

Deep learning encompasses a range of specialised models tailored to different tasks:

Feedforward Neural Networks (FNNs):

- The simplest type of deep learning model.

- Information flows in one direction, from the input to the output.

- Primarily used for structured data and simpler tasks.

Convolutional Neural Networks (CNNs):

- Designed for processing grid-like data, such as images.

- Convolutional Layers apply filters to input data, allowing the model to detect spatial hierarchies in images (e.g., edges, shapes, and more complex features).

- Used extensively in image and video recognition, object detection, and medical image analysis.

Recurrent Neural Networks (RNNs):

- Designed to handle sequential data, such as time series, audio, text, etc.

- Unlike traditional neural networks, RNNs have connections that form cycles, enabling them to maintain information about previous inputs.

- LSTM (Long Short-Term Memory) and GRU (Gated Recurrent Units) are special types of RNNs that solve the problem of vanishing gradients, to capture long-term dependencies in sequential data.

Transformer Models:

- A more recent innovation that excels in processing sequential data but is more efficient than traditional RNNs.

- Self-attention mechanisms in AI assess the importance of words or data in a sequence, regardless of their position.
- Widely used for natural language processing (NLP) tasks, including translation and text generation. Models like BERT (Bidirectional Encoder Representations from Transformers) and GPT (Generative Pre-trained Transformer) are based on transformers.

Autoencoders:

- Autoencoders are neural networks trained to reconstruct their input, typically used for unsupervised learning tasks such as dimensionality reduction, image denoising, and feature learning.
- Consists of two main components, which are:

  Encoder: Compresses input data into a lower-dimensional representation (latent space).

  Decoder: Reconstructs the original input from the compressed representation.

Generative Adversarial Networks (GANs):

- Consists of two neural networks—a generator and a discriminator—that compete against each other.
- The generator creates fake data (e.g., synthetic images) to fool the discriminator, which distinguishes between real and generated data. This competition drives both networks to improve.
- Used for image generation, deepfake creation, and data augmentation.

Deep Reinforcement Learning Models:

- Combine reinforcement learning (where an agent learns by interacting with its environment) with deep learning.
- Notable for achieving breakthroughs in games like chess, Go (AlphaGo), and video games (DeepMind's work with Atari).
- The agent uses deep neural networks to approximate the best actions it should take to maximise cumulative rewards.

Applications of Deep Learning Models:

- **Computer Vision:** Image recognition, object detection, facial recognition, and medical image diagnosis.
- **Natural Language Processing (NLP):** Language translation, text generation, sentiment analysis, chatbots, and more.

- **Speech and Audio Processing:** Speech recognition (e.g., Siri, Alexa), text-to-speech systems, and audio generation.
- **Autonomous Systems:** Self-driving cars, robotics, and drones.
- **Healthcare:** Predicting diseases, personalised treatment plans, drug discovery, and medical imaging.
- **Finance:** Fraud detection, algorithmic trading, and credit risk assessment.

Advantages of Deep Learning:

- **Data Requirements:** Deep learning typically requires vast amounts of labelled data for effective training, which can be difficult to obtain.
- **Computationally Intensive:** Training deep models demands significant computational power and time.
- **Interpretability:** Complex models like deep neural networks often function as "black boxes," making it hard to interpret their decision-making processes.
- **Overfitting:** Deep models can overfit training data if not properly regularised.

Natural Language Processing (NLP):

NLP is a field of artificial intelligence (AI) that focuses on the interaction between computers and human (natural) languages. The ultimate goal of NLP is to enable computers to understand, interpret, generate, and respond to human language in a way that is both meaningful and useful. NLP bridges the gap between human communication (text or speech) and machine understanding, making it possible for machines to process and analyse vast amounts of natural language data.

Key Components of NLP:

- **Syntax and Parsing:** This involves analysing the structure of sentences. Syntax helps computers understand the grammatical structure of a sentence (viz., identifying nouns, verbs, adjectives, etc.)
- **Semantics:** Focuses on the meaning of words, phrases, and sentences. Semantic analysis helps in understanding what the text conveys, such as identifying synonyms, antonyms, and word sense disambiguation (choosing the correct word meaning in the context).

- **Morphological Analysis:** This looks at the structure of words and their meaningful parts, such as prefixes, suffixes, and roots.

- **Named Entity Recognition (NER):** Identifies proper nouns in a text, such as names of people, organisations, dates, and locations.

- **Sentiment Analysis:** Determines the emotional tone behind a body of text. Sentiment analysis is often used to understand opinions or attitudes in social media posts, reviews, etc.

- **Tokenisation:** The process of breaking a text into smaller units called tokens (words, phrases, or symbols) for easier processing.

- **Speech Recognition:** Converts spoken language into text (e.g., virtual assistants like Siri or Alexa use NLP for voice commands).

- **Language Generation:** The ability of computers to generate human-like text. This can be seen in applications like automated content creation, summarisation, or chatbot responses.

- **Machine Translation:** Automatically translating text from one language to another (e.g., Google Translate).

How NLP Works:

NLP often relies on a combination of statistical, machine learning, and deep learning models to perform its tasks. Here's how NLP works:

- **Data Preprocessing:** Text data is often noisy and unstructured, so it needs to be cleaned and formatted (e.g., removing punctuation, converting to lowercase, and tokenising words).

- **Feature Extraction:** Converting text into numerical representations that a machine can understand. This includes techniques such as Bag of Words (BoW), Term Frequency-Inverse Document Frequency (TF-IDF), and Word Embeddings (like Word2Vec, GloVe, and Transformers).

- **Model Training:** Training an ML or deep learning model on labelled text data (for supervised learning tasks) or using unlabelled data for unsupervised tasks.

Applications of NLP:

- **Chatbots and Virtual Assistants:** Assistants like Siri, Alexa, and Google Assistant use NLP to understand spoken requests and provide relevant responses.

- **Sentiment Analysis:** Companies use NLP to analyse customer feedback, social media posts, or reviews to understand user sentiments about their products.

- **Machine Translation:** Tools like Google Translate use NLP to translate text between different languages.

- **Text Summarisation:** Extracts the most important information from large volumes of text and presents it in a concise form.

- **Spam Detection:** Email services use NLP to classify emails as spam or non-spam based on their content.

- **Named Entity Recognition (NER):** Extracting important entities from unstructured text (e.g., finding names, dates, or organisations in legal documents).

- **Search Engines:** NLP improves search engine performance by analysing and ranking search results based on the intent of a query and the context of the text.

- **Optical Character Recognition (OCR):** Extracting text from scanned documents, images, or handwritten notes and converting it into machine-readable text.

NLP Techniques and Models:

- **Rule-Based NLP Systems:** These systems use a set of hand-crafted linguistic rules to analyse text, but they often struggle with ambiguity and variations in language.

- **Statistical and Machine Learning-Based NLP:** Uses probabilistic models, algorithms, and statistical methods to learn from data (e.g., Naive Bayes, Support Vector Machines).

- **Deep Learning for NLP:** Recent advances rely heavily on deep neural networks and models like recurrent neural networks (RNNs), long short-term memory (LSTM) networks, and transformer models (e.g., BERT, GPT). These models can capture complex relationships in text, enabling state-of-the-art performance on tasks like text generation, translation, and sentiment analysis.

Challenges in NLP:

- **Ambiguity:** Human languages are inherently ambiguous; words and phrases can have multiple meanings based on context (e.g., "bank" can refer to a financial institution or the side of a river).

- **Context and Cultural Nuances:** Understanding context, slang, idiomatic expressions, and cultural references remains challenging.

- **Data Limitations:** Quality NLP models require vast amounts of data, and labelled datasets are often costly or difficult to obtain.

- **Bias in Language Models:** NLP models can inadvertently inherit biases present in training data, which can lead to biased or inappropriate responses.

Recent Advances in NLP:

- **Transformers and Large Language Models (LLMs):** Transformer-based models like BERT (Bidirectional Encoder Representations from Transformers) and GPT (Generative Pre-trained Transformer) have significantly advanced the field by providing high accuracy for various NLP tasks.

- **Pretrained Language Models:** Pretrained models allow developers to fine-tune general models for specific tasks with less data, improving accessibility and performance across NLP applications.

Generative AI (GAI):

Generative AI creates new content by producing novel outputs based on patterns learned from training data, unlike traditional AI, which analyses existing data or performs specific tasks.

How GAI Works:

Generative AI models learn complex patterns from large datasets during training and utilise this knowledge to create new, original outputs that are similar to, but not identical to, the training data.

Example Technologies and Models:

- **Generative Adversarial Networks (GANs):** GANs involve two neural networks: a generator that creates data samples and a discriminator that evaluates them. The generator strives to produce realistic data that deceives the discriminator, while the discriminator improves at detecting fake samples, resulting in more realistic outputs from the generator.

- **Variational Autoencoders (VAEs):** VAEs are a type of neural network that compresses data into a latent space representation and then generates new data samples by decoding the latent space.

Applications of Generative AI:

- **Text Generation:** AI-generated articles, poetry, dialogue, etc., using models like GPT (e.g., this conversation).

- **Image Creation:** AI can generate images from scratch or transform images into new styles (e.g., tools like DALL-E).

- **Music and Audio Creation:** AI can compose music, produce sound effects, or even synthesise human-like speech.

- **Coding Assistance:** Generative AI can generate, complete, or debug code snippets for software developers.

Agentic AI: This trend emphasises the creation of AI systems capable of acting independently. Such models can analyse situations, make informed decisions, and adapt to changing environments with minimal human intervention. Agentic AI can autonomously handle complex tasks such as booking appointments, managing emails, or navigating digital systems.

Large Language Models (LLMs):

Large Language Models are generative AI models that use deep learning to understand and generate human-like text, trained on extensive text data from books, articles, websites, and more.

Key Characteristics of LLMs:

- **Massive Scale:** LLMs are characterised by large parameters (tunable weights in the model). For example, GPT-3, a well-known LLM developed by OpenAI, has 175 billion parameters, enabling it to generate highly coherent and contextually relevant text.

- **Contextual Understanding:** Unlike smaller models, LLMs can capture the nuances and complexities of language, allowing them to understand context, generate coherent paragraphs, summarise long texts, and even engage in meaningful conversations.

- **Training:** LLMs are trained on large datasets using unsupervised or self-supervised learning techniques. During training, the model is exposed to vast amounts of text, predicting the next word in a sequence given its context, thereby learning grammar, facts, and nuances of human language.

Common LLMs:

- **GPT (Generative Pre-trained Transformer):** Developed by OpenAI, GPT models are transformer-based language models to generate human-like text. The models like GPT-2, GPT-3, and GPT-4.

- **BERT (Bidirectional Encoder Representations from Transformers):** Unlike GPT, which generates text unidirectionally, BERT is trained bidirectionally, considering both preceding and following context, making it highly effective for tasks like question answering and sentiment analysis.

Applications of Large Language Models:

- **Chatbots and Virtual Assistants:** LLMs power many conversational agents, enabling them to respond in human-like ways and provide useful information.

- **Text Summarisation:** LLMs can condense long documents into concise summaries.

- **Language Translation:** LLMs are used to improve machine translation systems (e.g., translating between languages).

- **Content Creation:** LLMs can generate articles, stories, scripts, and more, tailored to specific topics or styles.

- **Coding and Software Development:** Tools like GitHub Copilot, powered by LLMs, assist developers by suggesting code completions and debugging code.

- **Sentiment Analysis and Text Classification:** LLMs analyse customer reviews, social media posts, and other textual data to determine sentiments, classify topics, and provide actionable insights.

The Relationship Between Generative AI and LLMs:

- **LLMs as a Type of Generative AI:** LLMs are a specialised form of generative AI focused on processing and generating human-like text. While they excel in language tasks, generative AI can create diverse outputs like images, audio, and code.

- **Integration and Real-World Impact:** Generative AI (including LLMs) has revolutionised areas such as communication, creativity, customer service, education, and research, making it possible to automate complex tasks, generate creative content, and provide human-like interactions at scale.

Ethics in Artificial Intelligence:

Ethics in AI involves moral principles guiding the development and use of AI systems, ensuring they are responsible, fair, and beneficial to society as AI becomes more integrated into daily life.

Key Ethical Principles in AI:

Several key principles guide the ethical development and deployment of AI systems:

Fairness and Non-Discrimination

- AI systems should ensure equality and fairness, avoiding bias or discrimination based on race, gender, age, religion, disability, or other characteristics.
- AI models trained on biased data can perpetuate societal biases, leading to unfair outcomes such as discriminatory hiring algorithms or facial recognition errors targeting certain demographics.

Transparency and Explainability

- AI systems should be understandable and explainable to users. This means providing clear explanations for how and why an AI model makes certain decisions or predictions.
- Increasing transparency can improve trust, accountability, and user acceptance of AI systems, especially in critical areas like healthcare, finance, and law enforcement.

Privacy and Data Protection

- AI systems often rely on large amounts of personal data for training and operation. Ethical AI development must respect user privacy and protect sensitive information.
- Data collection should be transparent, consensual, and comply with relevant privacy laws (e.g., GDPR in Europe).

Accountability and Responsibility

- Developers, organisations, and users of AI systems should be accountable for their systems' behaviour and outcomes from the use of AI.
- This includes identifying who is responsible for AI decisions, especially when systems fail or cause harm.

Safety and Security

- AI systems should be designed to operate safely and should minimise the risk of unintended harm to humans or the environment.
- Ensuring AI security also involves protecting systems from malicious attacks (e.g., adversarial attacks that manipulate AI behaviour).

Autonomy and Human Control

- Ethical AI prioritises human autonomy, supporting decision-making rather than replacing it, especially in critical areas like healthcare and military applications.
- AI should allow humans to retain meaningful control over important decisions and processes.

Beneficence (Do No Harm)

- AI should be used to improve human well-being in all respects.
- Developers should strive to create systems that maximise positive outcomes and minimise harm.

Inclusivity and Accessibility

- AI systems should be inclusive and accessible to all, providing equal opportunities and accommodating diverse user needs.
- For example, accessibility features for people with disabilities can help ensure that everyone benefits from AI advancements.

Ethical Challenges and Issues in AI

While ethical principles provide a framework, real-world implementation presents challenges and raises complex questions:

Bias and Fairness

- AI systems learn and replicate biases present in training data, leading to unfair outcomes in areas such as hiring, lending, and healthcare.
- Ensuring fairness requires diverse and representative datasets, as well as techniques to identify and mitigate biases in models.

Lack of Transparency (Black Box Models)

- Many AI systems, particularly deep learning models, are complex and difficult to interpret, raising concerns about "black box" decision-making where the rationale behind predictions is unclear.
- This lack of transparency can undermine trust, especially in high-stakes applications.

Privacy Concerns

- AI systems often rely on collecting and analysing large amounts of user data. The potential for misuse, data breaches, or unauthorised surveillance raises serious privacy concerns.
- Clear policies, robust security measures, and user consent mechanisms are necessary to ensure data protection.

Job Displacement and Economic Impact

- AI-driven automation can lead to job displacement and economic disruption in certain industries (e.g., manufacturing and customer service).
- Ethical considerations should address the societal impact of AI on employment and economic inequality, including retraining and support for affected workers.

Autonomous Systems and Accountability

- As AI systems gain autonomy (e.g., self-driving cars, autonomous drones), questions arise about accountability and liability in cases of failure or harm.
- Determining who is responsible—manufacturers, users, or the AI itself—poses a challenge in legal and ethical frameworks.

Manipulation and Misinformation

- AI can be used to create and spread misinformation, such as deepfake videos or fake news, leading to potential harm and undermining trust in information sources.
- Ethical AI must involve safeguards to detect and mitigate such manipulative applications.

Human Rights and Social Justice

- The use of AI technologies (e.g., facial recognition for surveillance) can raise human rights concerns, such as potential violations of privacy and freedom of expression.
- Ethical frameworks should consider the broader societal impact of AI on fundamental human rights and social justice.

AI in Warfare and Defence

- The development of autonomous weapons and AI in military applications raises serious ethical concerns about human oversight, accountability, and the potential for unintended escalation.

The Future of AI:

The future of AI is promising, with several potential trends and directions likely to shape how it evolves and impacts society. Here are some key areas to consider:

Advancements in General AI: General AI (AGI) aims to create systems with human-like cognitive abilities across a wide range of tasks, unlike today's specialised AI. While it remains a long-term goal, research continues to bridge the gap between narrow AI and AGI.

Integration into Daily Life and Work: AI will increasingly integrate into daily life, transforming industries like work, healthcare, education, and entertainment by automating tasks and enhancing creativity and decision-making.

Explainability and Trustworthy AI: Efforts are increasing to make AI explainable and transparent in critical fields like finance, healthcare, and law, as trust is essential for adoption and risk reduction.

Human-AI Collaboration: AI will augment, not replace, human skills, fostering collaboration where AI supports and enhances creativity and productivity.

Advances in NLP and Conversational AI: Advances in AI language systems will enable more lifelike, context-aware interactions, revolutionising communication and human-machine interaction.

Robotics and Autonomous Systems: Autonomous vehicles, drones, and robots will transform industries like logistics, medicine, and agriculture, with AI-driven autonomy as a focus in their development.

Quantum Computing and AI: Integrating AI with quantum computing, which operates on the principles of quantum mechanics, to get super-fast processing, could revolutionise problem-solving, particularly in molecular modelling, cryptography, and large-scale data analytics.

Conclusion: *AI Algorithm vs Human Consciousness*

An AI-based Algorithm is a set of programmed rules and learned statistical patterns that allow machines to perform tasks without consciousness of existence, emotions, or feelings, and are not integrated with the environment and evolution, where Human consciousness has emotion, a realisation of self-existence and expansion, through its neural system, which has an interaction with the environment and nature's evolution process.

Chapter 17

Self-Management

A Key to Success

Chapter Objective:

★Introspection and reformation ★True man ★True woman ★Way of success ★Towards success ★Crowned by success ★Nature's rejection ★In sorrow how to be happy ★Love is wisdom ★Love is knowledge ★Effect of criticism ★Criticism as a barrier to success ★Removal of faults ★The wise and foolish ★Understanding character ★The aristocracy of imagination ★Vision as nature is ★Path of success ★Pauperism in the idle ★Friend of poverty ★Lust ★Win lust ★Win over anger ★Win over greed ★ Ego ★Suppression of complexes ★Save to serve ★Immortality and death ★Consciousness, environment, and Dharma ★Ideal master and his attachment ★Inner voice ★True love ★Lust and love ★Truth and false ★Effect and fate ★Fortune and effort ★Spiritualism ★The reality of God ★Coexistence of Science and God ★Ungratefulness to the past seers ★Regard others and be regardful ★Real service ★Service with love and in the name of love ★Work against Ideal ★Hate never the sinner, but sin ★Serving Ideal is the key to success ★True education and character building ★Complete education, 7 points ★Innovation ★Unemployment undone ★Memory retention ★Will of willpower ★Teaching technique ★Compatibility of man and woman ★Repent ★Kindness ★Mercy ★Glorify by becoming the centre of interest of all ★Achievement from an inferiority complex ★True success in Ideal centricity ★IndoAryan Existentialism ★Existentialism ★IndoAryanism ★Roadmap of Man-Making-Mission (IM3)

Introspection and reformation: It is only our mind that contains the infinite mystery of the whole creation of the universe, which could reveal the facts. From birth, continuous stimulation from our surroundings shapes our mindset, and according to our inner mechanisms and the arrangement of our complexes, we receive those external impulses and respond. The formation of complexes largely depends on psychogenic factors. To get rid of obsessions, one has to develop an uncoloured vision and learn the technique of introspection, and that is only possible by standing in front of a 'mirror' – the man of wisdom, the master, the man who can see beyond, the man who stays above the influence of complexes and having the ability of solve any problems of life. Let's find out a few major factors that often raise a barrier between us and our success, and introspect - view self deep inside with an X-ray eye, and also to rectify – removal of residue.

True man: *"Roll on like a flood, over the sorrows, sufferings, and calamities of the world, - with love, sympathy, and service and with the message of Beloved the Lord, - with knowledge and action that illuminates the path for the dull and the deterioratingly depressed; flow on – extremely un-resting and undisturbed; if a female wants to let her run after you, proclaiming admiration and worship, establishing the kingdom of peace and happiness with a wistful soothing gaze after her beloved; - but wish not for that at all !."* [Ref: 'The Message' Vol-I]

True woman: *"Your nursing, your gait, your imagination, your expression, produce within the common male like an essence, so that they, bending down the head meekly, with deference with full devotion and regards, could say – 'My Mother - My Mother'; They are fascinated, enlightened, satisfied, and gratified — only then do you become a daughter, a chaste, and a pleasing wife."* [Ref: 'Narir Niti', Bengali ver]

Way of success: Whether one knows how or not, he must continue to accelerate his effort – that will show him the path to success – and his success will surely establish his Ideal – the living embodiment of complete wisdom.

Towards success: The environment comes forward to protect, nurture, and uphold; when he becomes essential to the environment in his daily life process, no doubt he shall be crowned by glory and success.

Crowned by success: Who opens the doors of goodness and finds the path of success with faithfulness, gratitude, and activity even in opposition and obstacles, surely he would be crowned with success.

Nature's rejection: Nature neglects those who ignore certainty, embrace uncertainty, and allow ambiguity to colour their reality – indeed, they will go down into deep darkness.

In sorrow, how to be happy: One must not be sad about the incidents of sorrow, as sadness never makes one happy. Rather, he must try to think about how one becomes joyful, and he has to become active to find the way to make oneself cheerful.

Love is wisdom: Love (for great) and a balanced mind are the only sources of wisdom, well vision, and energetic character; but conflict, unfaith, and hatred give birth to foolishness, frustration, and fatigue.

Love is knowledge: Love is the supreme knowledge, it reveals how the lover, the Master, integrates into the environment through life, enjoyment, service, sympathy, and intelligence. So love is the mother of common sense, which enables one to sit in reality with efficiency.

Effect of criticism: If one wants to find the faults of others, he has to think and find the evil habits, and along with that, they has to activate the notion of unhappiness or disgust in their mind. And those make a home in his mind and tend to behave likewise, and gradually all of those get imbided in character. One must be cautious of dwelling on others' faults, as it can easily spoil one's character.

Criticism as a barrier to success: If one wants to grow, then he has to say goodbye to the habit of criticising others forever, and he has to practice thinking, saying, and discussing goodness; if possible, he has to be careful of the effect of badness.

Removal of faults: If one has been affected by the fault-finding attitude, then he has to find and analyse the cause and existence of this disease, and has to remove it from his mind sympathetically in such a manner so that he cannot be attacked anymore.

The wise and foolish: Those are wise observers who can find the golden chance of happiness and expansion even in sorrow, hazard, and hurdle! But those are foolish observers – easily find out the rubbish, inability, impossibility, and hopelessness; even in goodness.

Understanding character: One's attitude, intention, and taste tell what he is, what he wants, and what he can achieve.

The aristocracy of imagination: When one's thinking and way of life do not put him in action or never make him attached to the work of achievement, surely that thought is an aristocracy of imagination.

Vision as nature is: One's nature, which is made by his thoughts, acts, and behaviour; wherever he will be, surely he shall view his environment likewise (as his nature is).

Path of success: One comes at the door of success when they completely wipe out all the possible thoughts of 'no' or 'cannot do'. Thinking of negation or having doubts about success increases the chance of being unsuccessful.

Pauperism in the idle: One has to be very careful and alert from the thoughts of idle, can't do, impossible, difficult, because these characteristics rapidly transmit into heredity and infect the environment, spoil families, society, state, and collapse into pauperism.

Friend of poverty: Idle, unfaithfulness, egotism, and ungratefulness are the closest friends of poverty, and each of these characters always nurtures pauperism to be alive.

Lust: The most powerful passion is lust; it is also the mother of other passions like anger, greed, ego, etc. Lust makes one obsessed in such a manner that it locks all the entry points of finer thoughts and also takes out one's impartial vision, and one gets lost in the dark.

Win lust: Love for the higher Ideal and culture of knowledge to fulfill the greater cause of life – give victory over lust forever. This love generates normal motherhood feelings about women, and women never sacrifice their physical, mental, and spiritual chastity.

Win over anger: Anger mostly makes one selfish, irrational, and dull; and this madness also makes others unfortunate. So, to win over anger, if he practices thinking before it comes into effect, how to make anger profitable, and what is the ultimate gain of anger? In most cases, the reply comes into the void.

Win over greed: When one's need crosses over the boundary of sufficient need, then that becomes greed. So, one must be cautious not to cross the boundary of that 'need' because greed pulls one down into the grave, and may divert his greed towards the greed of making life meaningful for the greater cause of togetherness.

Suppression of complexes: One must not be too cautious to suppress the desires of complexes, because that abnormal attitude of 'carefulness' makes those more active and becomes the cause of turbulence. Instead, they should be moulded by engaging them in innovative, interesting, and purposeful activities aligned with the cause of life, so that they can rarely get a chance to rise.

Save to serve: One should save to serve – if saving does not serve the service, no doubt that saving will welcome the downfall. And service is that which makes a man grow, glowing, cheering, and loving.

Immortality and death: The more one is attached to many, the more he becomes a fluctuating personality. This dual personality makes one disintegrate, dull, and leads to death. When one is attached to an Ideal and embraces many through that connection, he transcends mortality and lives on eternally through his impact, because many impulses get materialised in 'one' and become everlasting wisdom.

Consciousness, environment, and Dharma: Receiving impulses from the environment proves that I'm conscious. This environmental impulse builds the idea, thought, and complexes that regulate life. So one must act and serve the environment in such a manner that one must continuously receive favourable impulses from there to lead a life and growth. And this existential behavioural act is called Dharma.

Ideal master and his attachment: The association of a 'man' - which enables one to exist, excel, and expand and the attachment to whom – never detaches one from being and becoming by any environmental pull, rather he rolls on with knowledge and activity by manipulating the environment enlightening the darkness of dullness – such a 'man' is actual Ideal master of whole mankind.

Inner voice: The constitution of memory and knowledge that has developed by the induction of the environment comes out in terms of the inner voice or Bibek.

Ego: 'I am existing' – this feeling of staying is a real ego. This stay-feeling comes while one responds to the impulse of surroundings. But when this feeling wants to override the stay of others to establish their stay, then satanic dullness locks up his existence. And to win over ego is to realise – 'I have been made for the supreme father for a supreme cause to uphold life and growth'.

Egoist pride: If one's success or efficiency tends to suppress, punish, or neglect others' success or efficiency, then he is a man of egoist pride. And the more he does the same, the more he falls into a vain.

True love: Love illuminating the heart serves the lover in the environment to establish him. Where this is not present, his love is very much doubtful. So, the greatest acid test of love is – love never makes any choice that may harm its lover physically, mentally, or spiritually.

Lust and love: Only sexuality never makes a couple husband and wife. But their common deep love for the Ideal becomes a 'cementing factor' to bind them together forever to enjoy heavenly bliss.

Truth and false: Truth is that which has existence, and evolution, and that never allows any deviation from this existential becoming. And which weakens self-existence and deviates the environment from being and becoming is false.

Effect and fate: Fate is the outcome of which has been compiled through variations by one's efforts and effect on the environment, and waiting beyond the horizon of knowledge.

Fortune and effort: Fortune (*daibya*) is that character that a man inherits by birth, and likewise, the environment also rewards him. And effort (*purusakar*) stands on inbuilt psychogenic characteristics, which he applies in the environment.

Spiritualism: Spiritualism is the cause-finding go-of-life, inspired by the idea or thought, and gets reflected in thinking, gait, and work.

The reality of 'God': It is not wise to conceptualise the existence of 'God' by mere imagination, which may lead to a void and make life unsuccessful. Rather, one must put all his love, devotion, and worship there only, in whom all his complexes get fulfilled to be and become in totality. HE is his living God in reality, as Arjuna had found God in Krishna, Mary Magdalene got the solutions to her complexes in her living God, Jesus, Swami Vivekananda realised his God in Sri Ramakrishna, etc., by which they gained mastery over goodness.

Coexistence of Science and 'God': We often think that Science and God-existence are antagonists, because God can't be scientifically explained. But science accepts that matter has an 'existential urge' — that leads to evolution from matter to life, and this 'urge' is God-ness.

Ungratefulness to the past seers: if we reject past seers or masters and focus only on promoting our ideas—without understanding or correcting past misinterpretations—we create division and dishonour tradition. Instead of making ancient wisdom relevant today, we try to disprove it, showing disloyalty and selfish motives. Such actions disrupt social harmony and lead to a culture of betrayal and disintegration, ignoring that the present is a continuation of the past.

Regard others and be regardful: One must not disregard the regardful people if he wants to be regardful to others. Often, one tries to bring others down who are regarded by many as mechanical to prove one's acceptance and importance. Sometimes, to put one down, they try to make them down whom he regards, loves, or follows. This is the character of a sign of pauperism.

Real service: It is more important to serve the mental need than to nourish physical needs. Because man gets more relaxation and comfort by serving the suffering mind. So to serve, one should first see the mental condition of the person and his immediate need; and accordingly serve him by word, idea, deed, and money, to make him enlightened, energised, and enthusiastic to enjoy life forever, along with all. This is service in reality.

Service with love and in the name of love: When service is done to satisfy the enticement of complexes, then it gets weakened by any feeble opposition; this indicates the hidden intention of the 'service'. But when service is done for the Master's interest, no doubt this becomes stronger, forceful, and enjoyable at any hurdle; and they only can realise the joy who has experienced it.

Work against Ideal: If one does something against the will of the Master or non-existential deeds, his hidden lust, ungratefulness, restricts his reach to his Master. But if he has normal and selfless love for his Master, then he cannot restrict himself to coming close to his love lord or Master to confess his weaknesses, which often drag him down into dullness and lead him into the darkness. So, be careful!

Hate never the sinner but sin: One must try to ignore and neglect the sin or dire, but never ignore or hate him who has committed a mistake. If one insults and punishes him for his sin, then surely all of those punishments will punish him too in due course of time.

Serving Ideal is the key to success: When one becomes keen to serve the Ideal out of loving affection, then he inquisitively looks around to collect the best things to offer for His pleasure and becomes alert to protect Him for any causality i.e. when he invests for the real existential becoming for individual and environment; the environment comes forward to honour him with rewards and recognition.

True education and character building: Education or efficiency-building out of jealousy, aggression, or an inferiority complex – that rarely affects the character and life, though it may let one reach the great height of disintegrated and extreme achievements! But, while education starts with a love of living-Ideal and effulging fulfilment tendency to the environment, which virtually strengthens the character and competency, and is transmitted into the heredity.

Complete education, 7 points: To get an effective and meaningful output of education, the emphasis should be given to the following seven objectives: **1.** *Concentricity:* One's every thought and activity should be dedicated to the pleasure of the superior Ideal. **2.** *Alertness:* None of the surrounding events should pass without close observation. **3.** *Agility:* Combination and coordination of fastness and perfection of the job should be adopted. **4.** *Inquisitiveness:* Attitude of cause finding tenacity of every incident must be practised, invest in favour of the greater interest of the surroundings. **5.** *Judicious Attitude:* Studying the cause of the events, the right application of the best solution must be in action. **6.** *Presence of Mind:* The development of a sense of behaviour in a positive direction to the immediate environment. **7.** *Cordial go of Life:* The loving attitude towards the surroundings and to make it in favour, even in adverse conditions.

Innovation: Where one stays, they should observe around and find out all the available resources there, and they should search how these can fulfill the needs of the people. Hence, within a short span of time, one would develop an innovative mindset and research spirit.

Unemployment undone: To exist, one needs to earn and have food, and to earn requires work. So they must see their surroundings and consistently give effort to find out the wants of the people, to meet them by any means. Gradually, this initiative would widen the scope and field, and once it gets adopted, then unemployment won't remain a problem anymore, but rather be undone.

Memory retention: If the mind is explored by two equal interests or desires, then both or any one of those gets lost from the memory forever. So, if one wants to retain their memory and wishes to make it sharp, healthy and bright, then they should allow an interest or a wish to enter their mind one after another.

Will of willpower: To keep the power of will active and alive, one must serve their environment, somehow, every day with an innovative and inquisitive mind. And while any goodwill comes to mind, it must be materialised without the least delay. Similarly, if any force of a complex like lust, anger, greed, etc., induces someone, that must be regulated immediately in favour of life and growth.

Teaching technique: To teach successfully to the learners, the teacher must enter into the mind of the student through his/her level of understanding. His "Yes" window. So firstly, the teacher has to discover where the student stands now, then has to enter just below that standpoint, but never penetrate, pointing out the unknown zone. And the more we could reveal the interrelationship of the subjects, the more we would solve the mystery of knowledge.

Compatibility of man and woman: Every man and woman is naturally independent, with distinct roles shaped by nature. Women are inclined to nurture, inspire, and bring new life, while men are geared toward fulfilling, protecting, and progressing. They complement each other, becoming whole through psychogenic compatibility. Each supports the other through their innate tendencies, creating a deep, loving bond that generates positive energy in nature.

Repent: If one(1) somehow hurts a person(2), then reviving his(1) sympathy and thinking by placing himself(1) in that situation from his(2) standpoint, he(1) must repent, assuming his(2) sorrow. And he(1) has to adjust himself(1) in such a manner that he(1) need not repent anymore. Then surely he shall be blessed by divine qualities.

Kindness: Those who are weak, poor, have no shelter, no food, whose life spirit has finished by frustration, begging for mercy to get a bit of support, looking with feeble eyes to save their hopeless life; if feelings don't arise immediately to extend hands towards them, then it is doubtful whether I am alive or dead. So one must come forward with a merciful heart at the beginning to pull them out from their grave condition, destroying all sorrow and continuing even if one's life comes under threat! His kindness will be honoured by heavenly bliss forever.

Mercy: If one wants to be powerful, then he has to be merciful, a sense of tolerance. He must be careful that – whom he is forgiving, i.e., the mistakes that made him weaken, he has to take him (who has committed a mistake) away in such a way with love, hope, support, and sympathy; so that – he could get a faithful shelter in him to be free from all of the faults. If it does not happen, then his mercy or forgiveness is a farce, false, and fake. So it is said – forgive the sinner, but not the sin.

Glorify by becoming the centre of interest of all: When needs arise, humans develop desires driven by self-interest. This selfishness, if not guided by awareness of how one's existence depends on the environment, drains one's life force. Ignoring the source of energy— the environment—leads to deprivation and failure. True joy and progress come when a person aligns their interests with those of their surroundings and becomes a positive centre of attention within it.

Achievement from an inferiority complex: One can achieve a lot of material gain, but if that is gained out of jealousy, aggression, or revenge; if one becomes popular as a poet, scientist, social worker, politician, but if this comes from wounded ego or damaged inferiority complex; then no doubt – this so-called success or achievement will produce nothing for the world, but only hopeless and degeneration.

True success in Ideal centricity: Whatever one is and however he is, his life and thought may be awful like anything; even though never mind, if he gets attached to a Master of wisdom by an unshakable adherence, and he never does anything which may distract him from the establishment of his master in the world. No doubt, he will be free from all sin very soon and glorified in all-around success forever.

IndoAryan Existentialism: This is probably the world's most advanced silent revolutionary roadmap of making humans based on genetic evolution, blended with the psycho-spiritual development of individuals. This idea has been derived from the facts perceived and practised by ancient Aryan Seers for thousands of years, and subsequently verified by scientific and sociological observations. It has now given rise to a new ideology, 'IndoAryan Existentialism'.

Existentialism is the existential urge, the common factor in each matter; this urge enables all the particles of the matter to be aligned with its centre (nucleus/sun) for existence, and it evolves according to the natural laws of becoming, balancing the total ecology.

IndoAryanism is Concentric go-of-life to adjust inner complexes, self-elevation with learning rules of life, and genetic enrichment through the application of psychogenic developmental laws of nature.

So, this is virtually IndoAryan Man Making Mission (**IM3**), and the objective of this mission is qualitative development of humans with the building of new psychogenic mechanisms. The goals of IM3 are to boost the missions of digital 'Global Citizenship' and to set a new divine world order, managed by divine (advanced psychogenic human-being) to cultivate humanity.

Roadmap of Man-Making-Mission (IM3): Let's dream of a divine world order, following 'IndoAryan Existentialism'.

Innate Urge: Each matter has an 'urge of existence' - the life throb. It wants to live and grow to keep its existence expanding. Such an urge in humans makes them conscious and active to control the environment in favour of their existence and surroundings. This prime driving force of the evolution of matter may be called 'Godness'. Hence, our final goal is existential realisation.

Ever Lasting Torch: In the course of life, to explore the inherent possibilities to their maximum degree and to apply the material possibilities with the all-inclusive spiritual knowledge profitably, we need a man of wisdom or a realised living Master. Such a personality as a human is 'God' himself, whose directions are inevitable to overcome all sorts of hurdles in the existential evolution of mankind.

All in One: Hence, God - 'the existential urge of matter' is One. Dharma - 'the science of existence is One. And all world teachers or Prophets are the messengers of the same, i.e., One God and One Dharma. This is the factor of the oneness of all in one.

Nature's Lesson: The result of biochemical and socio-cultural evolution is a grouping of similar characteristics of matter, followed by the division of labour according to the psychogenic instincts among species. Significantly, the same phenomena have also occurred in human beings. So, a grouping of similar psychogenic characteristics of humans should be protected and nurtured to transform individuals towards their highest grade of characteristics for the progress of civilisation, as human beings are the building blocks of civilisation, and their character is the factor of being-becoming of all.

Lift Law: Application of the natural laws of psychogenic growth, on the grouping of psychogenic potentials, would procure a better instinctive human resource by birth. On the contrary, awareness has to be built up to reject or restrict anti-natural 'incompatible' marriage (mating between higher instinctive females and less evolved males). A strong action program should be initiated to stop such marriages and to prevent a great loss of human potential and global humanity. And all must be connected to the Ideal-centric life, aligned to the living embodiment of the higher purpose of existence, to make a harmonious, conjugal, and peaceful family environment, a building block of a global society.

Self-Discovery: The education system must be modified with 'elevated intellectualism'. Here, knowledge is to be introduced on practical and industrial education from the primary level, by the disciplined teachers, who are disciples of the realised Master. This would reveal the cause-and-effect relation of all-natural phenomena, show the right application of lessons to fulfill social needs, and also unfurl the inter-subject relation, to break the compartmental barriers of the smooth flow of knowledge, and to reveal wisdom.

Social Change: Such educational enrichment would help humans to be transformed into a right socialist society that is free from unemployment, poverty, economic crisis, industrial downfall, uneven competition, capitalistic exploitation, state autocracy, loss of human resources, and discrimination, etc., and the state would play a leading role in the globalised economy. An economy sprouting up from such a system will only proliferate the ecology. The Indo-Aryan Soviet Socialist Republic (IASSR) is a model of such a socio-economic-political structure of greater India, extending it to the new world order.

People's Power: True democracy comes from the representatives of the conscious and better psycho-genic human resource, which is free from 'party politics' and runs under the guidance of the man of wisdom or the Ideal. So, in this alternative dynamic system, there will be no nominee, no political party, no police force, and no huge expenditure; but it comes from one representative from each family, who would select the best one from the village or ward. Such village representatives will select the best one at the district level. They would select the best representative at the state level. And from there, the country would get the best group of leaders to lead the country progressively.

Global Move: The path of becoming with the inseparability of Global humanity and all fulfilling philosophy is 'IndoAryan Existentialism'. It has an inherent potential to shape the world. Its mission is to transform each individual into the highest level of psychogenic characteristics, i.e. a 'Brahmin' by character. This is possible by following the fundamental program of human development, inspired by the theme of Indo-Aryanism. This was dreamed of and began in practice by the ancient Aryan Seers to make a divine World. This mission would lay a strong foundation for a unanimous Dharmik world order, having loyal coordination among the countries, following the leadership of a common, all-fulfilling Ideal. This is the background of the future World United States (WUS), the divine Communism.

Total Ecology: Human existence is directly connected to the coordination among biophysical existential urges of life. 'Everyone is essential for my existence' – this awareness auto-initiatively inspires to protect, nurture, and balance the Socio-Environmental-Ecology (SEE). In such a go-of-life under the leadership of the Master, one gradually discovers one's relationship with the total mechanism and attainment of self-realisation with a feeling of oneness with all. This realisation is the ultimate goal of life.

Testimonials

Prof (Dr) Itu Singh   *20/02/2026*
Department of Computer Science
BIT Mesra

The book discusses fundamental concepts of Python in a clear, simple, and highly expressive manner, making it particularly suitable for beginners and young learners. Its clarity of explanation and pedagogical design make it a valuable addition for students, educators, and anyone seeking a strong foundation in Python.

Key strengths of the book:

- Learner-friendly approach where complex topics have been introduced gradually.

- Logical progression of topics to enable readers to build confidence when they start with basic and advance to more complex topics

- Effective use of flowcharts and structured explanations. These increase the comprehensibility of complex concepts like file handling and database connectivity.

- Examples provided throughout the chapters are well-chosen and practical, offering a broad perspective, reinforcing theoretical concepts through hands-on learning, which is essential for mastering programming skills.

A noteworthy aspect of the book is its handling of data structures, from foundational concepts to modern concepts such as ensemble methods, with an introduction to explainable AI. The book reduces cognitive load and is an excellent and introductory resource for Python programming, along with Data Science, with powerful tools like Pandas and MySQL Database.

Prof (Dr) Manorama Patnaik   *02/04/2026*
Department of Computer Science
Amity University, Ranchi,
Jharkhand

Review on "Python for Beginners - The Easy Guide to Coding & Data Science"-The book is very helpful for Engineering students, students with a degree in computer science, and school students who are beginners in coding. It explains basic Python concepts in simple, clear language. Topics like variables, loops, and functions are taught using simple examples that show output, along with data science fundamentals.

The book also includes practice questions and exercises, which help students understand the Data science concepts better. The step-by-step explanations make learning interesting and less confusing.

One good thing about the book is that it does not use very difficult words, so even new learners can understand it easily. However, it has all the advanced topics, so it provides enough for higher-level learning.

Overall, this book is a very good choice for degree and engineering students, and class 12 students who want to start learning Python programming and the fundamental concepts of Data science.

Dr Sanjiv Kumar Sinha   *10/04/2026*
Former HOD, Department of Computers, DPS Ranchi
Research Scholar in BIT Mesra

"Python for Beginners – The Easy Guide to Coding and Data Science" authored by Dr Srikumar Mukherjee

In an era where computational thinking and data literacy are becoming essential life skills, "Python for Beginners – The Easy Guide to Coding and Data Science" by Dr Srikumar Mukherjee emerges as a timely and thoughtfully designed contribution to school and undergraduate computer science education.

Drawing upon more than two decades of rich classroom experience, Dr Mukherjee has crafted a text that beautifully balances conceptual clarity, practical application, and learner-friendly pedagogy. The book systematically introduces Python programming in a manner that is accessible to students of Classes XI & XII, BCA, MCA, and other beginners, without…

Affectionate, Sir. Greetings. Many more delightful content points can be mentioned for your high-quality, state-of-the-art writing. Wish Fly Up & High, always.

About the author

Dr Srikumar Mukherjee, the author of this book, has completed 25 years of teaching in the field of IT. He was awarded the 'Best Teacher' of the state, teaching Information Technology (IP/CS) at Delhi Public School, Ranchi, India. He is passionately involved as a 'Life & Lift Tutor' in an educational movement ", IndoAryan Man Making Mission" (IM3), aiming to make a better psychogenic mankind. He is the founder of the open-source virtual school 'IndoAryan School of H.R.D.' (ISHRD) to educate people about "IndoAryan Existentialism", which is an outcome of his research (PhD) work in Sociology, a new revelation in the field of HRD. He voluntarily serves in Psycho-Spiritual healing as an authorised instructor (SPR) and also an editor-publisher of an e-paper "The IndoARYAN Existentialism"

For further details, please contact

IndoAryan School of H.R.D.
Cell# +91- 9470932544 / 8210137153
Email: srikumar[dot]hrm[at]gmail[dot]com
Website: **www**[dot]**indoaryan**[dot]**in**

A few other books by the author

- **Science of Education** – *A Handbook for Parents, Teachers & Students*

- **Existential Quest** – *A key to life and lift*

- **IndoAryan Culture** – *A Historical Document of Global Consciousness*

- **Relevance of the Ideology of Sree Sree Anukulchandra in Modern Society** - *A Sociological Analysis*

- **Life and Ideology of Sree Sree Anukulchandra** – *A brief sketch*

- আর্যকৃষ্টি: *বিশ্বচেতনার এক ঐতিহাসিক দলিল*

- आर्यकृष्टि: *वैश्विक चेतना का एक ऐतिहासिक खोज*

- युवाचेतना और जीवनवृद्धिवाद

- श्रीश्रीअनुकूलचन्द्र के जीवनवृद्धिवादी सिद्धान्त का मूलतत्त्व: *एक समाज वैज्ञानिक अध्ययन*

NB. *All of the books are available in online stores*

www.ingramcontent.com/pod-product-compliance
Lightning Source LLC
Chambersburg PA
CBHW040735120726
48007CB00008B/91